Beiträge zur Indologie

Herausgegeben von Konrad Meisig

Begründet von Ulrich Schneider als
Freiburger Beiträge zur Indologie

Band 52

2024
Harrassowitz Verlag · Wiesbaden

Konrad Meisig, Marion Meisig

Tamil Temples

Traditional and Transcultural
Thirty-Three Sketches

2024
Harrassowitz Verlag · Wiesbaden

Bibliografische Information der Deutschen Nationalbibliothek
Die Deutsche Nationalbibliothek verzeichnet diese Publikation in der Deutschen Nationalbibliografie; detaillierte bibliografische Daten sind im Internet über https://dnb.de abrufbar.

Bibliographic information published by the Deutsche Nationalbibliothek
The Deutsche Nationalbibliothek lists this publication in the Deutsche Nationalbibliografie; detailed bibliographic data are available in the internet at https://dnb.de.

For further information about our publishing program consult our website https://www.harrassowitz-verlag.de

Printed on permanent/durable paper.
Printing and binding: Hubert & Co., Göttingen
Printed in Germany

ISSN 1432-6949
ISBN 978-3-447-12192-7
E ISBN 978-3-447-39526-7

Contents

Appendix

Preface

The following sketches are temporal spot-lights, about 20 years old; momentary shots and intentionally not updated. We aim to present the temples as we saw them, in the first years of the third millennium, unaffected by two decades of multifarious development.

We had considered the possibility of giving a brief introduction to each of the major deities, but soon rejected the idea. This book is about Tamil temples, it is not a general introduction to Hinduism. For those who want introductory information, or seek to refresh it, there are reliable compendia such as: U. Schneider: *Einführung in den Hinduismus*, 1989. – H. D. Smith/ N. Chary, M.: *Handbook of Hindu Gods, Goddesses and Saints*, 1991. – V. Moeller: *Die Mythologie der vedischen Religion und des Hinduismus*, [1966]. – J. Gonda: *Die Religionen Indiens: II Der jüngere Hinduismus*, 1963. – K. Meisig: *Shivas Tanz. Der Hinduismus*, 1996/2003; etc.

We have chosen three methods of presentation for our materials: text, picture and ground plan. All three are equally important. Notably, the text relies on the pictures and the ground plans, and *vice versā*. The pictures are printed as close to the relevant text as possible, and deliberately not in a separate section of the book. In addition, the reader is always asked to consult each temple's ground plan while looking at the text and pictures. These methods will fully convey the comprehensive religio-historical information. The pictures are printed in colour, as the colours are part of the liturgy.

Our thanks are due to the temple operators and staff, without whose cooperation these thirty-three sketches of Tamil temples wouldn't have been possible.

Hamm, January 2024 *Konrad Meisig* · *Marion Meisig*

Introduction

Pañcamukha – The Five Heads of Modern Hinduism

The five heads of modern Hinduism are: (1) traditional or orthodox Hinduism, (2) Neo-Hinduism, (3) commercial Hinduism, (4) political Hinduism, and (5) emigrant Hinduism.

(1) Traditional Hinduism

Traditional or orthodox Hinduism is characterised by: (1.1.) the folk-religious bonds with the cultural area of South Asia, (1.2.) the socio-religious affiliation to a caste and (1.3.) henotheism, i.e. devotion to a favourite god, an iṣṭadevatā.

(1.1) Traditional Hinduism as a folk religion. Hinduism has developed over the last three and half millennia in the cultural area of South Asia. It is a conglomeration of most heterogeneous religious beliefs and practices.

Traditional Hinduism consists of three strata:

Superstratum

Mainstream

Substratum

• *Substratum*: To begin at ground level, there are the innumerable autochthonous cults, represented by the varied village deities.

• *Mainstream*: The Vedic religion of the Indo-Arian immigrants superseded the indigenous cults in the middle of the second millennium B.C. The blending of both – of the autochthonous elements with the foreign Vedic beliefs and rituals – has created what we can observe today as *Mainstream Hinduism*. Even today there is still a marked difference between North Indian and South Indian Hinduism, characterised, roughly speaking, by a predominance of the indigenous elements in the south.

• *Superstratum*: On the intellectual level, we find the philosophical and cultic superstructure, represented by the texts of the Tāntric and Āgamic theological schools.

(1.2) The socio-religious affiliation to a caste. A person becomes a Hindu by being born into a caste. One cannot convert to traditional Hinduism so consequently there is no proselytising.

It is a fundamental right of the Indian constitution (part III, article 15, paragraph 2) that no person must be discriminated against on the grounds of caste affiliation.

On the other hand, no one will deny that the majority of Indians strictly follow the traditional caste rules concerning:

- food, cooking and eating
- marriage
- occupation

Abolition of the caste system is a claim, not a reality. It is comparable to the realisation of democracy, in India as well as in western countries. The Indian caste system is not waning but waxing. It is growing by cell division. Each of the Indian castes (around 3.000) tries to seal itself off in a downwards direction against the efforts of lower castes trying to climb up the hierarchy. In an upwards direction, each strives to join one of the higher castes above. As a result, new sub-castes emerge in the vertical transitional zones of the caste system.

(1.3) Henotheism. Thirdly, traditional Hinduism is marked by its henotheism, the devotion to a personal 'favourite deity,' called iṣṭadevatā (or iṣṭadeva) in Sanskrit. Such favourite gods are Kṛṣṇa, Rāma, Śiva, Gaṇeśa, his South Indian half-brother Murugan (Sanskrit Skanda), or goddesses like Kālī, Durgā, or Mīnākṣī, among others. Such devotion to a favourite god does not exclude the worship of extra deities in their special function, e.g., as 'Remover of Obstacles' (Vighneśvara = Gaṇeśa), who is the patron of business and science. Pure monotheism also exists as one of the varieties of Hinduism. It appeared for the first time in the first half of the second century B.C., namely in the *Bhagavadgītā*.

(2) Neo-Hinduism

Since the second half of the nineteenth century, traditional Hinduism has been complemented by Neo-Hinduism. The new Neo-Hindu movements like Ārya Samāj, or religious teachers like Vivekānanda and Aurobindo, originated during colonial times. Neo-Hinduism results from Indian thinkers being in contact with non-Indian religions, philosophies and egalitarian social teachings. The distinctive marks of Neo-Hinduism are

- missionary work in India and overseas
- social reforms and relaxation of precepts regarding caste, ritual and purity
- religious syncretism

(3) Commercial Hinduism

Commercial Hinduism is represented by organisations like 'Transcendental Meditation' founded by Maharishi Mahesh Yogi; the 'Rajneesh Foundation International' of 'Bhagwan' Shree Rajneesh (1931-1990, who changed his title into Oshō 和尚 in 1989, Japanese for 'Buddhist priest'); the Hare Krishna Mission or ISKCON ('International Society for Krishna Consciousness'), founded in 1966 by A. C. Bhaktivedanta Swami Prabhupada (1896-1977) or the organisation of Sai Baba, who is said to be worshipped by over five millions devotees worldwide. The distinctive features of commercial Hinduism are:

- missionary work, done by Indian founders, predominantly outside India
- business companies, including aggressive, profit-maximising marketing
- devotees' emotional naïveté and belief in miracles

(4) Political Hinduism

Political Hinduism is either non-violent or violent. Both forms are characterised by their mingling of the sacred and the secular, by the religious motivation behind profane goals.

(4.1) Political Hinduism: Non-Violent. The most prominent representative of non-violent political Hinduism is Mahatma Gandhi. It was he who transformed the ideals of the Old Indian warrior and ascetic ethics into methods of non-violent political argument. He adopted elements of traditional Yoga (cf. *Yogasūtra* 2,30) – like non-violence (*ahiṃsā*), truthfulness (*satya*), non-acquisitiveness (*aparigraha*), chastity (*brahmacārya*) and fasting (*upavāsa*) – and moulded them into political techniques like civil disobedience, non-cooperation and hunger strikes.

(4.2) Political Hinduism: Violent. The Hindu fundamentalists claim the absoluteness of Hindu dharma, the Hindu religion (also for non-Hindus). They demand validity of the sacred Hindu law in the secular sphere. They legitimate violence by reference to motifs and characters taken from Hindu mythology like Kṛṣṇa, Rāma of Ayodhyā or Hanumān. Their main organisation is the VHP (Viśva Hindū Pariṣad, founded in 1964) with its youth task force, the Bajrang Dal, named after Vajrāṅga, 'Whose muscles are as hard as diamond' (viz. Hanumān, the monkey general and Rāma's – the hero-god – helpmate). The Hindu fundamentalists' legal arm is the BJP (Bhāratīya Janatā Party), the largest party in the coalition of the National Democratic Alliance government in the 1999-2004 legislative period (and in 2023, leader of the present-day government).

With over 10 million members and even more followers, Hindu fundamentalism is the most powerful and predominant force in modern Hinduism. Like the business firms of commercial Hinduism, the VHP operates globally.

(5) Emigrant Hinduism

Hinduism, with approximately 800 million followers and globally, the third largest religious community after Christianity and Islam, is currently in the process of changing from a folk religion into a world religion. Traditionally limited to the region of Southern and South-eastern Asia, it was disseminated world-wide by modern migration. Since the 1980s, Tamil refugees from the civil war in Sri Lanka, in particular from Jaffna in the Northern region of the island, have settled in exile groups mostly in Europe and America by the hundreds of thousands. This process of migration is not limited to specific countries. It has a global perspective. In Germany, there are about 60.000 refugees from Sri Lanka living permanently in the country and in the Canadian Greater Toronto Area, a metropolis of immigrants, there are some 250.000.

Most of them had made a stopover during their flight, first in Germany, then in France, or some in Norway.

As a result of this process, Hinduism has become a tangible factor of Germany's, and of course other countries', cultural life. The South Asian religion is present in the German public conscience. This development is a novelty and it stirs up a growing attention among the local people. The press and the media cannot neglect this public desire for information. To a formerly unknown degree, press articles and leaflets appear in regional and national newspapers. Also, the Christian churches observe the alien religion with interest, if not concern.

In the meantime, many of the Tamil immigrants have gained official status as asylum seekers; more and more of them are acquiring German citizenship. They have found jobs and have settled, together with their families, in their new homes.

The more these immigrants are being integrated, the stronger their need to establish their religion overseas in their new homes. They hand it over to their children, to the second generation, which has started to become estranged to the customs and traditional way of life of their elders. In the beginning, the Hindu cult of Tamil immigrants took place in, for example, garages in front of tiny devotional pictures. Tamil migrants have, since the middle of the 1990s but mostly since the year 2000, built Śaiva temples. They have transferred the temple cult along with seasonal festivals and attained a vibrant community life – modelled after the pattern of their South Indian and Sri Lankan homeland but with significant modifications, transformations and altered functions resulting from new circumstances and pressures to accommodate to an immigrant status.

From 1994 to 2002, in the German North Rhine-Westphalian city of Hamm alone, three Hindu temples were founded: one for the elephant-headed god Gaṇeśa on the 12th of June 1994, one for his half-brother, the lance holder Murugan, on the 7th of February 2001 and one for the fertility goddess Kāmākṣī on the 7th of July 2002. The industrial town of Hamm, which was formerly considered interesting (at best) by the region due to having the second largest railway shunting yard in Europe, has unforeseeably become a hub of Tamil temple cult in Germany.

In the whole of Germany, there are currently (year 2004) 20 Hindu Tamil temples, with an increase in industrial areas like the Ruhr area ('Ruhrgebiet' around Dortmund), and the North (Lower Saxony, Hannover and Bremen). There are two temples in Frankfurt and others in the South, in Munich for example. Outside Germany, we find important temples in Paris (for Gaṇeśa) and London (the Murugan Highgate Hill Temple in London Archway), also in Switzerland (Basle) and Scandinavia (Oslo).

We have stated that Hinduism is currently in the process of changing from a folk religion into a world religion. It must be stressed that it is emigrant Hinduism which is essentially responsible for this epoch-making transformation. The religious metamorphosis of traditional Hinduism does not take place in India itself, but overseas. This makes expat-Hinduism an important object of research for Indologists. Significant changes of present-day Hinduism – alterations which influence the type of Hinduism as a whole, becoming not only a world religion, but rather a universal religion

– cannot be observed in the province of Uṛīṣā, but overseas, outside India and outside Asia, in the kālāpānī, beyond the 'black waters' of the Indian Ocean, in exile. In this situation, the comparison of Hinduism abroad with original Hinduism in India and Sri Lanka enables predictions of the potential chances of development back in the home countries. Overseas Hinduism can only be properly understood by careful comparison with its Indian and Sri Lankan traditional models.

The Layout of Śaiva Tamil Temples

Our description of the layout of Śaiva Tamil temples is based on observations. It does not depend on the rules that traditional scriptures or textbooks (*śilpaśāstra*) would impose. But of course, it will not necessarily contradict them.

We base the following sketches on four categories of temples, depending on whether their principal deity is Gaṇeśa, Murugan, a goddess (Devī) or Śiva.

Gaṇeśa Temple
(Ideal Type)

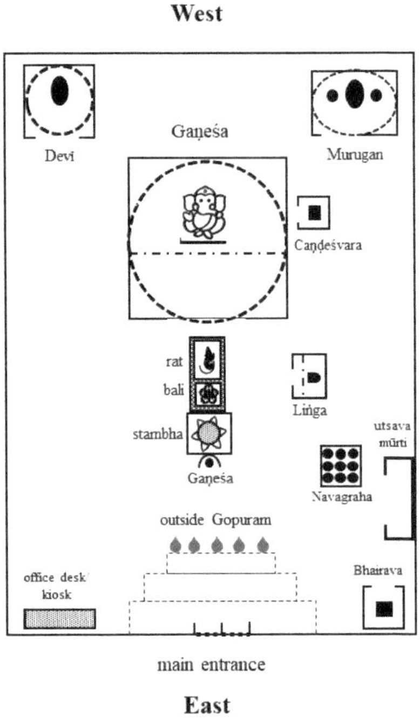

Murugan Temple
(Ideal Type)

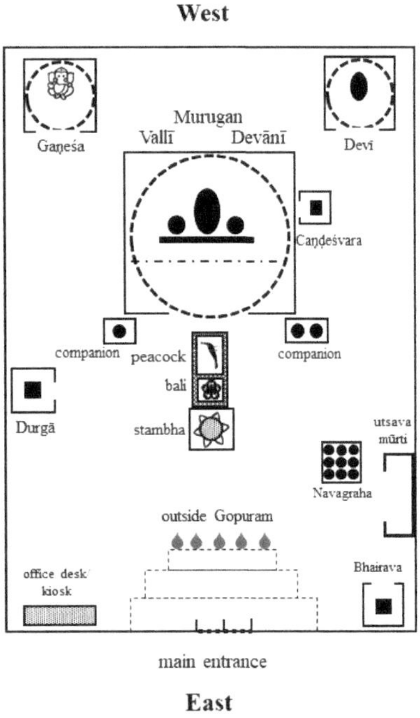

There are several features that these four kinds have in common. Firstly, the main divinity resides in the sanctissimum (*mūlagarbha* or *mūlasthāna*), in the centre of the western part of the temple hall. If possible, the chief deity must face east; except the Devī temples: typically, they are orientated to the south. Accordingly, in our descriptions, we will give all directions, as to right or left, in the perspective of the deity (not that of the observer!) so, when the god looks to the east, right means south and left means north.

Secondly, the statue of the chief god – or goddess – is made of black granite. Through the inauguration ceremony (*kumbhābhiṣeka*), this sculpture becomes a sthalamūrti, a 'locally fixed statue,' which must never be removed from its place.

Thirdly, immediately in front of the main statue watches its mount (*vāhana*): a rat for Gaṇeśa, a peacock for Murugan, the Devī commands a lion and Śiva a zebu bull. These 'mūrtis' (sculptures) consist of black granite too. Behind the animal, we will find another granite object, namely an egg-shaped lotus bud, the balipīṭha, literally 'bench for offerings,' because it rests on a pedestal that can be used as a devotional table. Mount and lotus bud are completed by the towering metal flagpole (*dhvajastambha*) behind, which will be missing only if the temple roof is too low (as is quite often the case in emigrant temple buildings).

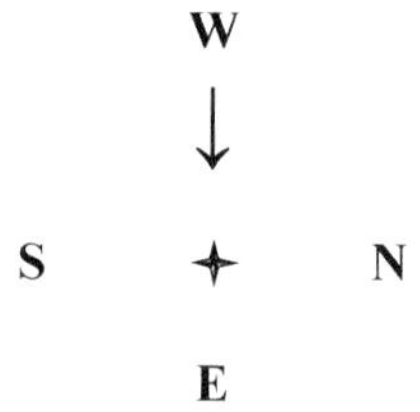

Ideally, this main entrance is where the main deity looks, in the east. On the left side of the entrance gate, to the north, stands a shrine (*maṇḍapa*) for the chief guard of the temple, i.e. for Śiva Bhairava. Śiva is in his awe-inspiring manifestation, recognisable by a trident and his dog, which usually peeps around from behind his right lower leg.

The northern wall. Moreover, along the north wall, we will come across two more shrines, one for the Nine Planets (Navagraha), astrological bodies that are believed by pious devotees to possess forceful, even dangerous powers. They are made of granite, too. The other shrine is the 'spring pavilion' (*vasantamaṇḍapa*), which houses the 'festival statues' (*utsavamūrti*). These are made of bronze – often extremely valuable – and unlike the sthalamūrtis, they *may* be removed from their places, especially during the great annual temple festival (*mahotsava*) in June/July, when the bronze effigy of the chief deity is carried in a solemn procession through the streets and alleys around the temple.

Devī Temple
(Ideal Type)
North

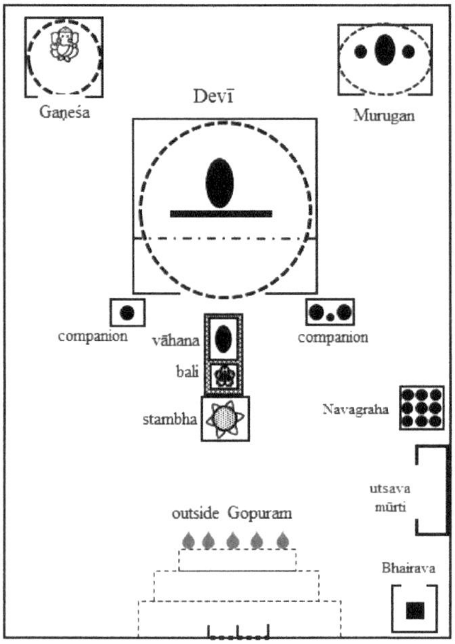

main entrance
South

Liṅga Temple
(Ideal Type)
West

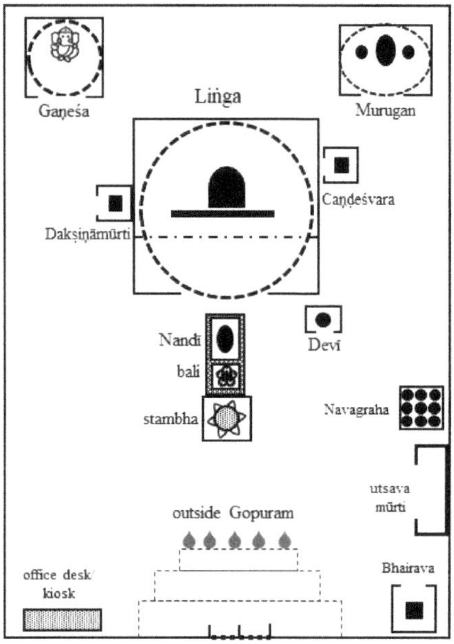

main entrance
East

And now to the differences between the four varieties of Śaiva Tamil temples. It must be underlined in the first place, that all these temples belong to the middle level of what we have termed *mainstream* Hinduism at the outset of this introduction. And this classification will explain many peculiarities. Therefore Gaṇeśa and Murugan are not regarded as divine beings with a quite heterogeneous religious-historical background in the *substratum*, but (according to *mainstream* legends from the Sanskrit epics, chiefly the *Purāṇas*) as brothers. To be exact, as half-brothers, for only Gaṇeśa is said to be Pārvatī's son. Śiva's spouse modelled him out of the remnants of the beauty-paste for her body and breathed him to life; whereas Murugan, who became the god of war, emerged from the semen of his father Śiva and was nourished by his wet-nurses and foster-mothers, the Pleiades. This is why he is also called Ṣaṇmukha, the 'Six-headed One,' because in India and Sri Lanka, people appear to see only *six* Pleiades.

The shrines behind the sanctissimum. This also explains why, in the south-west corner behind the sanctissimum, in a Gaṇeśa temple, there is the shrine of a Devī, thought of – in the *mainstream* – as Gaṇeśa's mother, who deserves a place on the right side; and why, in a Murugan temple, the mother must be content with the left side behind the dominant god Murugan (usually, however, there is an additional pavilion for Durgā at the south wall in the war-god's temples). The respective half-brother, Murugan or Gaṇeśa, has his pavilion in the opposite corner: Murugan in the north-east, Gaṇeśa in the south-west. In a temple dedicated to one of their parents, be it Śiva or Pārvatī, the half-brothers both have their place behind mother or father, Gaṇeśa to the right and Murugan with his two consorts to the left.

The shrines in front of the sanctissimum. Now we turn to the area in front of the main shrine. In the north-eastern direction, in front of the sanctissimum of a Gaṇeśa temple, we will perceive a shrine or an altar with Śiva's symbol, the Liṅga. In a Śiva temple, there is a shrine for Śiva's spouse, the Devī, on this spot. In the temples of Murugan and those of the Devī, we find pedestals, altars or pavilions with quite different companions on both sides before the sanctum sanctorum.

The smallest shrine in a temple is reserved for the general of Śiva's demonic hordes. He is named Caṇḍeśvara, the 'Fierce Lord.' He keeps watch at the outer side of the northern wall of the sanctissimum. In Śiva temples, sometimes also in kōvils (Tamil for 'temple') of Murugan, there will be, at the opposite, southern wall, a niche for the preaching Śiva Dakṣiṇāmūrti ('Śiva, the Southern Sculpture').

The south-eastern corner of a temple would be vacant for practical purposes. Usually, there is a small kiosk, where the visitors can buy devotional items such as pūjā tickets, incense, oil lamps, coconuts, pictures of saints, etc. This would also be the place of residence for the porter or temple warden.

Tamil Śaiva temples thus reflect a popular motif, namely that of the peaceful family life of god Śiva as *pater familiās*. He resides on the mountain Kailāsa in the Himālayas, together with his consort Umā (also called Pārvatī, 'Daughter of the mountains') and both their sons, Gaṇeśa and Murugan. Each of the four deities is usually accompanied by the respective mount. Not only the mural (opposite page) in the Kāmākṣī temple in Māṅgāḍu, South India, but also many devotional pictures, or a frieze on the Murugan-Kārttikeya temple in Mādampē, Sri Lankā, present this still-life of the 'holy family.'

Gaṇeśa Temples

‘Gaṇeśa in the Fig Tree’
The Āśvattha-Vṛkṣa-Vināyaka Kōvil in T. Nagar

A bird’s eye view of the Āśvattha-Vṛkṣa-Vināyaka Kōvil

Typically, a Śaiva temple is constructed around a natural sanctuary, for example a conspicuous-looking piece of stone which might be interpreted as a Śivaliṅga. Therefore, Śaiva temples more often than not, are built upon ancient places of worship which were already considered as holy sites in the cults and rituals of the substratum and have maintained their position in today’s mainstream Hinduism.

Let us take as an example, a relatively recent temple dedicated to the popular elephant-headed god Gaṇeśa. This is located in T. Nagar, a suburb of Chennai, capital of the South Indian state of Tamil Nadu. The small temple is situated on a lively shopping street (96, Usman Road). Inaugurated in the year 1992, it is known under the name of *Āśvattha-Vṛkṣa-Vināyaka Kōvil*, the ‘Temple of Gaṇeśa in the Fig Tree.’

Temple roof and fig tree
from the inside

The temple is built around a magnificent fig tree, which rises through an aperture out of the roof of the temple hall. It is right behind the sanctissimum, where the granite statue of Lord Gaṇeśa is placed, overshadowing the whole temple structure.

The special feature of this fig tree is a branch knot – or 'bulge' in the trunk – which reminds the spectator of the head of an elephant. In addition, ancient snake stones, called nāgakkals, are placed around the trunk of the tree. The veneration of trees, as well as of snakes, especially cobras, is a well-known part of the archaic cult of fertility of substratum Hinduism. Up to the present day, such nāgakkals can frequently be seen all over India and Sri Lanka.

The branch knot resembling an elephant's head, however, predestined this place of worship to become the site for a temple dedicated to the elephant-headed god, Gaṇeśa.

Prior to the construction of the temple, the fig tree and its fork, which looks like an elephant's head and trunk, were in all probability worshipped at the street corner. It is a common custom all over India, especially in big cities like Chennai, to place pictures or statues of deities at road sides or in alleys, thus creating microplaces of veneration. The devotees offer fresh flowers and fruits on a daily basis, light oil lamps, burn incense and decorate the statues with paint. The same custom can be observed in Mauritius for example, where, quite unexpectedly, one will find little Gaṇeśa shrines on the beach next to the Indian Ocean (see p. 287).

'One day,' a member of the temple trust informs us, 'a picture of Gaṇeśa was found in the fig tree.' This event seems to have been the reason for actually building the present-day temple, integrating the fig tree into the kōvil structure by letting it grow out of the temple roof.

Branch knot or bulge resembling
an elephant's trunk

Nāgakkal – snake stones in the T. Nagar fig tree temple

Thus, the temple structure clearly gives evidence of the first level in the development of Śaivism, i. e. the folk-religious substratum.

This neighbourhood temple is smoothly integrated into a flourishing shopping area with shops offering jewellery, textiles like saris and articles for everyday use. Proprietors and customers are mainly Muslims rather than Hindus. There are also a lot of restaurants. The temple is situated right opposite the *Guruprakasa Hotel and Restaurant*. There are temples of Śiva and Veṅkateśvara at a distance of only 200 metres.

Gaṇeśa is the patron of merchants; accordingly, the temple is frequented by businessmen and clerks of the local shopping mall. These visitors, in the late afternoon, after business hours, use to complete a quick clockwise circumambulation (*pradakṣiṇā*) around Gaṇeśa's statue to request economic success from the god in his manifestation as Vināyaka, 'Remover of obstacles.'

Opening hours are daily between sunrise and sunset. At nights, the huge double gate of the sanctum is closed. The temple trust is called *A.V.V.-Bhakta Jana Sabhā* ('Society of Devotees of Vināyaka/Gaṇeśa in the Fig Tree'). The main sponsor is said to be a rich businessman from the immediate neighbourhood.

Our guides were an elderly gentleman who introduced himself as a member of the temple trust and a courteous brahmin of around thirty years old. The brahmin disapproved of us taking direct photographs of the main statue of Gaṇeśa. This also made a frontal picture of the whole temple interior impossible.

Times of visit: February 26 and 27, 2002, around 17.45 – 18.30 hrs.
Address: Ashvattha Vriksha Vinayagar Kōvil, 96, Usman Road, T. Nagar, Chennai 600017, Tamil Nadu, India.

Temple brahmin
Āśvattha-Vṛkṣa-Vināyaka Kōvil, Chennai

Āśvattha-Vṛkṣa-Vināyaka Kōvil, Chennai

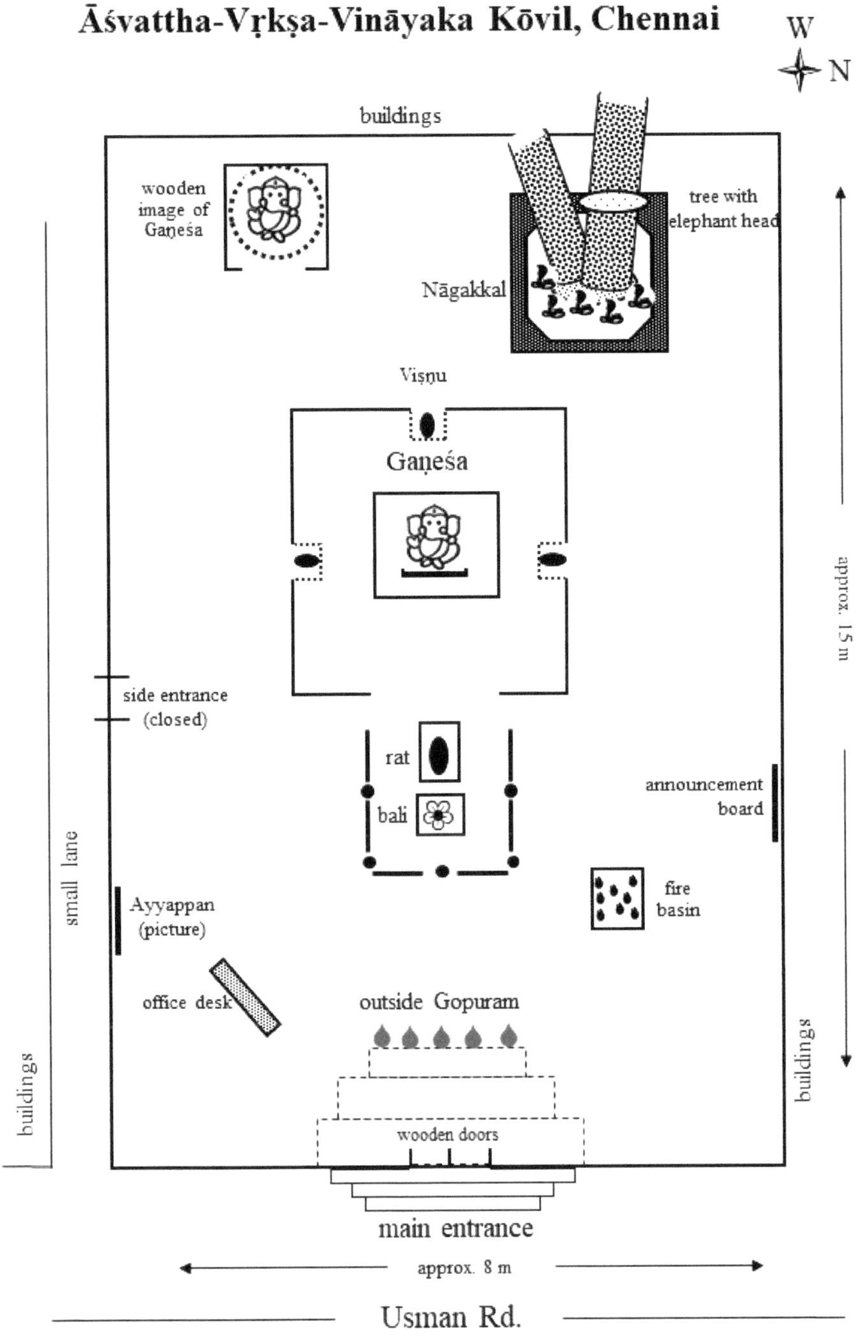

‘Gaṇeśa in Germany’
A Tour of the Siddhi-Vināyaka Temple in Hamm

Temple entrance

Temple History and Organisation

The Siddhi-Vināyaka Temple in Hamm, Germany, is dedicated to the elephant-headed, single-tusked, pot-bellied god Gaṇeśa in his manifestation as Siddhi-Vināyaka, the ‘Leader to Success (who removes the obstacles)’ or Vighneśvara, the ‘Lord who removes the obstacles.’ The temple society or temple trust was founded by the constitutional meeting on January 12, 1994. On May 10, 1994, it was registered as a public charity, as ‘Sri Sithivinayagar-Tempel Hamm e. V.’ (e. V. for ‘eingetragener Verein’, ‘registered society’).

The consecration ceremony (or *kumbhābhiṣeka*, its Sanskrit designation) was celebrated on June 12, 1994, which makes the Siddhi-Vināyaka temple in Hamm the oldest Tamil temple in Germany.

After the municipal building control office in Hamm had given permission for a conversion of the building (which had previously been used as a warehouse by the local haulage contractor, 'Spediteur' Drewitz), the consecration was possible. The consecration ritual was celebrated by two brahmins, Satkuru Sivaya Subramuniya Swami from Kuwei in Hawai (who had also presented the central cult statue of god Gaṇeśa to the temple society) and by Sivachariya Thilagam Siva Srirathina Somaskanda Kurukkal from Denmark, a former priest of the Selvavinayagar Kōvil in Kandy, Sri Lanka.

The flagpole (*dhvajhastambha*) in front of the central shrine of Gaṇeśa was erected on August 19, 1996.

The temple society or trust, an officially acknowledged charity, employs a temple custodian and a temple priest, a brahmin. The priests work in a Tamil temple for a limited period of time, normally four years, and return to their home temples afterwards. At present (2001), the former auxiliary priest, Sivasri Sandrasegara Ravindranatha Kurukkal, is permanently employed as the main priest.

The temple is financed exclusively by donations, either from members of the temple trust, or from devotees who pay for the temple services and rituals of worship.

The temple society appoints a committee for the management of the temple. One of the founding members of the temple society was Mr. Nataraja Paskaradas who also acted as elected chairman of the temple committee from January 1997 to December 1998. Mr. Paskaradas had been one of the very first Tamil refugees in Germany. He was soon granted the status of an asylum seeker, attained German citizenship and has settled in Hamm with his wife and three children. In the meantime, like many other Tamil refugees in Hamm, he has fully integrated into the local population and has acquired many social contacts. His wife works as an administrative and jurisdictional translator, the children have completed their higher education and they all have a perfect knowledge of the German language.

For Tamil immigrants like the Paskaradas family, the temple is a symbol of their original culture. It is a piece of their home country in foreign surroundings. By means of the cultivation of their temples, they wish to make it

Gaṇeśa – frieze

clear to the local German population – but also to their own children who are born, brought up and educated in Germany – that their Hindu religion must be taken as seriously and earnestly as the Christian faith. Indeed, Śaivism and Śāktism, through their thousands of years of tradition, the intensity of their spirituality and the sophisticated intellectual level of their Āgamic rituals and Śaiva Siddhāntic theologems, offer the devotees spiritual possibilities which need not shy away from any comparison with Christianity.

The flagpole (*dhvajastambha*) in front of the sanctissimum

Pantheon and Iconography

As previously noted, the god Gaṇeśa forms the centre of devotion in this temple. In his manifestation as Vighneśvara, 'the Lord who removes the obstacles,' he functions as the patron of business and science. But Gaṇeśa is not the one and only god to be venerated in this temple.

Tamil Śaivism is neither monotheistic nor polytheistic. It belongs to a type of religion which is termed 'henotheistic,' meaning that a devotee worships one special god as his favourite deity, his iṣṭadeva, literally his 'desired god.' This devotion does not exclude other gods and goddesses. For special reasons the devotee would also pray to a goddess for example, a Devī, if she or he desires children. Thus, in each and every Tamil Śaiva temple, there are a lot of other gods and goddesses positioned in their shrines around the main shrine, the sanctissimum (Sanskrit *mūlagarbha* or *garbhagṛha*).

Flagpole (detail)

Gaṇeśa – utsavamūrti

There are two types of statues to be found in these temples. The more important ones, the sthalamūrtis ('place-statues') are immovable and made of black granite. They are implanted permanently during the initial consecration of the temple and must never be removed from their shrines. The other type is represented by the mobile ones, made of bronze, which, during the 'great festival' are carried around the temple through the streets and alleys in the neighbourhood.

That is why they are called utsavamūrti, 'festival statue.' Both kinds, granite and bronze statues, are manufactured by highly specialised artists in prominent workshops in South India, like those in Mahābalipuram or Kumbhakonam. The larger sculptures cost approximately between 3.000 and 5.000 Euro.

The traditional direction which the main deity of a Śaiva temple faces is the east. The Siddhi-Vināyaka temple, however, is orientated towards the north-east. This is because the building in which it is set up was not newly constructed but is a rented former warehouse, the rent being 1.000 Euro per month. Thus, the orientation of the whole temple setup was pre-directed.

Gaṇeśa's sthalamūrti in the main shrine

The following description and pictures document the state of the temple on January 14, 2001, at about 7 p.m., after the conclusion of the pūjā ceremonies of the Taipoṅkal festival which is comparable with the western Thanksgiving Day. *Tai-p-poṅkal* is the name of the first day of *Tai* (the ninth Tamil month, Sanskrit *pauṣa*, about January/February). It is celebrated by eating *poṅkal*, sweetened rice, which is 'seasoned with salt, pepper, cumin seeds and ghee' (*Tamil Lexicon*, s. v. *poṅkal*). It is a 'solar festival when the sun enters Capricorn and takes a northward course, being the first day of the month Tai, when *poṅkal* is prepared as an offering' (loc. cit.).

Immediately in front of the sanctissimum we can see the abovementioned flagpole (*dhvajastambha*), the granite lotus bud (*balipīṭha*) and Gaṇeśa's mount (*vāhana*), the rat, facing its lord.

The black granite statue of Gaṇeśa himself, in his manifestation as Siddhi-Vināyaka or Vighneśvara, resides in the centre of the temple, in the central maṇḍapa or shrine, the garbhagṛha (sanctissimum). It is flanked to the right and left by a painted image of a door-keeper.

Gaṇeśa's door-keeper in front of the sanctissimum

The granite lotus bud and Gaṇeśa's mount, the rat, in front of the sanctissimum

Now, after the pūjā ceremony, the god is surrounded by burning oil-lamps, incense, food and beverages, flowers and Bilva leaves. The god stands (compare picture on p. 13) beneath a wreath of flames; a silver plate serves as his halo. The sthalamūrti of the elephant-headed deity is adorned over and over until it is beyond recognisability.

His tummy (Gaṇeśa is fond of sweet laḍḍūs) is draped with a scarlet-red silken sash; silk clothes in diverse shades of red hang around his shoulders, even decorating the wreath of flames behind him; a garland (*mālā*) of yellow and white petals, accentuated by green leaves, falls downwards right to his knees; around his neck he wears a heavy gold chain.

On his black trunk we observe several yantras (magical diagrams) painted in yellow saffron and red colour – most noticeably the three horizontal streaks of the Śaiva forehead mark (*tripuṇḍra*). The small elephant-eyes are colourfully accentuated as well. A red semi-precious stone, the forehead-jewel, is resplendent in the middle of a golden (or perhaps gilded?) crown (*ratnamukuṭa*).

Granite statue of goddess Durgā

Durgā's yantra

Vighneśvara's accompanying deities – or rather their sthalamūrtis – are also housed in their own, though smaller, maṇḍapas in the round of the temple hall. To the left and right of the main shrine – in the south and the west – we come across the most important of them, as far as the divine hierarchy is concerned.

When we walk around the main shrine of Gaṇeśa, keeping it on the righthand side, thus performing a traditional pradakṣiṇā or circumambulation, we first pass, in the south, the shrine of the goddess Durgā, holding a trident. She wears an orange flowered silk dress, a long chain of pearls in front of her body, a shorter golden necklace and a mālā of white asters. Behind her, again, we observe a silvery shining wreath of flames.

The goddess's yantra of beaten copper, leaning against her knees, is remarkable. A yantra is a diagram, the microcosmic representation of a temple. By means of magical formulas, called mantra in Sanskrit, a chosen deity, in this case Durgā, can be captivated and kept spell-bound (cf. U. Schneider, *Einführung in den Hinduismus*, 1989, pp. 197f). On Durgā's rather common yantra, we can see, starting from the periphery, the square area of the temple walls. There are apertures on all four sides, representing the temple gates. Extending inwards are three concentric circle lines, then a round of sixteen lotus petals, another circle line, eight further lotus petals, then a last circle which encompasses the inner third of the diameter. The centre of the yantra is covered by a tangle of major and minor triangles laid one on top of the other, which intersect each other regularly, until a triangular centre emerges at the core – the microcosmic heart of the macrocosmic temple as the seat of the goddess.

Mural of the eight-armed Durgā

On the wall behind and above her shrine there is a mural of Durgā: the goddess as a beautiful young woman, with eight arms, riding a tiger. Her right, lower, front hand is held out to the observer in the gesture of providing shelter (*abhayadamudrā*), the palm to the front with fingers upright. With the remaining seven hands, she holds (counted clock-wise from the right lower hand): a trident, a sword, a disk, a lotus and a mace, in addition to a bow and finally, the conch.

The next shrine, in the west behind the sanctissimum, belongs to Gaṇeśa's half-brother, Murugan.

Murugan Ṣaṇmukha, the 'Six-headed One'

Murugan with his consorts

He is easily recognised by his lance (Tamil *vēl*), which he holds in his right hand, rested on the ground. The four-armed young god of war is wrapped in marvellous, colourful, red-orange-green garments. He wears a heavy chain of pearls around his neck, covered by a garland of white and yellow asters. His two consorts stand by his sides: on his left (in the god's perspective) Vallī (also called Mahāvallī) and on his right Devānī (or Devasenā). The mural on the wall beside the shrine depicts Murugan, here with six heads (Ṣaṇmukha) and twelve arms, riding his mount, the peacock.

On our tour of the Vighneśvara temple we pass the entrance door to our left and approach the shrine of the Śivaliṅga, containing two stone statues. The larger one represents the god Śiva in the form of the Liṅga, i. e. the phallus, crowned by a metal cobra, its hood dilated. The Liṅga is decorated by the white-painted tripuṇḍra, the Śaiva emblem. It is draped with red and yellow clothes and adorned by a mālā of white asters. At the front lie the green aster leaves, food on a thālī and a banana. On the god's left hand side stands the four-armed goddess Umā (aka Pārvatī), who is much less groomed than her spouse.

Śivaliṅga with Umā

The next shrine, to the right, presents the Nine Planets (Navagraha), which will very rarely be missed out of a Tamil temple.

The appellation Nine 'Planets' must not be misunderstood in an astronomical sense; they are purely astrological bodies. They consist of the five planets: Mercury, Venus, Mars, Jupiter and Saturn, visible with the naked eye. In addition there is the Sun god, the Moon god and the demon Rāhu, who causes the solar and lunar eclipses by swallowing the sun and the moon, and finally the demon of the comets and meteors, Ketu. The Sun god always occupies the centre, facing east. He is surrounded squarely by the other figures; none of them must look at another.

The Nine Planets (Navagraha)

Śiva Bhairava

On the left side of the wall opposite the sanctissimum, in the north-east, stands the shrine of Bhairava, a fearsome manifestation of Śiva. His symbols are a trident and a dog. The trident is leaning against the statue, which is nearly covered up with gold and blue garments. The dog is supposed to peep out behind the god's right leg, but is unfortunately hidden by the costume.

We have already mentioned some of the colourful murals of the gods and goddesses, which decorate the temple walls (Gaṇeśa, Durgā and Murugan). There are several others, for instance of Saturn, of Śiva and Pārvatī, the androgynous Śiva Ardhanārīśvara, the five-headed Gaṇeśa Pañcamukha, the South Indian village-god Ayyappan and the four Tamil saints: Tirujñānasaṃbandha, Appar, Sundaramūrti and Mānikkavacagar.

Saturn, the ominous planet; clad in a black dhotī; holding a bow and arrow,
a half-opened lotus flower and showing the gesture of granting boons (*varada*).
Mural behind the shrine of the Nine Planets

The androgynous Śiva Ardhanārīśvara
'Śiva who is half woman'

The South Indian vill age-god Ayyappan

'Five-headed' Gaṇeśa Pañcamukha

All these murals were painted by the artist Arul Joseph.

Part of the temple is also a refectory or dining hall, a bathroom and toilets, and the adjacent quarters of the brahmin and the custodian.

Spacious shelves contain the pūjā utensils like banana leaves, silk shawls, coconuts, camphor, incense, ghee and metal vessels, thus completing the temple equipment.

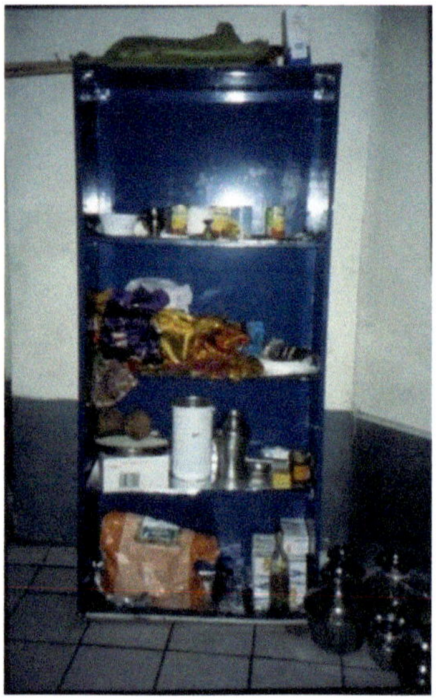

Shelves containing pūjā utensils

As to the cult of the temple, there are three kinds of ceremonies: the everyday rituals of worship (*pūjā*), consecration (*abhiṣeka*) and service to the statues (*upacāra*). Also, there are more significant and more expensive ceremonies, which demand more costly donations. These are important for the maintenance of the temple, like weddings and wedding meals. There are other *rites de passages*, like name-giving ceremonies or the receiving of the sacred thread. There are festivals over the course of the year, like the harvest festival Taipoṅkal (see above, p. 13), the Great Night of Śiva, Mahāśivarātri, in March and the festival of lights, Divālī, at the end of Navarātri in October. The mahotsava ('Great Festival') of the year – the culmination of all festivals – is when the great procession around the temple takes place. On this occasion, a multitude of pilgrims from all over Germany and even from foreign countries visit this Gaṇeśa temple.

However, these exotic spectacles are not why the Siddhi-Vināyaka kōvil in Hamm has such special importance. It is not the intention of this temple's society to draw attention to itself unnecessarily – this temple flourishes in the background; it is not noticed very much by the German public, but it is revered by the Tamil refugees all over Europe. This temple cultivates an orthodox Śaiva Hinduism, in an authentic and unadulterated manner. It builds bridges between the old home in Sri Lanka and the new home in Germany, and thus satisfies the elementary spiritual needs of the Tamil immigrants.

Time of visit: January 14, 2001.
Address: Sri Sithivinayagar Tempel, Ferdinand Poggel-Str. 25, Hamm, Germany.

Siddhi-Vināyaka Temple, Hamm

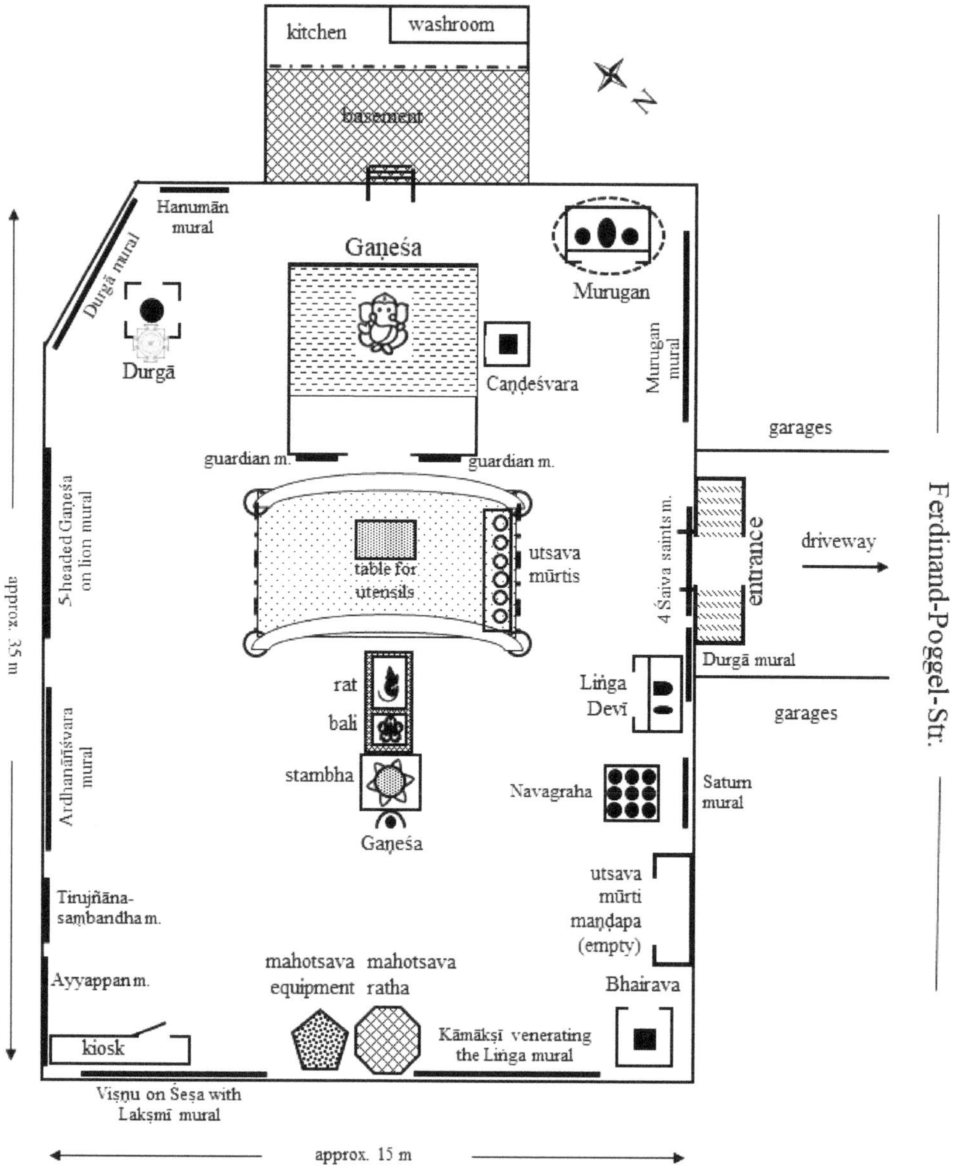

‘Gaṇeśa with the Ruby’
The Śrī Māṇikya-Vināyaka Kōvil in Bambalapiṭiya

Temple interior

In order to set up and install their own temples overseas, Sri Lankan Tamils may use the ‘Vorbildtempel’ (model-temple) of Śrī Māṇikya-Vināyaka Kōvil in Bambalapiṭiya, a busy suburb of Colombo, the capital of Sri Lanka. The temple is also known as Sri Manikka-pillair Temple, and formerly as Sri Siddhivinayagar Temple. The name can be translated as ‘The Temple (*kōvil*) of the Lord (*śrī*) with the Ruby (*māṇikya*), Who Clears away (*vināyaka*) the Obstacles.’

The original temple was founded in 1910. Rebuilding started in 1996, when a seven-storied gopuram – a temple tower above the main entrance gate – was erected with the help of renowned temple architects (*sthapati* or *śilpaśāstrī*) from South India, and the work was completed by the inauguration ceremony (*kumbhābhiṣeka*) in 2001.

The gopuram

Signs advertising the name of the architect (*sthapati*)
of the gopuram in Tamil and English

Entering the front hall, used for weddings

Our visit took place on a Tuesday morning, on a public holiday (not of the Hindu, but the Muslim calendar as it was the prophet's birthday). Banks were closed and the temple was swarming with devotees, for whom a variety of ceremonies were being officiated. During our nearly three-hour visit, approximately 300 devotees came, paid homage and left again. The temple seems to be a centre of the Gaṇeśa cult in Bambalapiṭiya and especially in the adjoining suburb of Vällawatta, which is also called 'Little Jaffna' because of the many Tamils residing there.

When entering the temple, the visitor first crosses a front hall. (Compare ground plan at the end of this chapter.) This foyer, used by the temple society for major celebrations – mostly weddings – is nearly as spacious as the temple hall itself. The ceiling is richly ornamented with large open lotus blossoms. Friezes on the next wall, above the connecting door to the temple interior, depict varied manifestations of Gaṇeśa (*Gaṇa-īśa*, 'Lord of Śiva's troops'). Two large murals, to the left and the right, illustrate legends taken from his mythology. The fresco on the opposite wall, behind us, to the right (south-west corner) shows the wedding of Śiva and his spouse Umā, also called Pārvatī ('Daughter of the Mountain').

Gaṇeśa as Dvāra-Gaṇapati
Gaṇeśa as doorkeeper'

Murugan as Daṇḍāyudhapāṇi
'With a stick as weapon in his hand'

We now enter the actual temple hall and stand right in the middle, between two shrines housing the gods Gaṇeśa and Murugan. The maṇḍapa ('shrine') to our right (south-west) is dedicated to Gaṇeśa in his function as door-keeper. As such, he is called Dvāra-Gaṇapati (*dvāra*, 'door', or 'gate,' *Gaṇapati* is the same as *Gaṇeśa*). It is evident that Dvāra-Gaṇapati is located at the entrance, to have the maximum impact on the visitors.

The shrine on the other side, to our left (north-west) is dedicated to Murugan as Daṇḍāyudhapāṇi, Murugan in his manifestation as the god 'Who carries a stick as weapon in his hand,' a weapon he can use to assist his half-brother Gaṇeśa to keep watch over the entrance. The stick here is not to be confused with the lance (*vēl*), the main symbol of the god Murugan.

In addition to the watch-keepers Gaṇeśa and Murugan we see a third guardian deity near the entrance. It is Bhairava, Lord Śiva in his 'Dreadful' manifestation, who is generally to be found directly beyond the entrance to the temple hall; here, his pavilion stands in front of Gaṇeśa's.

The pavilion houses, beside Śiva-Bhairava, the demon Iṭumpaṉ. Having been slain and immediately revived by Murugan, Iṭumpaṉ became Murugan's most obedient servant and faithful devotee. The statue of Iṭumpaṉ carries a pole on his shoulders with jugs resembling calabashes hanging down from each side. Iṭumpaṉ is escorted on his right and left by two huge mastiff-like dogs. Sometimes these hounds complement Bhairava's symbol, the dog, which regularly peeps out from behind the god's legs to the right side.

Iṭumpaṉ

Whereas the entrance of a Tamil Śaiva temple is normally guarded by just one figure, namely Bhairava, here we find – and this is a special feature of this temple – four watchkeepers altogether: Gaṇeśa, Murugan, Bhairava and Iṭumpaṉ.

Let us now turn to the main maṇḍapa, which is the abode of Śrī Māṇikya-Vināyaka, the 'Lord with the Ruby, Who Clears away the Obstacles.' The sanctissimum is located in a raised pavilion at the centre of the eastern half of the temple hall. The main statue inside is adored by Lord Gaṇeśa's mount (*vāhana*), a rat, a small granite figure immediately in front of him.

Mani Iyer, one of the temple brahmins, stated that the 'very powerful' main statue (*sthalamūrti*) of Gaṇeśa was once found by fishermen 'in the sea,' in the immediate vicinity of the present temple. Similar to the temple of Gaṇeśa in the Fig Tree in T. Nagar, Chennai, which initiated the present series of sketches of Tamil temples, an object of nature (in this case a stone, which looked strikingly like a statue of Gaṇeśa), was taken and made the centre of a Śaiva temple and the temple was built around it. This tradition can be understood as a reflection of the original idea that a Śaiva temple is built around a remarkable natural object – be it a stone in the shape of a Liṅga, or a tree.

From its outward appearance, it seems that the present statue in the main maṇḍapa is not the original stone image of Gaṇeśa found in the sea. The sthalamūrti of Śrī Māṇikya-Vināyaka in the temple appears to be a granite statue, like the other stone images, which originate from Tamil Nadu. Mr. A. Nadarajah, a member of the temple trust, thinks that they came from the town of 'Tirupur' (= Tiruppūr), but Mani Iyer gave us different information, viz. Mahābalipuram, famous for its sculptures and artwork.

Sanctissimum with the statue of Gaṇeśa

Sthalamūrti of Gaṇeśa
His mount, the rat, in the foreground

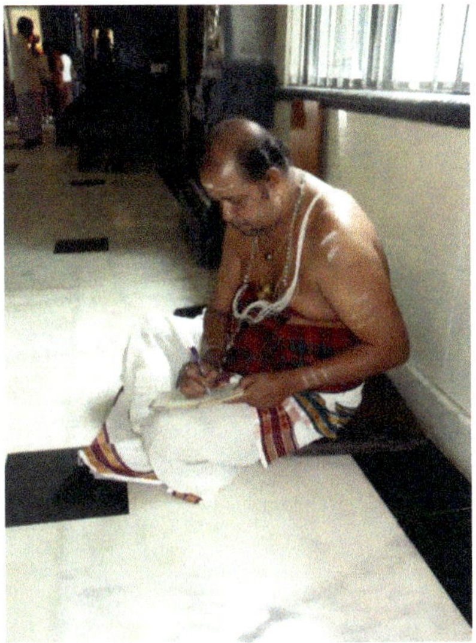

Mani Iyer

Mani Iyer, according to his self-introduction, is one of the leading brahmins of the temple. His full name reads Sivasri B. Sitsabesa Kurukkal, 'Sivacharyamani' (*Śivācāryamaṇi*), 'Agama Soodamani' (*Āgama-cūḍāmaṇi*). Usually, he practices astrology while sitting beside the main maṇḍapa of the temple. He turned out to be very cooperative and obliging, and was so kind as to function as our guide and contact during our visit. Mani Iyer visited Berlin to participate in the consecration ceremony of a Tamil temple in 2000.

During our visit we learned some details about the family tradition in this temple. One of Mani Iyer's sons was also in charge of a temple duty: he performed the pūjā in front of the Nine Planets. Although it was a Tuesday, special honour was given to Sūrya, the sun god, patron saint of Sunday.

The layout of the temple is somewhat puzzling and does not correspond with the orthodox arrangements of traditional Śivaïte Gaṇeśa temples. The main statue of Gaṇeśa in the sanctissimum does not face east, but west, the direction of the busy Galle Road and the sea. To be precise, it faces west with a slight turn to the south, by approximately 10 degrees.

Mr. Nadarajah explains this abnormality by the necessity of embedding the temple in the neighbourhood premises. There was no other possibility except the present orientation. Mani Iyer assured us that the god had been asked in a ceremony about his altered position and had graciously declared his consent. Two other temples in the neighbourhood on Galle Road also look west.

The frescoes on the roof of the sanctissimum do follow the traditional order: Brahmā to the north, Gaṇeśa accompanied by Viṣṇu and Śiva to the east and Śiva Dakṣiṇāmūrti, as his name ('the Southern Statue') requires, to the south.

In order to complete our tour of this temple, we now start a circumambulation (*pradakṣiṇā*) around the sanctissimum. The northern wall is decorated with the festival statues (*utsavamūrti*), which will be carried in a solemn procession around the temple during the annual Great Festival, the mahotsava. These are mainly the bronze statues of Gaṇeśa, here depicted as Gaṇeśa Pañcamukha, 'Five Heads,' and Murugan Ṣaṇmukha, 'Six Heads.' His festival statue is accompanied by his consorts, the dark-complexioned Vallī and the fair Devānī.

Brahmā

Gaṇeśa accompanied by Śiva and Viṣṇu

Śiva Dakṣiṇāmūrti

Altar of the Nine Planets (Navagraha)

We keep walking to the rear of the temple, eastwards, and come across the altar of the Nine Planets in the north-east corner.

It is remarkable that the Navagrahas always stand in the correct corner. The laws of magic concerning the location of the Nine Planets seem to have innate dynamics which must not be neglected under any circumstances. For a stout believer, a dialogue on an important issue, such as the place of residence, between the gracious iṣṭa-devatā Gaṇeśa and the devotees seems possible, but not with the dreaded Nine Planets.

On the opposite southern wall, we find, beside the fire basin, the shrine of the goddess Durgā. She has the main maṇḍapa of Gaṇeśa in her immediate view.

Sūrya in the centre of the Nine Planets

Durgā Mahiṣamardinī

An exceptional decorative feature of the Māṇikya-Vināyaka Kōvil is the six pillars in the southern part of the inner temple hall. At a height of approximately 1.50 meters, they carry the sculptures of Apsarases, the heavenly maidens. All of them are different, from the colour of their saris, the type of hairstyle, the objects in their hands even to the number of arms they have.

Before we could complete our tour, the temple was closed rather abruptly at 11:30 a.m. The shrines were quickly cleaned and swept, their wooden doors as well as the heavy main temple gate were shut, and the priests were eager to get to their lunch.

The heavy wooden temple door

Time of visit: April 11, 2006, 8:50-11:30 a.m.
Address: Sri Manikka Vinayagar Kōvil Colombo, 359, Galle Road, Bambalapitiya, Colombo-04, Sri Lanka.
Phone: 2583315.

Śrī Māṇikya-Vināyaka Kōvil, Bambalapiṭiya

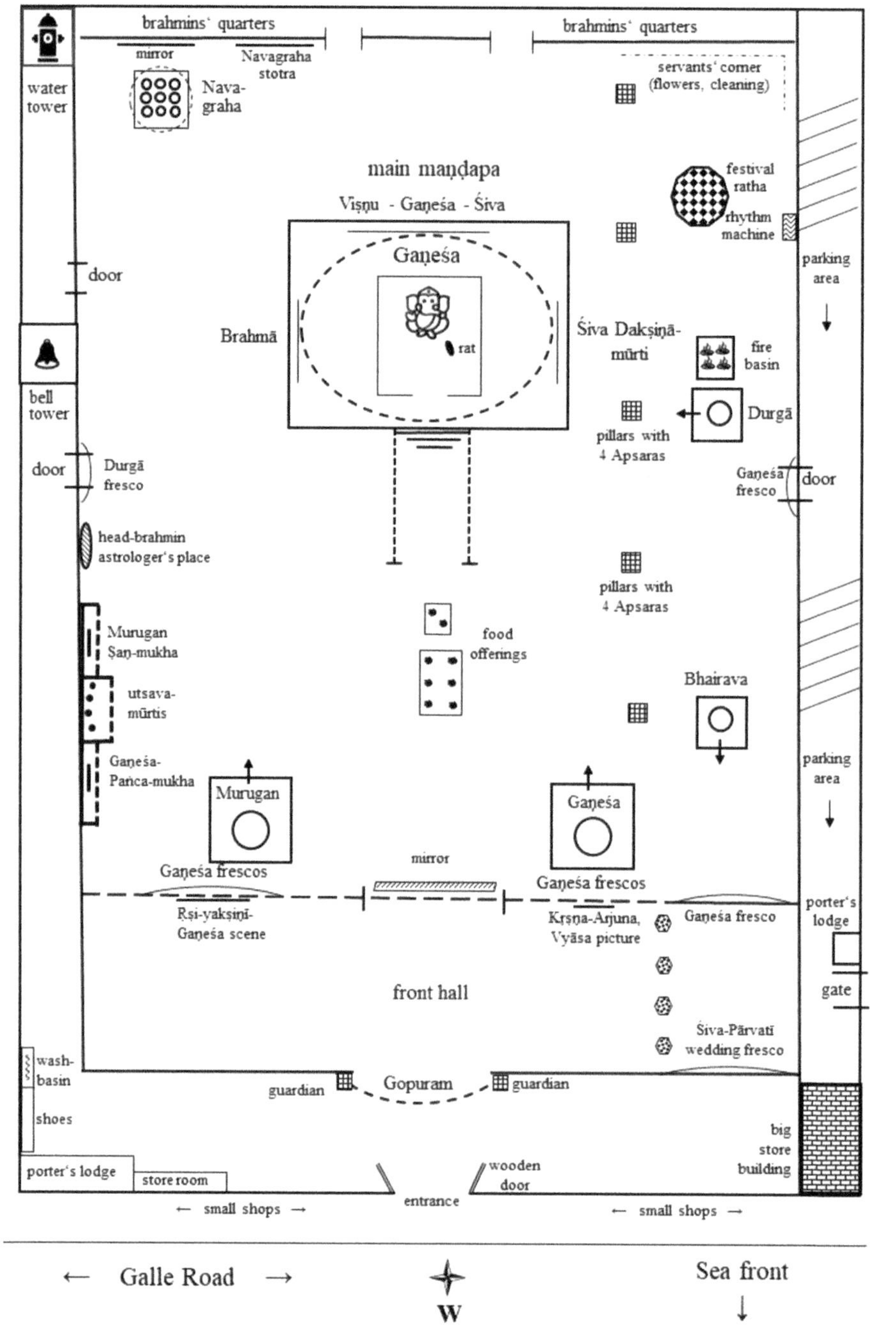

‘Gaṇeśa in Scarborough’
The Śrī Varasiddhi-Vināyaka Devasthānam in Toronto

The temple in a former truck depot

The temple is located in a former depot of heavy trucks, the juggernauts (from Sanskrit *jagan-nātha*, the colossal procession wagon in Purī, Orissa, India). The unit belongs to a row of commercial warehouses situated on an industrial site in Scarborough, a suburb of the Greater Toronto Area, Canada. In Scarborough, a large number of Sri Lankan Tamil refugees have settled. The temple’s ground plan measures approximately 60 x 25 meters. The conception and interior decoration of the temple was designed by a specialist architect named ‘Sirpakalaiyarasan’ Saravanamuththu Jeyaraja, principal of the ‘Saravanas Kalaikoodam.’ The inauguration ceremony, the Mahākumbhābhiṣeka, was held on September 19, 1999.

The Building Permit

On November 9, 1999, the Toronto East District Urban Planning and Development Services granted the building permit, consenting to carry out

The main idol of Śrī Gaṇeśa

structural alterations. The document reads:

> 'Project Description: Non-Residential Building Permit; Place of Worship; Alteration to Existing Building.'

The unit is leased. At the time of our visit the temple trust was engaged in negotiations to purchase it.

There is always the danger of the contract for the unit being terminated, if the worst comes to the worst. In such a case, the temple would have to be closed and perhaps rebuilt at another place. The temple trusts of many smaller temples must live with this kind of threat, especially those who do not have the money to buy a plot of land or a building big enough for the installation of a Hindu temple.

Mahālakṣmī

The 'Maha Kumbhabhishega Yagasala Poojas & Pratishda traditionals' were celebrated as a big event. Famous brahmins were invited for the ceremonies. These were performed by 'Viyakarana Siromani' Sivasri Poorana, 'Professor of Hindu Culture' of the 'Sri Sivananda Vidyalayam,' Batticaloa, Sri Lanka and Thiyagaraja Kurukkal, B.A. (Hons), of the Annamalai University in Chidambaram, Tamil Nadu, India.

The statues were carved from black granite stone by a noted artist, Dr. Muthaiya Sthapati, Visvabhramasri Thevasenathipati, from the famous centre of the art of sculpture, the town of Mahābalipuram in Tamil Nadu. They were installed as sthalamūrti in accordance with the ritual of the Śaiva Āgamas under the supervision of the āgamic advisor Dr. Somaskandak Kurukkal from Australia.

Murugan with consorts

Nāgabhūṣaṇī
Frieze in the roof of her maṇḍapa

Nāgabhūṣaṇī
Dressed as Sarasvatī

Our visit of the Śrī Varasiddhi-Vināyaka Devasthānam in Scarborough was on October 21st, 2004, one day before the end of the Navarātri festival, which took place that year on October, 22nd. The statues of the main deities: Gaṇeśa, Mahālakṣmī and Murugan (with his consorts Vallī and Devānī) were painted with fragrant yellow sandal paste, donned with elaborately draped saris and precious garments, and adorned with valuable jewellery and multicoloured flower garlands. The other idols were smartened up, too; the maṇḍapas of the deities as well as the whole temple were thoroughly cleaned and tidied.

The statue of Nāgabhūṣaṇī Devī, a snake-goddess, worshipped originally in a temple at Nainativu (a small island near Jaffna, Sri Lanka), was beautifully dressed and made up as Sarasvatī, goddess of wisdom, education and fine arts. The Devī was equipped with a papier-mâché image of her mount (*vāhana*), the wild goose (*haṃsa*) or the peacock (*mayūra*, in Tamil *mayi*) behind her, and her instrument, the vīṇā (the Indian lute), on her lap. This arrangement was made on the occasion of Pañcamī, the fifth day of the Navarātri festivities, when Durgā is worshipped in her aspect of Sarasvatī. Nāgabhūṣaṇī Devī, in her manifestation of the great goddess, receives the same devotion as Durgā.

At the time of the Navarātri festival, a golu is installed for nine days, a custom mostly celebrated in South India, and now transferred to the expats' community in Canada.

Golu arrangement

In their homes and temples, the devotees arrange a kind of temporary maṇḍapa with decorations of gods, goddesses, vāhanas (attributes or mounts), saints and other celestial beings. In general the objects are not expensive or of great artistic merit, but one can admire the colourful individualistic compilations. The items are blessed in the temple and carried home again when Navarātri is over.

Because of the layout of the former truck depository, the partition of the available area into the temple as well as a festivity hall was not feasible. Therefore, behind the entrance and the bathroom with the announcement board, on the right (eastern) side within the temple complex, a temporary stage for musical performances during the celebrations of Navarātri was erected.

Sitting Nandī as drummer

Music stage

Cow with electrical percussion machine

Here, too, the organisers demonstrated a special gift for lovingly detailed decorations. Even the places for putting down the musical instruments were of unique design: a standing cow carried on her back an electrical percussion machine; and an anthropomorphic Nandī, sitting with crossed legs, held the drum.

'...the sound of the drum, happily beaten by the hand of Nandī during Śiva's wild dance' – *sânandaṃ Nandi-hastâhata-muraja-rava-... Tāṇḍave Śūlapāṇer* (Bhavabhūti, *Mālatī-Mādhava*, I 1; the Sanskrit play was written about 700 A. D.)

Temple Organisation

The temple community includes approximately 10.000 individuals. The temple committee has between nine and eleven members. The founder and, at the time of our visit, chairman of the 'Temple Management Committee' is Mr. 'Sivacharya Kulabooshanam Sivasri Panchara' Vijayakumara Kurukkal, called Iyamanu Iyar by the community. He supervises and manages all of the more important or special pūjā ceremonies, thus functioning as a kind of *purohita* (Sanskrit designation of the Old Indian family priest).

Price list for pūjā services in Canadian Dollars

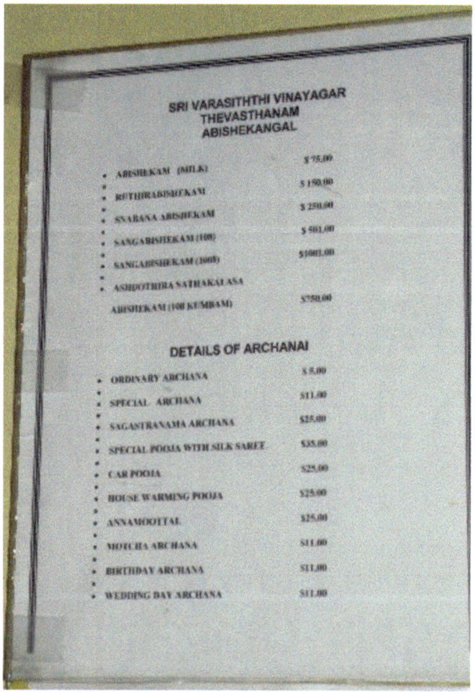

Sivasri Thiyaga Muruganantha Kurukkal is an 'extraordinary' 'Uthsava Sivacharyar (*utsava śivācārya*)', a Śaiva priest for festivities (*utsava*), who always performs the 'Alangara Kalaimani' (*Alaṃkāra Kalāmaṇi*), on Tuesdays and Fridays, and on the occasion of the Chathurthi day (*caturthī*), the annual festival in honour of Gaṇeśa, also called 'Gaṇeśa's Birthday.'

Brahmins on duty

In addition, the temple trust permanently employs three brahmins, two younger ones and a senior. The elder brahmin speaks only Tamil.

Besides the regular pūjā ceremonies for the iṣṭadevatā, the favourite and main god Lord Gaṇeśa, the brahmins also celebrate particular rituals in honour of his half-brother, the god Murugan.

A large number of devotees visit the Śrī Varasiddhi-Vināyaka temple on January, 1st. As this day is a public National Holiday, the community takes the opportunity to assemble in the temple and meet relatives and friends. Also prominently observed is the Hindu Tamil festival of Tai Pongal (*tai-p-poṅgal*). Originally a harvest festival in South India, Tai Pongal in Canada falls in the winter season, in the month of January/February. On this occasion the chief brahmin, Iyamani Iyar, usually invites a Canadian farmer to help him with his cow to perform a special pūjā for cattle.

At the time of the annual carriage festival, the rathotsava, the temple cart is drawn by a pair of horses. On this occasion, an aśvapūjā – a ceremony which has its roots in the old Vedic horse sacrifice (*aśvamedha*) – is performed on behalf of the temple.

A special gajapūjā ('elephant worship') is celebrated on Gaṇeśa caturthī, Gaṇeśa's birthday. In the evening of September 17, 2004, this event was crowned by an extraordinary highlight. A tame and very well trained elephant, named Cesar, from the Toronto zoo, was led into the temple right through the spacious entrance gates (which formerly had let the juggernauts in). Wrapped in adornments in traditional Tamil style, the animal was told to bless the devotees with his raised trunk as part of the ceremony.

Frontpage of a local newspaper showing Cesar, the elephant, during the pūjā ceremony

SATURDAY S

DON'T HAVE A COW

DEAR NHL....

A massive celebration for Lord Ganesha

Time of visit: October 21, 2004, 10:30-12:20 a.m.

Address: 3025 Kennedy Road, Scarborough, ON M1V 1S3, Canada.

Phone 416-291 8500 www.vinaayagar.com

Śrī Varasiddhi-Vināyaka Temple, Toronto

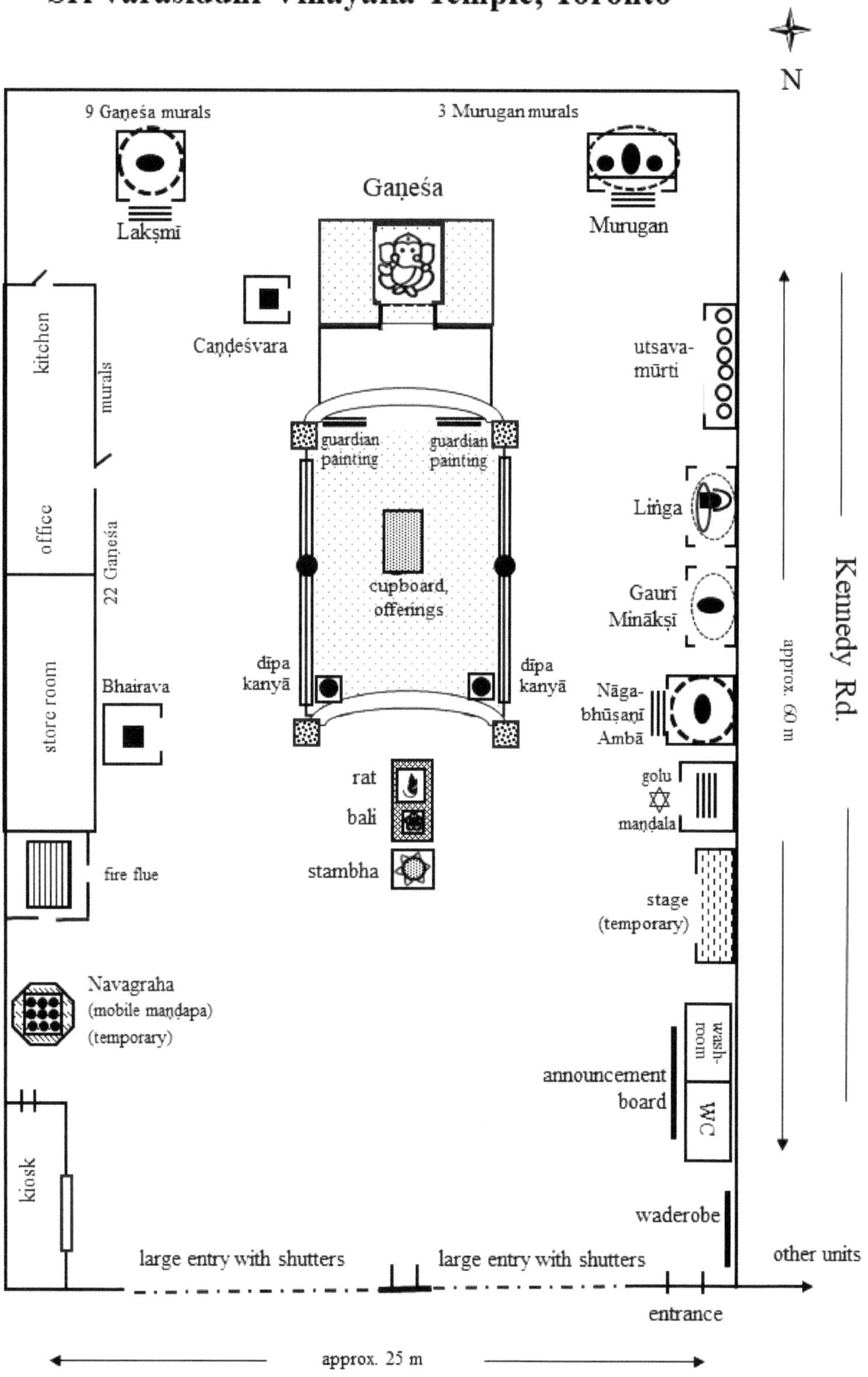

‘Gaṇeśa in Brampton’
The Kalpaka-Vināyaka Devasthānam near Toronto

The temple in a department store unit

The ‘Temple (*devasthānam*) of [Gaṇeśa] the Fulfiller (*kalpaka*, Tamil *kaṟpaka*) [of wishes] and Remover (*vināyaka*) [of obstacles]’ is located at one of the crossroads of two enormous highways, which are very common on the outskirts of Canada’s large cities. Compared with the Śrī Varasiddhi-Vināyaka Devasthānam in Scarborough, Toronto, this abode of Gaṇeśa, situated in Brampton in the vicinity of the Greater Toronto Area, makes a much more modest impression. Embedded in a corner between the Banquet Hall of an Indian restaurant called ‘Bombay Palace’ and the exhibition area of a ‘Fabulous Flea Market,’ the elephant-headed god occupies a smallish single-storied unit. Here, the statue of the main deity, Śrī Gaṇeśa, is installed according to the traditional rules, facing east.

The rent for the somewhat remote, roughly about 40 x 10 square meters unit was 3.800 Canadian Dollars per month in 2004. The inauguration ceremony (*mahākumbhābhiṣeka*) was celebrated in July 2001.

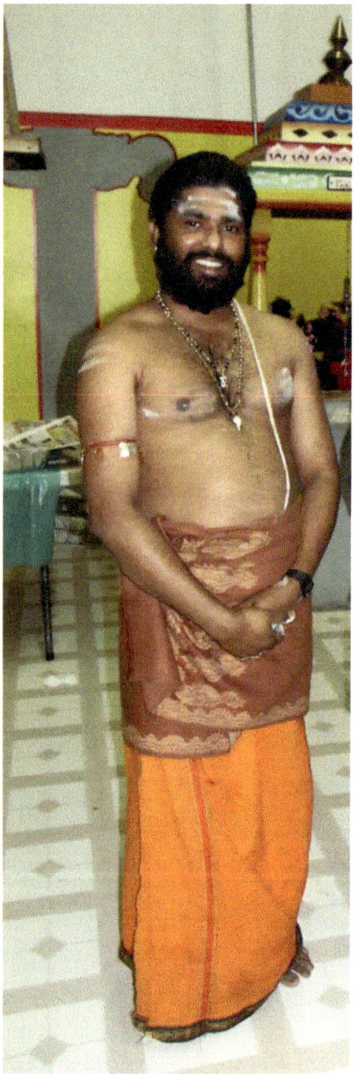

Brahmin Īsan Kurukkal

The Temple and its Management

We arrived at the temple shortly before the official opening time at 6:15 p.m. The brahmin was already present, busy with the necessary preparations for the daily pūjā. He introduced himself as Īsan Kurukkal, born in Jaffna, Sri Lanka. His native temple is dedicated to the god Murugan, half-brother of the god Gaṇeśa. It is situated in the town of Point Pedro, in the very north of the Jaffna peninsula. Īsan Kurukkal had lived in Canada for 12 years at his home in Scarborough, around 30-40 kilometres from Brampton. He speaks English fluently and seems to have enjoyed some kind of higher education. Since the foundation of the temple in 2001 he had been employed as the only brahmin most of the time.

On occasions of important ceremonies, like a mahākumbhābhiṣeka for instance, temples with affluent sponsors invite brahmins from all over the world to participate in the event. Thus Īsan Kurukkal, together with other brahmins from Canada, attended the inauguration ceremony of a Murugan temple in August 2004 in Oslo, Norway.

After a short while the brahmin excused himself because he did not want to fall behind with his pūjā preparations.

Brahmin Īsan Kurukkal
Performing the pūjā

Vijaya Rāmanātha
Owner of the temple

Not long afterwards the temple manager arrived, a bit breathless. At once he lent the brahmin a helping hand in his preparations while he was talking to us. His name is Vijaya Rāmanātha. When he left Sri Lanka in 1995, he arrived first at the town of Soest, in the western part of Germany and remained there for six months before emigrating to Canada. Some of his relatives still lived in Germany, in some of the big cities of the Ruhr Area ('Ruhrgebiet').

He helped the brahmin during the pūjā ceremony, too, handed him the necessary utensils, like small water vessels, candelabrums, flowers, joss sticks, coloured paste etc. In a small kitchen, adjoining the temple's main room, he prepared some plain food to be eaten after the pūjā. During the ceremony, he also attended to the music, followed the brahmin during his pradakṣiṇā (circumambulation) around the main shrine with a colourful umbrella and assisted in the ritual.

The manager, Mr. Rāmanātha, stated that the foundation, installation and equipment of the temple were all his own idea. Lord Gaṇeśa, he confessed, is his pronounced iṣṭadevatā (chosen deity). When he was a little boy, he spent a lot of time in the Gaṇeśa temple of his home village on the Jaffna peninsula and helped out here and there.

During the pūjā
ceremony

Main shrine with Lord Gaṇeśa

Kalpaka-Vināyaka Devasthānam in Brampton

Viṣṇu with spouses

Murugan with consorts

He told us about his previous financial sorrows which had diminished considerably after the installation of his temple. They became bearable, psychologically and in reality.

The temple with its maṇḍapas was tastefully rather than opulently furnished. The community of this recently-established devasthānam was made up of a few, not very rich, members.

The big chariot used to carry the statue of Lord Gaṇeśa around the temple area during the annual mahotsava ('great festival') was manufactured in Sri Lanka at a price of 45.000 Canadian Dollars. The decoration of the festival chariot consists of eight statues, which are each nearly 1.60 metres high. They depict mythical creatures (*vyālaka* in Sanskrit), hybrid beasts of prey like lions, elephants, snakes or tigers. They serve as atlantes, supporting roofs or pillars. In Tamil they are termed *yāḷi*, 'a mythological lion-faced animal with elephantine proboscis and tusks.' (*Tamil Lexicon*) We came across similar statues in Mauritius, too, in the *Arul Migu Sockalingum Meenatchee Amman Tirukkōvil* in Port Louis (see p. 283). Here, in the Brampton Gaṇeśa temple, they resemble lions with horns standing on their hind legs and holding their long rolling tongue sticking out of their mouths between their forelegs. The figures were fabricated in Sri Lanka, too. When not used for the mahotsava, the statues decorate the southern wall of the temple hall, serving as atlantes supporting the roof.

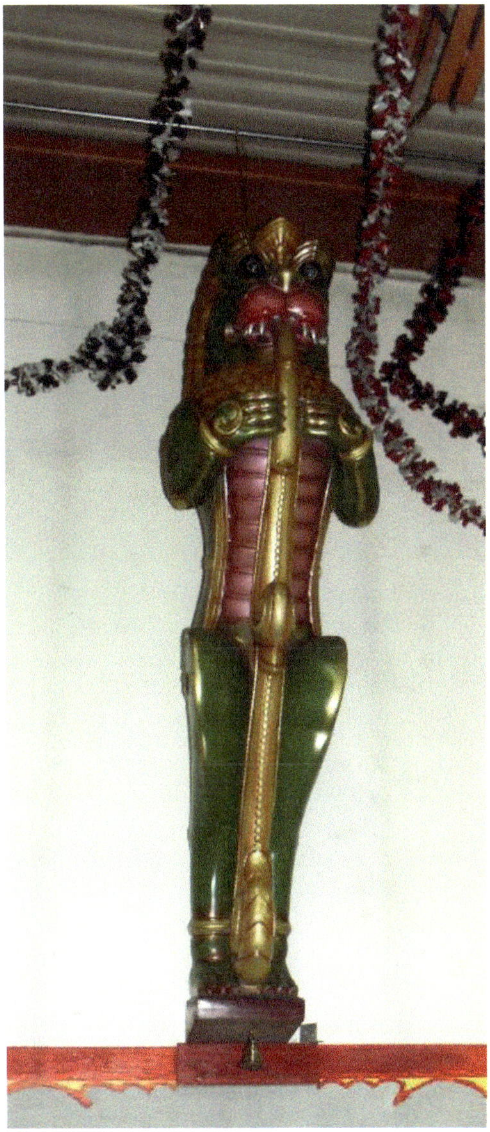

Statue of a mythical creature (*vyālaka*) on the wall of the temple hall

View along the southern side of the temple hall

At the regular evening pūjā while we were visiting the temple, only a few devotees were present; among them a young couple with two little children. On special holidays, the manager assured us, there are more than fifty people. One of the reasons for the small amount of visitors to this Gaṇeśa temple is surely the remote location of Brampton, a district, as already mentioned above, at the very north-western outskirts of the Greater Toronto Area.

The temple's website shows pictures of the mahotsava in 2009. Obviously the number of participating devotees has grown considerably since 2004.

Visit card

Time of visit: October 28, 2004, 18:15-19:30 hrs.

Address: 200 Advance Boulevard, Unit #21, Brampton, ON L6T 4V4.

Phone: 905-458 9701 or 416-471 0255 – www.srikatpagavinayagar.ca/home.html.

Sri Katpaka Vinayagar Hindu Temple, Toronto

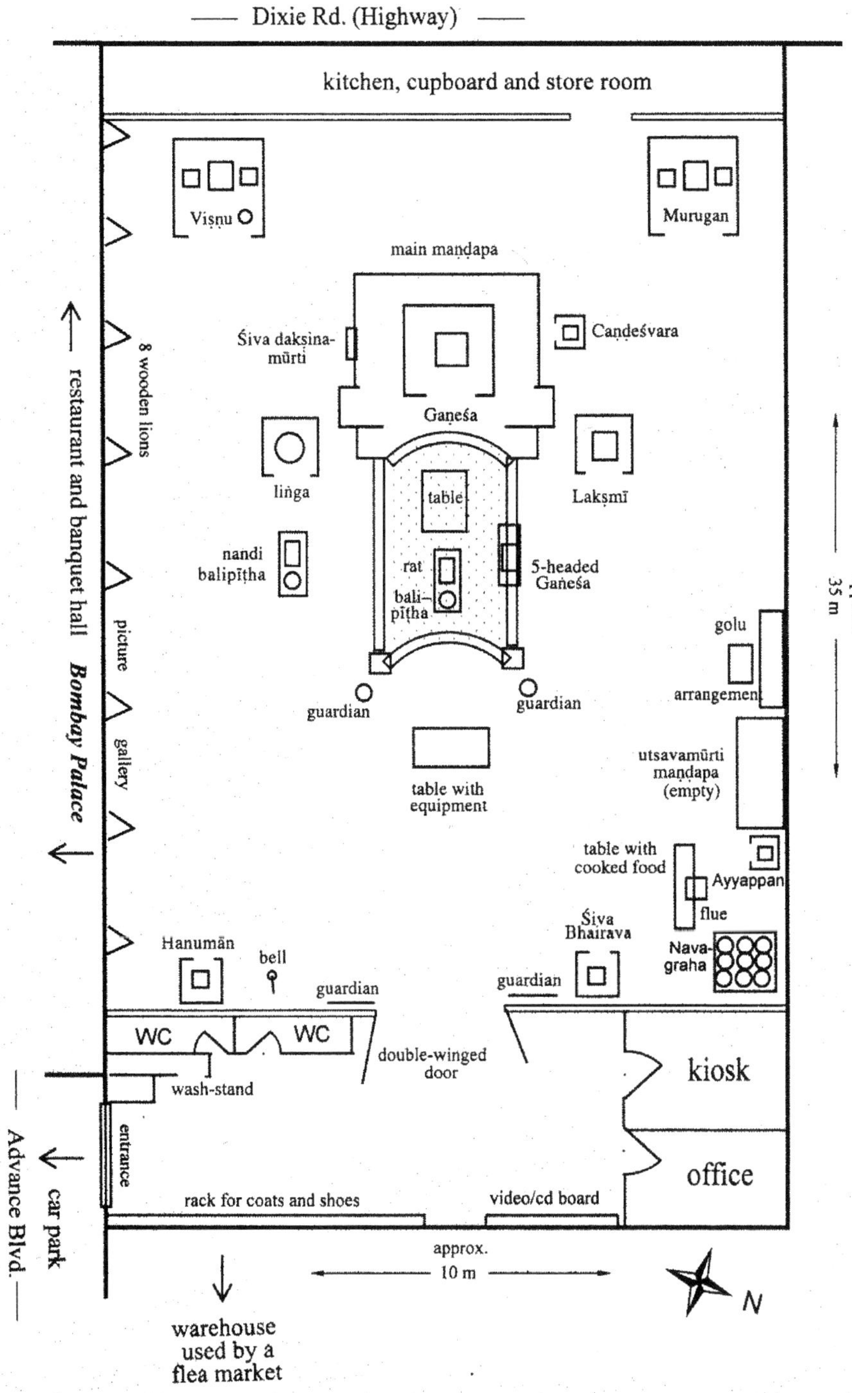

‘Gaṇeśa in Richmond’
The Hindu Temple Society of Canada

A temple in the open country

Situated at the entrance to Richmond, a suburb some 30 kilometres north of Toronto city centre, the white structure of a temple surrounded by an extensive car park stands out in the rural countryside. This place of worship differs from all the other establishments included in our research. Firstly, there is no iṣṭadevatā (lit. ‘chosen deity’), after which the temple would be named. Officially the temple is called *The Hindu Temple*, belonging to the *Hindu Temple Society of Canada*. While visiting the premises and talking to one of the brahmins on duty, Mr. Sri Ketheeswaranatha Kurukkal, we got the impression that the temple was originally dedicated to Gaṇeśa, in his manifestation as Varasiddhi Vināyaka.

Sign at the roadside of the highway from Toronto to Richmond

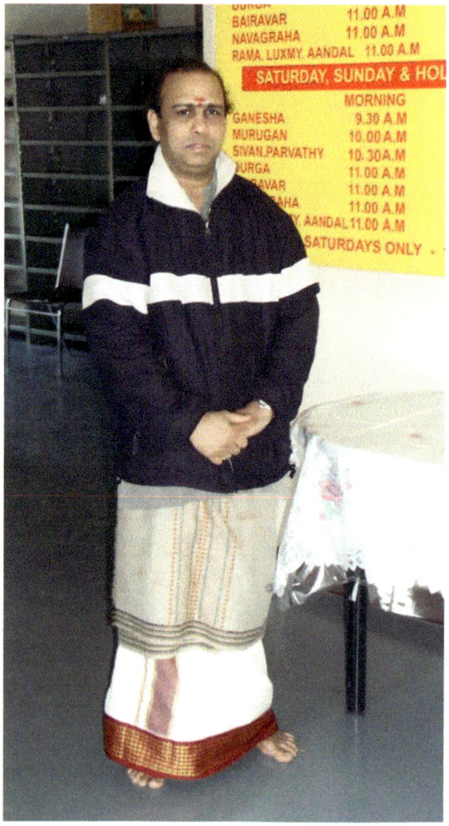

The temple brahmin
Sri Ketheeswaranātha Kurukkal

This view is corroborated by the outline of the temple's history in the Mahākumbhābhiṣeka (inauguration ceremony, August 30, 2001) commemoration booklet (www.thehindutemple.ca), where it is said (p. 14): 'After much search, a land was bought in the town of Richmond, north of Toronto… The site was consecrated in October 1983. The difficult but rewarding task of building the Temple was launched with the installation of the Premier deity of Hinduism – Lord Ganesa – at a temporary altar in April 1984. Then a "Trailer Temple" – again a temporary interim temple built on two flat-bed trailers – was constructed… to house Lord Ganesa and Goddess Durga, by October 1984.'

In the current temple building (in 2004), Gaṇeśa's shrine is the smallest between a very large one of Veṅkaṭeśvara (here called Bālājī) on his right side and of Murugan to the left. Veṅkaṭeśvara is believed to be a manifestation of Viṣṇu; his pilgrimage centre lies by the town of Tirupati, Andhra Pradesh. Both statues, of Veṅkaṭeśvara and of Murugan, are life-sized, dwarfing that of Gaṇeśa, which measures the usual size, about 1.20 meters tall. These three maṇḍapas are lined up nearly in a row at the rear of the temple hall, all of them facing west.

Opposite Veṅkaṭeśvara lie the maṇḍapas of Lakṣmī and Bhūdevī, the spouses of Viṣṇu. Murugan faces his consorts Vallī and Devānī. The statues of the goddesses are also of above-average proportions and they are separated from their male companions by nearly the entire space of the temple hall.

The temple area also houses other groups of deities. For example, the statue of Rāma in the south-west corner, in a little partitioned room together with his entourage. The high god Viṣṇu manifests himself in ten Avatāras (lit. 'descent'), in order to save the dharma, the Hindu religion. The seventh of these Avatāras is Rāma, the hero of the Sanskrit epic *Rāmāyaṇa*. Many Hindus consider Rāma as an independent high god. Mahatma Gandhi, for example, died with the words 'he Rāma!' on his lips.

Interior of the temple hall

The goddess Durgā has found her place of worship in the opposite north-west corner.

The north-eastern part of the temple-complex assembles maṇḍapas for the worship of Pārvatī (here called Tripurā Sundarī); of Śiva represented by a Liṅga and a statue of Śiva Naṭarāja; and the group of the Navagraha, the Nine Planets. The temple combines a large variety of Śaiva and Vaiṣṇava deities.

The temple building is *not* orientated in the orthodox manner to the east. The main statues of Veṅkaṭeśvara, Gaṇeśa and Murugan are facing west. The possibility of constructing the temple layout in the traditional way had existed, since the purpose-built structure was newly erected. One explanation might be that the whole complex faces the highway and a spacious parking lot lies in front of it, which provides ample space for the visitors during the mahotsava and other occasions.

Nevertheless, the magically effective and therefore much dreaded Navagraha, the Nine Planets, still have their pavilion in the north-east.

The *Hindu Temple* in Richmond is predominantly frequented by Telugu-speaking Indians immigrated from Andhra Pradesh, and less by Tamils from India or Sri Lanka. Because of its mixed Śaiva-Vaiṣṇava tradition, the temple turns out to only be partially relevant for our subject, the *Tamil Temples*.

Be this as it may, the Richmond Hill temple is an illustrative example of Hindu syncretism amongst South Indian emigrants.

Time of visit: October 28, 2004, 11:30-13:30 am.
Address: 10865 Bay View Avenue, Richmond Hill, ON L4S 1M1, Canada.
www.thehindutemple.ca

Porter's lodge and kiosk

Richmond Hill Temple, Toronto

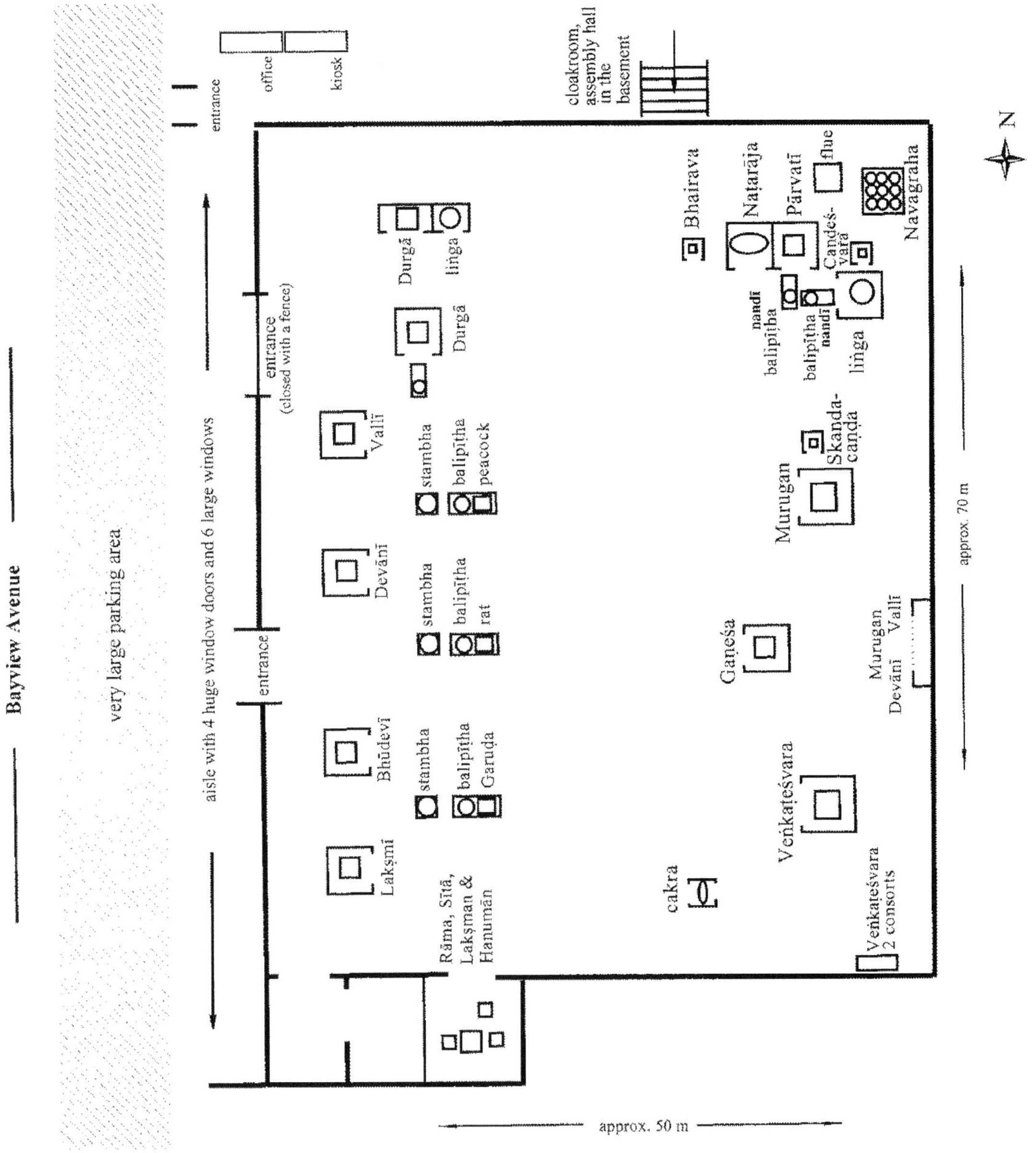

‘Gaṇeśa in the Neighbourhood’
The Śrī Siddhi-Vināyaka Ālayam in Negombo

Front view of the temple from the east, Sea Street

Gaṇeśa Siddhi-Vināyaka has his abode here on Sea Street, one of the busiest streets in the town of Negombo, a centre of fishing on the west coast of Sri Lanka, about 40 kilometres north of the capital Colombo. On the same road, in the immediate vicinity of this temple, are two other kōvils, that of the goddess Kālī to the north and, nearly opposite the Siddhi-Vināyaka temple on the other side of the street, southwards, the temple of Mārī-Ambā.

The current building of the Siddhi-Vināyaka temple is fairly recent. The consecration ceremony (*mahākumbhābhiṣeka*) took place on July 13, 1981. Mr. S. Navaratnarajah, the secretary of the Temple Trust Board, showed us an official booklet that was printed on this occasion under the title *Nīrkomumpu Śrī Cittivināyakar Ālayam Kumpāpiṣeka* (Negombo Śrī Siddhivināyaka Ālaya-Kumbhābhiṣeka). This brochure, describing the temple’s history, provides the information that a much smaller Gaṇeśa shrine existed before. This original shrine now serves as the main maṇḍapa on the same spot.

Lord Gaṇeśa, utsavamūrti

The former shrine is depicted in the abovementioned booklet. The little sanctuary is said to have been erected in the year 1880. The last consecration ceremony was thus celebrating the centenary jubilee of the original place of worship.

Although the consecration dates back nearly 30 years, the temple structure is far from being completed. The elaborate gopuram for example was installed and inaugurated in 1998. Some of the frescoes and murals are unfinished or the colour is still missing. We were also told that the flagpole (*dhvajastambha*) in front of the main maṇḍapa (the pedestal was already installed) is planned to be erected shortly. With the necessary repair works and some extensions, the temple looked a little bit like a construction site in some places.

Lord Gaṇeśa's abode in Negombo does not seem to be a centre of pilgrimage, it is more akin to a popular neighbourhood shrine. An uninterrupted flow of visitors did their obeisance during our visit on a Saturday morning, all of them very likely living in the vicinity of the temple.

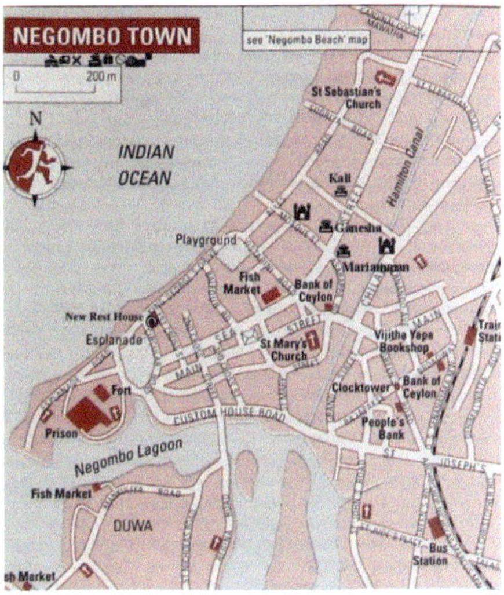

Location of the Gaṇeśa Siddhi-Vināyaka temple: Sea Street (second street parallel to the sea front), second temple south of St. Sebastian's Church (Map taken from: Gavin Thomas: *The Rough Guide to Sri Lanka.* New York, London, Delhi, 2nd ed., 2006, p. 132.)

Temple Layout

Considering all its features, this Siddhi-Vināyaka temple in the Sri Lankan town of Negombo can justifiably be compared with the Siddhi-Vināyaka temple of the Sri Lankan emigrant community in the city of Hamm, North Rhine-Westphalia, Germany. However, there are noteworthy differences concerning both temple layouts. Here are some examples:

(1) The Devī-maṇḍapa is installed in both temples in the same traditional location, the south-west corner behind the sanctissimum, to the right side of the main deity. But while in Hamm we find a shrine for the goddess Durgā, it is Gajalakṣmī ('Lakṣmī with elephants') who adorns the Negombo temple. Lakṣmī, usually associated with Viṣṇu as his spouse, represents in Śaiva temples, like Gajalakṣmī, an independent manifestation of the great goddess.

Gajalakṣmī with two elephants
Black granite statue

Three snake stones (*nāgakkal*)

(2) A small shrine for Caṇḍeśvara, a fervent devotee (*bhakta*) and worshipper of Lord Śiva and commander of his troops (*gaṇa*), can normally be found on the left side of the main maṇḍapa, looking towards the shrine. This regular member of Śiva's entourage, Caṇḍeśvara, is missing in Negombo.

(3) On the other hand, close to the shrine of Lord Murugan, there is a smaller shrine containing three snake stones (*nāgakkal*), which has no correspondence in the temple in Hamm.

(4) In addition to the platform with the festival statues (*utsavamūrti*) in front of the main maṇḍapa, there is another shrine containing a bronze of Naṭeśvara (i.e. Śiva Naṭarāja, 'Lord of dance'), together with a bronze of a Devī, which looks exactly like the bronze of Vaḍivāmbikā in the inner sanctum of the famous Munneśvara temple in Chilaw. The gestures of the goddess's hands are identical and the right hand holds a lotus flower, the left hanging loosely down to her side (which is the usual iconographical gesture of Śiva's spouse Pārvatī).

Śiva Naṭarāja and the goddess Vaḍivāmbikā

Viṣṇu on Śeṣa with spouses

Upon the dome above the main shrine, we find a fresco of Gaṇeśa, the foremost deity of the temple, at the front. Other depictions of Gaṇeśa follow clockwise: we see him five-headed (Pañcamukha) in the south, on the west side it shows Viṣṇu sitting on Śeṣa, the king of snakes, between his two spouses and finally, in the north, there is Gaṇeśa again, here with *his* two spouses. Obviously, the iṣṭadevatā Gaṇeśa has ousted the otherwise predominant Trimūrti (except Viṣṇu), consisting of Brahmā the creator, Viṣṇu the preserver and Śiva the destroyer.

Sanctissimum
Lord Gaṇeśa, sthalamūrti

Mr. S. Navaratnarajah with brahmins and temple servants

Time of visit: April 8, 2006, about 9-11 a.m.
Address: 135 Sea Street, Negombo, Sri Lanka.
Phone: 0777-788937.

Śrī Siddhi-Vināyaka Ālayam, Negombo

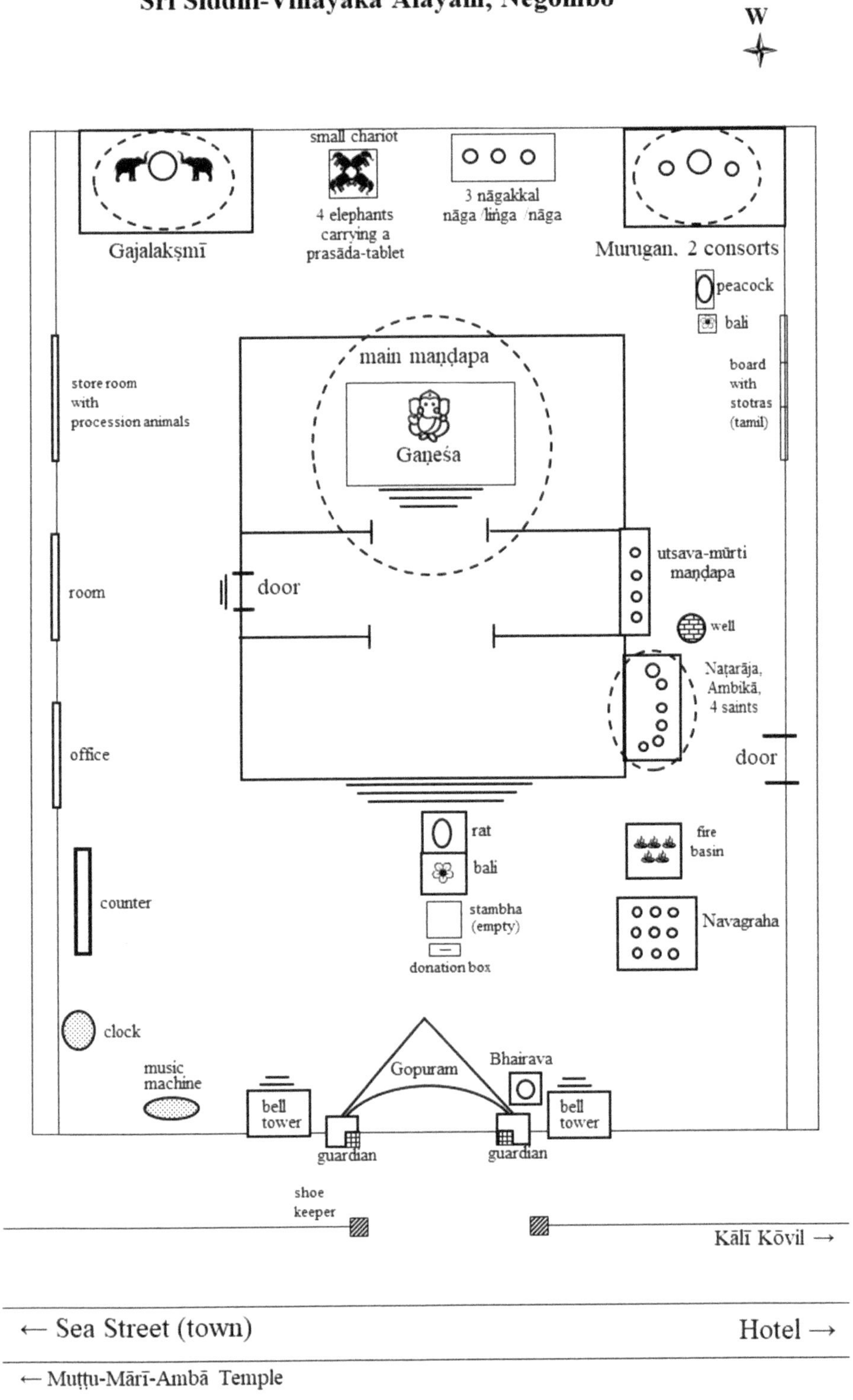

‘Gaṇeśa in the Paddy-Fields’
The Muṭṭu-Vināyaka Kōvil in Negombo

Front view of the temple entrance

Building and Priest

The kōvil is situated on the fringes of the harbour town of Negombo, about 40 kilometres north of Colombo, Sri Lanka. The name of the temple reads in its anglicised version *Sri Muthuvinayagar Kōvil* (Sanskrit *Śrī Vighna-Vināyaka* Temple), ‘The Temple of the Lord, the Remover of Obstacles (= Gaṇeśa).’

This is a traditional temple in a timeworn building which must once have been quite magnificent but has seen its best years. It is said to be 250 years old. It comprises only two maṇḍapas: a bigger one in the main building for Gaṇeśa and one small shrine dedicated to both Viṣṇu (‘Mahāviṣṇu’) and Kālī, in a separate edifice, outside to the north.

Temple interior, front view of the main shrine

On the first floor of the main building is a dusty hall, which does not seem to have been in use for a long time. It is a location for weddings and celebrations, now inhabited by pigeons.

K. Lokanathan Swamy
Temple priest
In front of the main shrine

Our interviewee is K. Lokanathan Swamy, the temple priest. Mr Lokanathan, who does not wear a sacred thread, is descended from a traditional family of priests (father and grandfather) who looked after this same place of worship. His forefathers came from Mahārāṣṭra, India. Mr Lokanathan cannot speak English, nor write his name and address. The conversation is conducted with the help of our three-wheeler driver who translates from Tamil into English.

Temple Layout and Pantheon

The temple orientation is to the east with a slight turn to the north, in order to enable Gaṇeśa to face the country road in front. His granite statue was made in Mahābalipuram and appears to be rather old.

All the other minor deities which are also worshipped in the temple are only represented by tiny statuettes, murals, wall-carpets, paintings or devotional pictures.

We enter the temple premises, passing the belltower to our right, crossing a porch and a spacious verandah, past a sacrificial basin (*homapīṭha*). Gajalakṣmī, the goddess of fortune, blesses the visitor from above the door that leads into the interior of the temple hall. She is flanked by Durgā and Murugan functioning as guardian deities. Having entered the temple hall we approach the sanctissimum (*mūlagarbha*) first.

On top Gajalakṣmī
Durgā and Murugan on both sides of the main entrance

Gaṇeśa in the sanctissimum

On the exterior walls of the sanctissimum there are murals which are rather darkened by old age. We can recognise a deity with a flute (not Kṛṣṇa) on the right wall and a picture of the lance holder Murugan on the opposite side (depicted as a baby – Bāla-Murugan).

Behind the main shrine hang wall carpets portraying the goddess Pattinī to Gaṇeśa's right side and the god Viṣṇu on the other.

Murugan as a baby balancing upon his peacock

Goddess Pattinī

Viṣṇu on his mount, the vulture king Garuḍa

Pattinī and Viṣṇu both belong to the well-known quartet of Ceylon's guardian deities – the other two being the gods Kataragama (who can be identified with Murugan) and Nātha (who is none other than the local variety of the Buddhist Bodhisattva Avalokiteśvara).

These deities are usually venerated in Hindu devasthānas affiliated to Buddhist monasteries in Sri Lanka. In the direct vicinity of the temple lies a

Buddhist monastery, the *Śrī Hariścandra Vihāraya*. So this Hindu temple might be influenced by its Buddhist neighbourhood.

On the painting of the goddess Pattinī we read beside her right foot in Sinhala script the blessing: *Rōhiṇi gē graha apala vē vā*, 'The [personified fourth] lunar mansion of Rōhiṇī (considered wife of the moon) may keep away [from you] the evil influences of the planets!', (followed by the undecipherable name of the artist on the opposite side). It appears that the temple is visited not only by Tamil but also Sinhala devotees, which is not at all unusual for a Tamil temple in Sri Lanka.

We now walk around Gaṇeśa's main maṇḍapa, passing the wall-carpets of Pattinī and Viṣṇu to our left and reach the northern side wall of the temple hall. Here stands a table with a collection of small statuettes and pictures of a wide variety of gods and goddesses.

Table with statuettes and paintings

We notice, among others, the paintings of three goddesses: Sarasvatī, goddess of science and arts; Gajalakṣmī, goddess of fortune, whom we have met already above the entrance door and to the right, Kāmākṣī, a vegetation goddess of the substratum, originating from the South Indian pilgrimage centre, Kāñcīpuram. She can easily be recognised by the green sugarcane plant in her left hand.

Paintings of Sarasvatī, Gajalakṣmī and Kāmākṣī with a figurine of Śiva in meditation

Figurine of a Samādhi Buddha

The statuette of a Meditating Buddha (*Samādhi Buddha*) is placed just on top of a devotional picture of Ayyappan (a local South Indian god), on the very end on the right side of the table.

A very similar small statue which looks as if it had been carved by the same artist, is part of the collection too. However, it is not a Buddha but a meditating Śiva, recognisable by the snake around his neck, the matted hair of an ascetic and the antelope skin, yellow with speckled black dots, around his shoulders.

Figurine of a meditating Śiva

Śālagrāma stones under the table

On the floor at the north side, we count 15 stones, each about 30 cm long. These ominous Śālagrāma stones are 'said to be typical of Viṣṇu, as the Phallus is of Śiva.' (Apte) One could call them 'Vaiṣṇava Liṅgas.' Mr Lokanathan explains that they are used for 'ritual.' They are subjected to a 'prescribed set of rituals which must be utilised in the worship of the stone… It is considered "unsafe" for most persons to worship a śālagrāma identified with a ferocious aspect of Viṣṇu… and, in order to avert "danger," such a stone, if it comes into one's possession, must be handed over permanently to a holy man willing to use his spiritual power to tame the beast, or to a temple where the dangerous potential of the stone will be offset by the overabundant presence of pacific powers pulsating throughout the place (Smith/ Narasimha Chary: *Handbook of Hindu Gods…*, 1991, pp. 130-133, with more strikingly relevant details).

Outside the temple building, to the north, stands a small shack which serves as a shrine dedicated to both Viṣṇu and Kālī. The board above the entrance door reads, (at the top) in Sinhala: '*Śrī Mahāviṣṇu saha Kāli Kōvila*', (in the middle) in English: '*Sri Mahavishnu and Kali Temple*,' and (at the bottom) in Tamil: '*Śrī Makāvisn̲u Kōvil – Kāli Amman Kōvil*. The priest and his family seem to live in the quarters behind the temple hall in the same building.

A bull, a mother cow and a very young calf also belong to the inhabitants of the temple premises.

Time of visit: April 30, 2006, Sunday, approximately 8:50-9:30 a.m.
Address: Sri Muthuvinayagar Kōvil, Dawatha Gaha Watt, Divulapitiya Road, Negombo.

Shrine for Viṣṇu and Kālī

Muṭṭu-Vināyaka Kōvil, Negombo

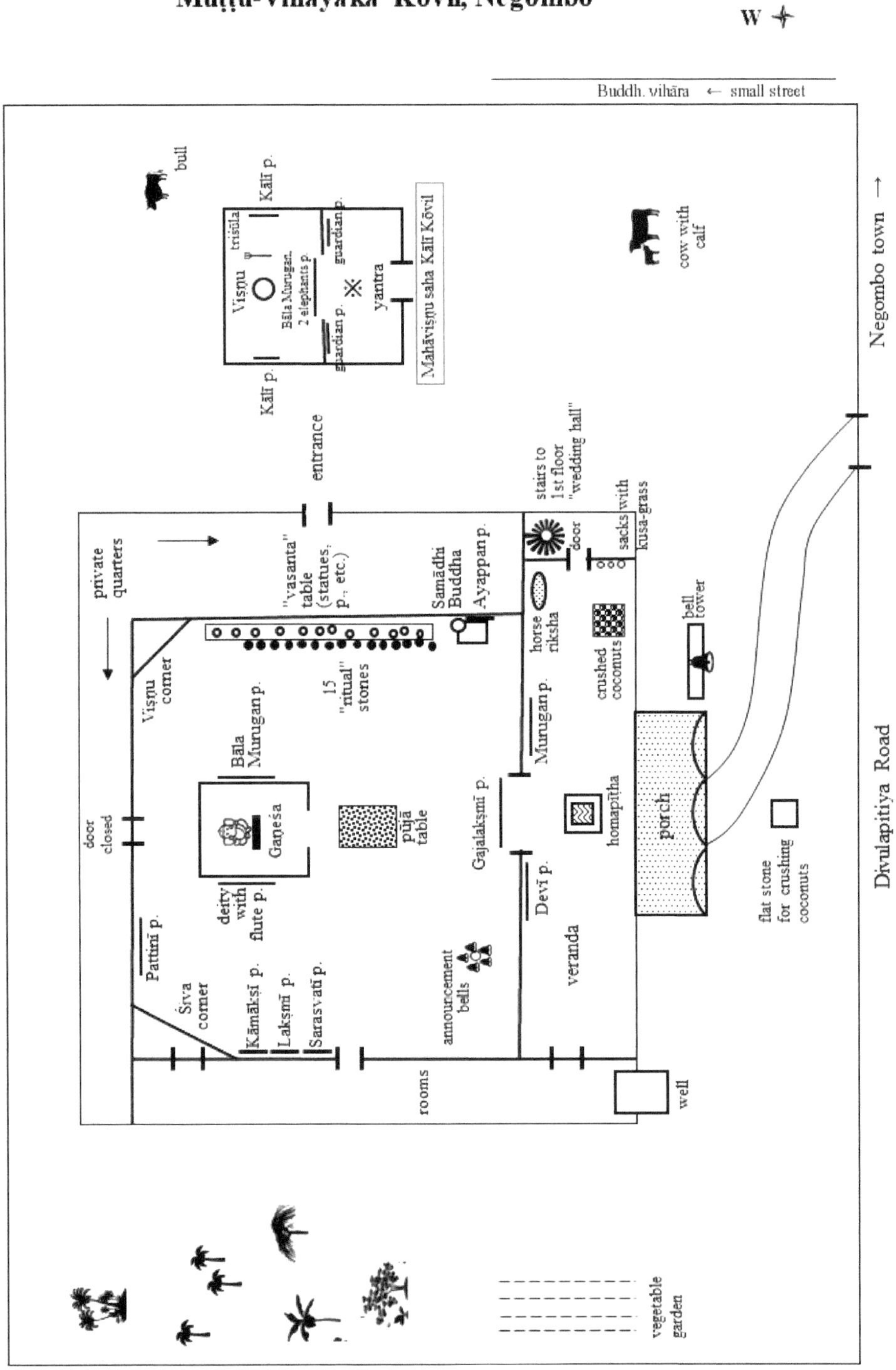

'Gaṇeśa in Frankfurt'
The Śrī Kalpaka-Vināyaka Kōvil

Sri Katpaka Vinayagar Kōvil, Frankfurt, north-west front

This modest temple is situated in an industrial area of the Frankfurt metropolis, in Intzestr. 26a. It goes under the name of the 'Temple of (Gaṇeśa) the Fulfiller (of wishes) and Remover (of obstacles).'

This is the only place of worship incorporated in the present collection that we did not visit personally. One of our students took useful pictures of this sanctum, by which we would like to wind up the section on Gaṇeśa temples. Our thanks are due to Felix Eickelbeck for kindly making his photographs available. He visited the temple in May, 2004. Thanks to his instructions and photographs we were able to draw a ground plan of the temple setup as well.

Temple Layout and Pantheon

The temple faces northwards due to the fixed orientation of the rented building. 'North is second best,' the brahmin of the Mīnākṣī-Ambā temple in Scarborough would say. The entrance from Intzestraße leads the visitor into a spacious assembly room surrounded by a kitchen corner, kiosk/office, storeroom and toilets.

Gaṇeśa in the main maṇḍapa, his mount, the rat and the obligatory lotus bud (*balipīṭha*) are represented by black granite stones. The god has donned a white and yellow robe and is decorated with a luxuriant garland of white, yellow, orange and red flowers, mostly asters. He wears a necklace of jewels; his forehead is covered by a diadem, his head helmed by a gilded

Gaṇeśa
Granite statue in the sanctissimum

basket-crown (*karaṇḍamukuṭa*). His face is painted with three white horizontal lines, the Śaiva sign (*tripuṇḍra*). Face, trunk and flapping ears are furthermore decorated by yellow and red round tilakas.

The southern wall directly behind him is occupied by the two shrines of his accompanying deities. Their figurines are not carved out of granite, but cast in bronze. The shrine in the southeast corner houses Mīnākṣī, the famous goddess of the pilgrimage centre Madurai in Tamil Nadu. She is easily recognised by the parrot that sits on a flower bud in her right hand.

The goddess Mīnākṣī
Bronze statuette

Murugan with his two consorts
Bronze statuettes

To her left, in the opposite corner, stands Gaṇeśa's half-brother, Murugan, the youthful god of war, with his consorts, Vallī and Devānī. Dark complexioned Vallī is believed to be a wild hunter's daughter while fair Devānī is an offspring of the god Indra.

Vallī Murugan Devānī

At the wall to the west, one perceives the shrine of the Nine Planets (Navagraha). Many devotees believe that these demigods are so powerful that they deserve to be worshipped first. Some believers come to venerate only them.

The Nine Planets
Granite statues

The Nine Planets,
and their appropriate places

The temple provides a sign on which their names and positions are noted. The Sun always deserves the central place. Since these are mythical bodies, belonging not to astronomy, but astrology, Sun and Moon are counted among the planets too, Rāhu and Ketu as well. Rāhu devours the Sun and Moon during the eclipses – Ketu is the demon of comets and meteors. The remaining five positions are occupied by the astronomical planets that are visible with the naked eye.

Bhairava
Granite statue

The pavilion in the north-western corner accommodates a granite statue of Bhairava, a manifestation of Śiva in his terrible form. He is always accompanied, on his right side, by a huge dog.

Gaṇeśa, utsavamūrti
Bronze statue

The last shrine on our survey is the place of the bronze festival statues (*utsavamūrti*). Traditionally, it can be found on the north side, between the Nine Planets and Bhairava, where the entrance is in this building. Therefore, it was moved directly to the opposite wall.

Besides the festival statue of Gaṇeśa, we find an exquisite figure of a Dancing Śiva (Naṭarāja, the King of Dance), who concludes our virtual visit to the Frankfurt Gaṇeśa temple and of the Gaṇeśa section as well.

Dancing Śiva Naṭarāja
Utsavamūrti, bronze statue

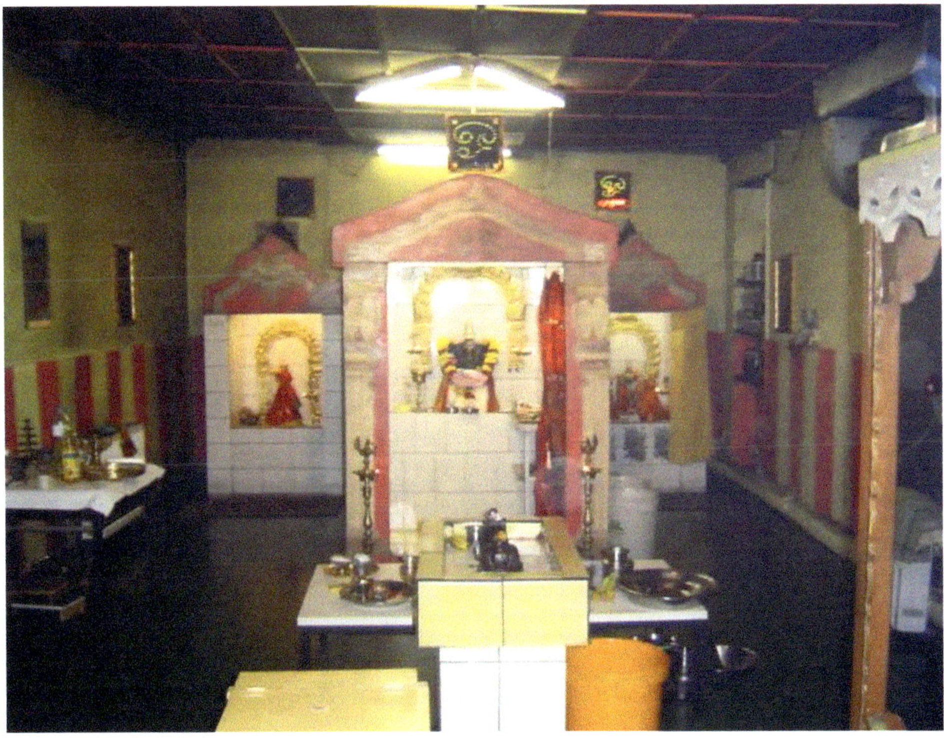

Temple hall interior
seen from the north

Śrī Kalpaka-Vināyaka Temple, Frankfurt

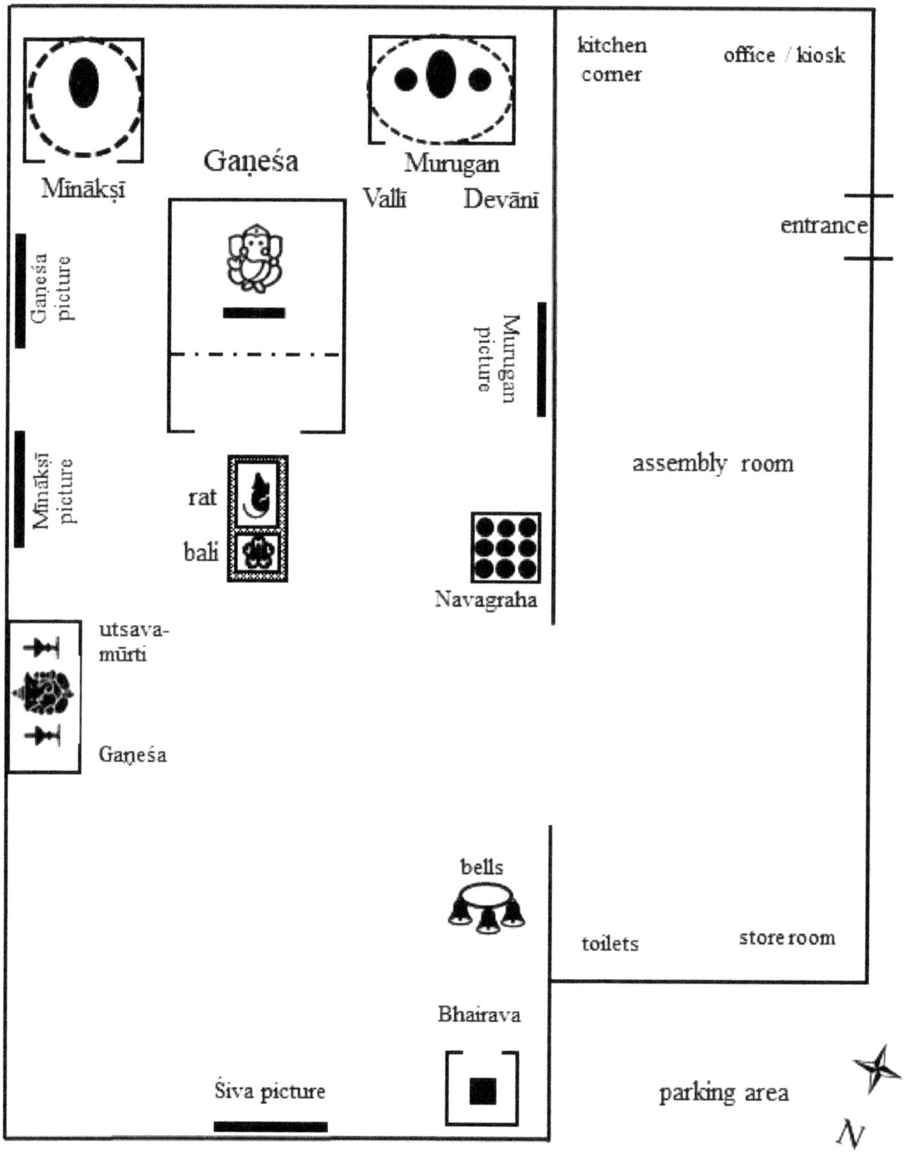

Murugan Temples

‘Murugan in London.’ The Highgate Hill Temple. A Centre of Emigrant Hinduism

Highgate Hill Murugan temple, main entrance, west front

The *Tamil Pages*[1] (see notes at the end of this chapter) from 2003 (p. 342) list 24 Tamil Hindu temples in Great Britain altogether, 14 of which are in London. Five of the London temples are dedicated to diverse goddesses like Durgā, Lakṣmī or Muthumārī (the goddess of smallpox), four to Gaṇeśa, three to Murugan and one to Śiva. In addition, there is one temple of Ayyappan (p. 362), who is venerated in Kerala and Tamil Nadu as the son of Śiva and Mohinī, the female manifestation of Viṣṇu.

The most prominent place among these temples occupies the Highgate Hill Murugan temple in London Arch-

Temple hall, looking to the west

way. It describes itself as 'the oldest established Saiva (Hindu) Temple in London.' (*Tamil Pages*, p. 350) Its history is most intimately linked with the fate of the Tamil immigrants from Ceylon and South India since the nineteen sixties. Up to the present day it has a formative influence on the life of the Tamil Hindu community in London and the whole of Great Britain. The temple itself, as well as the 'Brittannia Hindu (Shiva) Temple Trust,' which operates the temple, function as a paradigmatic example for half a dozen younger 'mushroom temples' (K. Nagarajah, temple administrator), which have sprung up in Great Britain, since about 1990, after the influx of Sri Lankan Tamil refugees from the civil war. The trust, with its 2.500 plus members, permanently employs no less than three temple brahmins, who fashion the temple and its 'parish' life. Until the completion of the Śrī Svāmī Nārāyaṇa temple in Neasden (Willesden), London, inaugurated on July 29, 1988 (which belongs to a modernistic, mission-oriented Vaiṣṇavism, anchored in the London Gujarātī community), the Highgate Hill Murugan temple was, as far as its architecture is concerned, the biggest Hindu temple in Europe. Therefore, it seems appropriate to let it initiate the major section on six Murugan temples in the present volume.

Temple hall, looking to the east

God Murugan: His Origins and Iconography

Murugan,[2] the main deity of this temple, is the most popular god of substratum Hinduism in South India (with the exception, perhaps, of Veṅkaṭeśvara). Murugan, the god of war, under his Sanskrit epithets: Skanda, Subrahmaṇya, Kumāra or Kārttikeya, was integrated into mainstream Śivaïsm. Here, he is venerated as Śiva's sole son (whereas Gaṇeśa, as legend has it, was created by Pārvatī alone). But already in the substratum, Murugan is obviously of heterogeneous origins. A couple of different local deities seem to have met in the god's personality. Murugan is young, handsome and strong. The name Murugan means 'The Good-Looking-One.' He is the youthful lover of the Great Goddess. His sign, the lance or spear (Tamil *vēl*), is a phallus symbol. He grants children. In his manifestation as Bāla-Murugan, he is venerated as a cute baby – like Kṛṣṇa or Śiva. He is a deity of vegetation, responsible for the correct course of the sun. As a deity of hills, he relates to the mountain cult. He is also associated with the snake cult. He is the god of hunting and the god of healing. As to his iconography, he is depicted either alone, or together with his two consorts, Vallī and Devānī. As a single figure, he will be standing upright, or riding his mount, the peacock. The god appears with one or six heads (Sanskrit Ṣaṇmukha), and has two, four or twelve arms.

Sthalamūrti of Murugan, central cult statue in the Highgate Hill temple

He always holds the lance in the inside of his right elbow, while his right hand shows the gesture of providing shelter (*abhayada*) and the left of fulfilling wishes (*varada*). He wears dhotī, bracelets, necklaces, earrings and the sacred thread (*yajñopavīta*). His hair flows long from under his basket-helmet (*karaṇḍamukuṭa*) backwards over his shoulders. His mount, the peacock, has its place behind the god: The peacock symbolises māyā, the cosmic illusion and Murugan stands between this phantasmagoria and the observer, thus providing shelter for him against the deception of the cycle of reincarnation (*saṃsāra*). In

Murugan with his two consorts and a sage (*ṛṣi*)

the company of his consorts, we recognise to his right (from the perspective of the statue) Vallī ('Creeper' or 'Liana'), the dark-complexioned daughter of a chief of hunters and to his left, Devānī, with a rosy complexion (like Murugan himself), daughter of the king of gods, Indra.

Murugan's cult shows ecstatic features. The devotees lie on their faces, prostrate in front of him. Some induce a trance, twitching and yelling. Having small lances – Murugan's symbol – stung through one's cheeks or tongue, swinging while hanging on hooks pierced through one's back muscles or 'fire walking,' running over blazing charcoals are some of the cult-like actions appealing to tourists. Murugan's devotees come from all social strata.

S. Sabbapathipillai
Photo in the Highgate Hill temple

Temple History

The[3] pre-history of the Highgate Hill Murugan temple starts with the arrival of its founding father, S. Sabapathipillai in England on board the S.S. Himalayas P&O Liner towards the end of 1965. Sri Sabapathipillai, a barrister by profession, commanded over an additional, spiritual background. He had passed the 'Triple Theedchais' (Sanskrit *śikṣā*), a rite that authorised him to perform Śaiva rituals (*Śaiva-pūjā*). His spiritual teacher was Easana Sivachariar, the Principal of the Śaiva Siddhānta College of Palani in Tamil Nadu, who is regarded as one of the most eminent scholars of South Indian Śaiva Siddhānta. Sabapathipillai found few Tamil Hindus in Great Britain – there were no priests or an organised cult. The Tamil emigrants had no opportunity of having performances of basic traditional Hindu rituals on the occasions of marriage, death or house consecrations. In order to consolidate the religious and cultural activities of Tamils in Great Britain, Sabapathipillai founded the *Hindu Association of Great Britain* on October 23, 1966, in London. This society dedicated itself to the task of bringing together the spiritual and cultural affairs of emigrated Tamils not only in Great Britain, but also world-wide in Malaysia, Singapore, Mauritius and South Africa, with support from the South Indian and Ceylonese native countries. The society's first committee therefore consisted of one representative from each of those countries. It was the declared objective of this society to offer the emigrants' children the possibility to come together in a Hindu-religious atmosphere

Fire ruin of the former synogogue (temple brochure)

and to become acquainted with, cultivate and revive their parents' religion and culture despite all the constraints of 'fitting in' to foreign surroundings.

In October 1973, in the Wimbledon Coronation Hall, seat of the *Hindu Association of Great Britain*, a statue (*vigraha*) of the god Murugan was consecrated which had been carved especially in Kumbhakonam, South India, by the temple architect (*sthapati*) A. R. Mohanram for the London emigrant community. The regular consecrations (*abhiṣeka*) and veneration rituals (*pūjā*) for this statue encouraged the desire of the London Tamil community to build a temple. And as is customary in traditional Tamil Hinduism, in order to accomplish this aim, a temple trust had to be founded. Therefore in the inaugural meeting on August 17, 1974, the *Brittannia Hindu (Siva) Temple Trust* (BHTT) emerged (charity no. 269067), a daughter organisation of the *Hindu Association of Great Britain*. The trust is managed by seven trustees and an advisory council, commanding a couple of sub-bodies. In the beginning, it consisted of 650 members, who committed themselves to pay 100 £ each over four years into the society's cash register. The society inaugurated four committees, for membership, religious education, social and cultural affairs and temple building. Their members, as well as all the other officials, e. g. the treasurer, are elected or confirmed, respectively, at the annual general meeting. The first chairman of the temple society was S. Sabapathipillai. He served in this office until his demise in the year 1989. Still today, his portrait adorns the temple's entrance hall.

It is a characteristic of a Śaiva temple, that it is (as opposed to Vaiṣṇava sacral buildings) built around a natural shrine, for example a conspicuously-moulded stone which is interpreted as a Śiva-liṅga. This explains why Śaiva temples are often erected upon ancient places of worship which have already been considered as holy sites in the cults of the substratum. We refer to two examples (also incorporated in the opening and final chapters, in the present volume), the Āśvattha-Vṛkṣa-Vināyaka Kōvil, the 'Temple of Gaṇeśa in the Fig Tree,' in T. Nagar, Chennai and the Jyotirliṅga temple in Mauritius. It is understandable why the London temple society decided in favour of a site which looked back to a religious tradition – from the perspective of Tamil emigrants it is a cult of the substratum. The temple society chose the fire ruin of an abandoned former synagogue. The fact that it could be purchased for a favourable price, around £12.500 (although its real value was more likely to be £140.000), would naturally have made the decision easier. In addition, there is its location upon a hill which links with the god Murugan being traditionally connected with mountain cults. The temple building is – here we cite from the brochure which the temple society edited on the occasion of the celebrations of its 25th anniversary on December 4, 1999: '[...] located on a hilltop – a favourite residence for Lord Murugan – and overlooking and guarding the City of London with grace.'

After clearing away the debris with the help of volunteers, the *Śramadāna volunteer force* ('Those who donate [not money, but] their labour'), now, in the first place, a temple annex with a subsidiary shrine and the lodging for the temple brahmin was completed (cost £3.000) and inaugurated on December 2, 1979 in the presence of 700 devotees.

The metal 'festival statues' (*utsava-mūrti*) which are carried through the streets around the temple – as opposed to the immovable granite statues (*sthalamūrti*) which always remain in their shrines – were ordered by the temple society to be made by an artist of the Koneswarar temple in Trincomalee, on the east coast of Sri Lanka. They represent a six-headed Murugan (Ṣaṇmukha) with his consorts Vallī and Devānī. The inauguration rituals (*prāṇa-pratiṣṭhā*) devoted to them were performed by the registrar of the Bhāratīya Vidyā Bhavan, Shri Mathoor Krishnamurthi, on the day of the Hindu New Year 1980. In the same year the temple society permanently employed a temple brahmin. To find the right candidate, a selection committee travelled to Colombo where it interviewed 45 applicants before it finally decided in favour of the former chief priest of the Koneswarar temple in Trincomalee.

Thereafter the temple society attracted many new members and, through them, further financial support, so that in 1982 it was able to finally start the construction of the two-storied temple building. In order to cover the expenses of £160.000, 400 donators acquired a *unit block* with each unit worth £400. The construction firm McGee & Co., from Ealing, was awarded the contract for the steelworks, concrete floors,

Utsavamūrti of a Six-headed Murugan with consorts in front of a mirror

walls and roof. The original annex was also enlarged.

Therefore, besides the actual temple hall, an additional hall was built which accommodates about 500 guests for weddings and other festivities. There is also a library, more lodgings for the temple brahmins, office rooms for the temple society, cloakrooms and toilets for the visitors.

For the traditional structuring of the temple layout, six architects (*sthapati*) arrived in 1983 from Madras (today Chennai), led by the abovementioned A. R. Mohanram (the same artist who had already made the central statue in 1973 in Kumbhakonam), meeting a six-month contract in order to construct the shrines for the numerous deities in the temple hall. After their departure, another team from Madras (under the direction of Sthapati M. Muruganandam and consulted by the Principal of the Government College of Architecture and Sculpture – Madras) completed the finishing touches.

The Great Inauguration Ceremony (*mahākumbhābhiṣeka*) was celebrated on July, 9-13, 1986 (Wednesday through to Saturday), performed by eleven brahmins and three assistants. Nearly 5.000 devotees are said to have participated.

A central event of the public temple life – as in every South Indian Śaiva temple – is the Great Temple Festival (*mahotsava*) which was celebrated in 2003 from Monday, June 30, through to Tuesday July 15.

However, the political climax of the temple's history was marked by the visit of Queen Elisabeth on June 6, 2002, during her *jubilee tour* on the occasion of her 50th anniversary of her coronation when she chose the Highgate Hill Murugan Temple for her very first visit to a Hindu temple in Great Britain. We quote from the internet announcement of the BBC, which acknowledges the religious-political importance of this visit:

'*The Queen visited a Hindu temple for the first time in Britain and did so in her stocking feet. She removed her shoes as a sign of respect as she and the Duke of Edinburgh entered the Highgate Hill Murugan Temple in Archway, north London…*'

'After being welcomed with garlands of yellow flowers, the Royal couple were blessed with peace and long life by four high priests. The visit was intended to show the inclusive nature of the monarchy and the Queen's respect for all religions in Britain, not just the Church of England, of which she is head. She has previously visited Hindu temples in India but it is the first time she has been to one in this country. Temple leader Suganya Naveenan said: "It's made people feel valued and we are honoured she chose to come here." The Queen slipped on thin slippers over her tights, while the Duke padded around the temple chatting to worshippers in his socks. In typical style, he asked a Tamil priest if he was a Tamil Tiger, the militant fighters in Sri Lanka. The priest replied: "No, we're priests. We're not associated with violence." The priest later added: "It was just friendly, just a joke. We were not offended. We blessed him with a long life and health and peace."' (BBC)

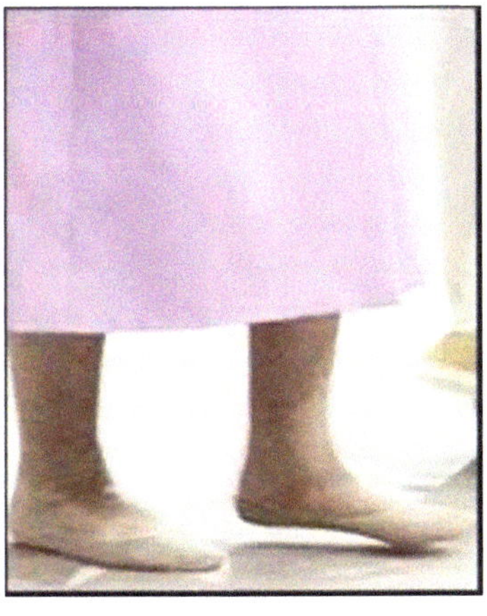

The Queen in her stocking feet

The Queen in the Highgate Hill Murugan temple
June 6, 2002
BBC homepage

The Temple Hall and its Shrines; the Pantheon

The temple hall is situated in the upper storey of the building above the celebration and meeting room. The visitor proceeds from the staircase through the entrance in the north-west corner. The temple is orientated according to tradition. The sanctissimum (*garbhagṛha*) is located in the middle of the western half of the rectangular room, so that the main deity Murugan nearly exactly faces east, – the mansion is slightly turned to east-north-east. During the conversion of the temple, a wide window was especially broken to make it possible for Murugan to view the rising sun. From the perspective of the statue, on the right side in the sanctissimum stands the dark-complexioned Vallī, on the left is Murugan's other consort, Devānī.

Murugan with his consorts Vallī and Devānī
Sthalamūrtis in the sanctissimum

Murugan with his consorts Vallī and Devānī
A frieze in the temple hall

Murugan's mount, the peacock and – like in all the other South Indian and Sri Lankan Śaiva temples – the lotus and the gilded flagpole (*dhvaja-stambha*) have their place in front of them.

In addition, there is a small shrine of Murugan's half-brother Gaṇeśa at the base of the flagpole. Close to the northern wall, open to the sanctissimum, is positioned the tiny shrine of Caṇḍeśvara.

The gilded flagpole (*dhvajastambha*)

Durgā, sthalamūrti

When we now circle the sanctissimum in a pradakṣiṇā, i. e. in a clockwise motion, we come across the maṇḍapa of Durgā at the southern wall. The shrine of Gaṇeśa is in the southwestern corner of the western wall – Gaṇeśa in his manifestation as Vināyaka, the 'Remover of Obstacles.' In mainstream Śaivism, Gaṇeśa is considered as the half-brother of Skandakumāra (the Sanskrit equivalent of Murugan). The two deities in the middle of the western wall are quite exceptional however. These are shrines of the Liṅga of Kāśī-Viśvanātha (i. e. Śiva in the 'Golden Temple' in Benares) and his spouse Kāśī-Viśālākṣī (a manifestation of Umā). Just beside her, near the entrance, we find Bāla-Murugan, i. e. Murugan in his appearance as a baby.

Bāla-Murugan, sthalamūrti

Proceeding along the northern wall to the east, we encounter a shrine with another incarnation of Murugan, appearing as Arumuga-Svāmī, here again with both his consorts, six-headed and also depicted in a frieze of this maṇḍapa as a plaster statue. The next shrine houses Viṣṇu; then Śiva the god of dance (Śiva Naṭarāja), in a frieze is Śiva with Pārvatī and Skandakumāra. We walk through a passage into the corridor, running parallel behind the northern wall. The frieze above the passage gate shows the wedding of Śiva and Pārvatī, and we stand in front of the place that accommodates the metal procession statues.

Gaṇeśa, sthalamūrti

Among these, we discern a six-headed Murugan (Ṣaṇmukha), also a figure of Murugan with one head; both statues are accompanied by the consorts Vallī and Devānī. In a corner we see a magnificent statue of the saint Appar, recognisable by his staff and another Gaṇeśa. Back again in the temple hall, we pass a basin with oil lights and arrive at the shrine of the Nine Planets (Navagraha). Another passageway in the north-eastern corner leads to an annex which hides a maṇḍapa with a Śivaliṅga; in front of it is Śiva's mount, the white zebu bull Nandī and a shrine with a mūrti of the ominous planet Saturn. A relief of the goddess Gajalakṣmī who, as her name proclaims, is accompanied by elephants, adorns the frieze above this passageway. We pass the shrines of two heroes (*vīra*) at the eastern wall: one a hero with a sword, and one of the hero Vīrabhadra, master of two lions. Two paintings of the half-brothers Murugan and Gaṇeśa hang high on the eastern wall. Our tour of the temple hall ends in the south-eastern corner, in front of a procession waggon transporting a papier-mâché figure of Gaṇeśa's mount, the rat.

Viṣṇu and his spouses,
Lakṣmī and Bhūdevī
Temple frieze

On a final closer examination of the sanctissimum, inside the exterior wall niches and on the south side, we see one of Gaṇeśa and another of Śiva Dakṣiṇāmūrti as spiritual advisor, in the north the sun god Sūrya and Murugan himself. The dome-shaped roof is embellished by coloured reliefs of the three high-gods (Trimūrti): to the south Śiva Vidyādhara, to the west Viṣṇu upon the cobra Śeṣa, and to the north Brahmā with his spouses Sāvitrī and Gāyatrī. On the roof beam sits Murugan between Vallī and Devānī, who are each surrounded by sages (*ṛṣi*) as custodians and peacocks.

Conclusion

The Highgate Hill Murugan temple plays a central part in the religious and even more importantly, the cultural self-definition of the Tamils who migrated to Great Britain.

Murugan's mount, the peacock, and the lotus bud, granite statues in front of the sanctissimum

Tamil immigrants from India or Sri Lanka do of course have their roots in their Asian homelands. The religion they brought with them cannot remain identical overseas. 'Exile' Hinduism or rather 'emigrant' Hinduism – as opposed to traditional inner-Indian Hinduism – is marked by fast and deep-reaching modifications. Here, outside the South-Asian homeland, Hinduism is presently changing from a folk religion into a universal religion. It is the function of the Highgate Hill Murugan temple and particularly its temple society, to protect, even safeguard, Indian traditions in this process of transcultural metamorphosis. British society is, to a much greater degree than German for example, enriched by Asian, notably Indian, influences. Transversally, the Tamils who have emigrated to Britain do not want to stay one hundred percent Indian at all, they want to integrate into British society. Therefore, the function of an emigrant Hindu temple is to help keep the balance amidst the cultural appropriation. The Highgate Hill Murugan temple seems to live up to this difficult task.

Time of visit: Saturday, May 24, 2003, 11:00-13:30 hrs.
Address: 200A, Archway Road, London N6 5BA, Great Britain.
www.highgatehillmurugan.org.

Notes

1 Tamil *Pages 2003. Social and Commercial Directory of Tamils 2003-2004.* Managing editors: T. Srikantha Rajah, A. Gnanendran. Published by British Tamil Directories, 52 Kingsley Road, Wimbledon, London, SW19 8HF, UK.
www.tamilpages.org.

2 As to this section cf. H.D. Smith, / M.N. Chary: *Handbook of Hindu Gods, Goddesses and Saints*, 1991, pp. 227-235; and J. Gonda: *Die Religionen Indiens: II Der jüngere Hinduismus,* 1963, p. 15.

3 The following remarks concerning the temple history are based on three sources: (1) The brochure *Maha Kumbabishekam. Consecration Ceremony 9-13 July 1986*. Ed. Brittannia Hindu (Shiva) Temple Trust, Highgate Hill, Murugan Temple. (2) The brochure *Millennium & Silver Jubilee Celebrations, 4.12.1999*, by the same editor. (3) A detailed conversation with Mr K. Nagarajah, administrator of the temple, whom we thank warmly for his kind information.

Gajalakṣmī, goddess of fortune with two elephants, temple frieze

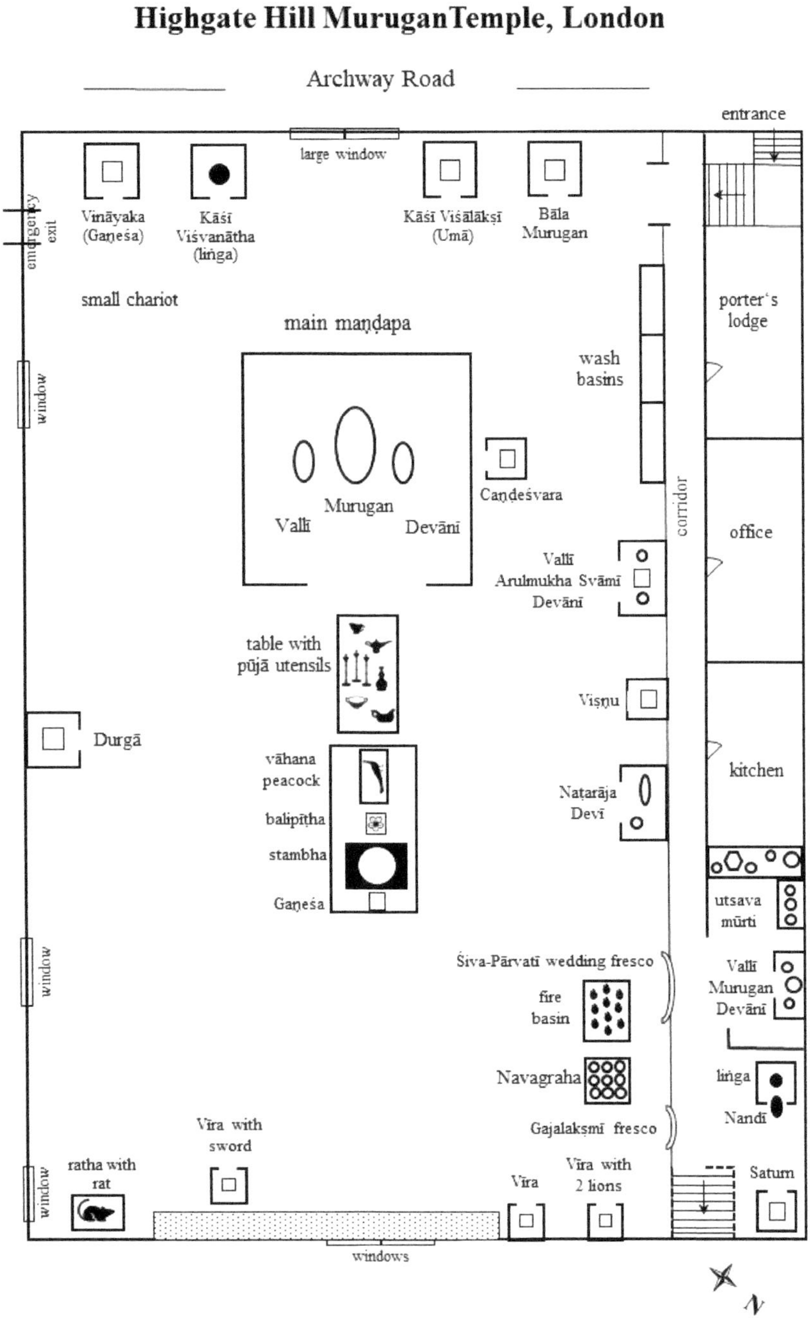
Highgate Hill MuruganTemple, London
Archway Road
entrance
large window
emergency exit
Vināyaka (Gaṇeśa)
Kāśī Viśvanātha (liṅga)
Kāśī Viśālākṣī (Umā)
Bāla Murugan
small chariot
main maṇḍapa
porter's lodge
wash basins
Murugan
Vallī
Devānī
Caṇḍeśvara
corridor
office
window
Vallī
Arulmukha Svāmī
Devānī
table with pūjā utensils
Viṣṇu
Durgā
vāhana peacock
balipīṭha
stambha
Gaṇeśa
Naṭarāja
Devī
kitchen
utsava mūrti
Śiva-Pārvatī wedding fresco
fire basin
Vallī
Murugan
Devānī
Navagraha
liṅga
Nandī
Gajalakṣmī fresco
Vīra with sword
ratha with rat
Vīra
Vīra with 2 lions
Saturn
windows
N

Highgate Hill MuruganTemple, London
Sanctissimum
(Dome Structure)

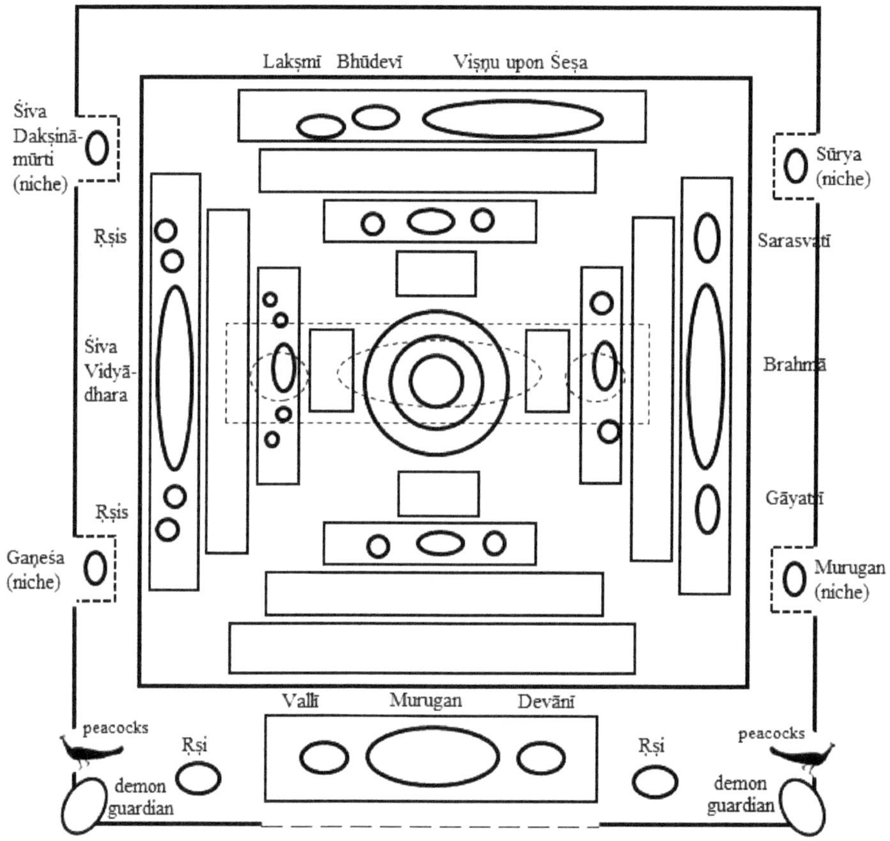

‘Murugan in Germany’
The Inauguration of the Murugan Temple in Hamm

Temple entrance from the east

The Inauguration

On February 7, 2001, the Murugan temple in the city of Hamm, Germany, was solemnly inaugurated. It was the second consecration of a Tamil temple in Hamm; the first had been that of the Siddhi-Vināyaka Gaṇeśa kōvil, which is situated in the immediate neighbourhood, downtown, near the railway station.

The full name reads *Thiru Nallur Sri Arumuka Velalakan Hindu Tempel Hamm e.V. (Europa)*. This is what one might call a transcultural writing for Tamil திருநல்லூர் ஸ்ரீ அருமுக வேலழகன் ஆலயம் *tirunallūr śrī arumuka vēlal̲akan̲ ālayam, ham*, ‘the Home (*ālayam*) of the Lord (*śrī*) Arumuka (Murugan), the Lance-Bearer (*vēlal̲akan̲*) from the Eminent (*tiru*) [Town of] Nallūr, [in] Hamm.’

Peacock and devotees in adoration

The outstanding ceremony, which can be observed nowadays more often overseas than in its homelands of India or Sri Lanka, was officiated by distinguished foreign brahmins. The temple hall was filled with devotees and the smoke of incense, – to such an extent that the quality of the pictures we took turned out to be rather foggy.

Temple musicians

Two musicians accompanied the event appropriately by blowing the Nādasvaram and beating the drum.

Donations prepared in advance

Brahmin consecrating the sanctissimum

Consecration of the sanctissimum from the outside. In this temple, Murugan, the main god and his subsidiary deities, Gaṇeśa and Lakṣmī, are not housed, as usual, in separate shrines. Instead, they are accommodated in one big pavilion with three apartments. Murugan, of course, is located in the middle. For the sake of simplicity, we call this collective shrine-of-three the sanctissimum.

The sanctissimum from the inside

It is a most essential part of the veneration ritual for the main god, to perform a clockwise circumambulation around the honoured deity. To make this possible, two doors have been installed in the west wall of the temple hall, to the right and left of the sanctissimum, leading to a small backyard. Therefore the brahmins and adoring laymen can walk around the main god. These doors are added to the already existing entrances in the north and the east (which is the main gate, but practically always locked).

The three domes of the sanctissimum during consecration

Since the sanctissimum also needed to be anointed from the outside, the performing brahmin, during the ceremony, climbed, with the help of a ladder, from the backyard up to the roof, which is – quite erratically among the houses of this neighbourhood – crowned by three shining domes. A spiritual and practical assistant came to his aid – spiritual, when providing devotional vessels, offerings or incense and practical, when giving a helping hand during critical moments on the ladder.

Anointing the pavilion of the Navagraha. The pavilion of the Nine Planets (Navagraha) had to be consecrated in a similar way but from the inside of the temple hall, which made the procedure less dangerous. But again, the ladder was indispensable.

Anointing the pavilion of the Nine Planets

Oblation on top of the shrine
of the Nine Planets

Welcome ceremony for the god Murugan. The salutations to the newly installed god were a moment of the highest spiritual importance for the Śivaïtic devotees. The recital lasted at least a quarter of an hour, whilst the believers were absorbed in prayers.

Suddenly one of them fell into a trance. Lying on the floor with twitching limbs, he kept on yelling the name of God until some of his companions succeeded in calming him down so much that he returned to comparative normalcy. Such states of unconsciousness are said to be not unusual in the devotional practice for Murugan.

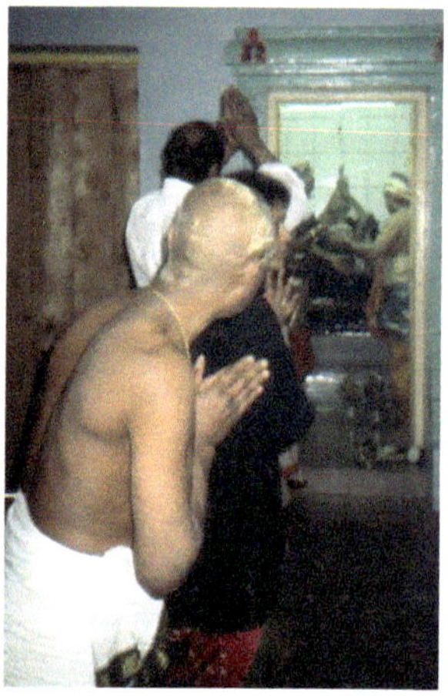

Welcoming Murugan

Venerating Murugan

Murugan, main shrine, granite statue

Iconography and Pantheon

The pantheon of the Murugan temple in Hamm is certainly not overcrowded but it represents all the significant deities expected in a temple of Śiva's son. The temple hall roughly faces the east (with a negligible turn to the east-north-east). The visitor, when he looks to the west in front of the main shrine, will have a square view of the god Murugan with his two consorts, Vallī to his right (from the god's perspective) and Devānī to his left.

Murugan and his consorts, main shrine

The god's sthalamūrti of black granite has three heads, which is quite an extraordinary feature for Murugan. Each head wears a basket-crown (*karaṇḍamukuṭa*) and the three of them culminate in one single point. Depictions of the god Śiva with three heads are renowned in his manifestation as Maheśamūrti, e. g. in the famous cave-temple in Elephanta, an island off the coast of Bombay; or of Brahmā with his four heads (occasionally three, as the one to the back might not be visible to the on-looker), each representing one of the four Vedas. But Brahmā's heads are bearded, as is one of the three heads of Śiva Maheśamūrti, his face with the wild, barbarous (*raudra*) aspect (see U. Schneider, *Opera Minora*, 2002, pp. 232-243). Murugan, however, is a handsome youth with clean features.

Therefore, there can be no doubt that we are looking at a statue of Murugan, particularly since he half sits on and half leans upon his mount, the peacock (Śiva rides a bull, Brahmā a goose). The peacock's white, painted, shining left eye peeks out under the god's lowest right hand.

Murugan has twelve arms. It is hard to say which objects he holds in his hands, because the black dark granite makes any identification virtually impossible. But at least both his lowest hands show discernible gestures: the right one grants freedom from fear (*a-bhayada*), on the left he indicates his willingness to grant wishes (*varada*). A metal lance, his symbol, leans against the inside of his right shoulder.

Murugan wears a white cummerbund with an orange hem and an orange shawl in the same pattern. The forehead and the helmet, his lance, also the palms of his front hands, are each decorated with a yellow mark (*tilaka*) with a red point in the middle. A heavy necklace fastened to a six-pointed jewelled star adorns his chest.

His consorts wear the same basket-helmet as their lord. Vallī is draped in orange clothes, Devānī in green. Vallī is additionally decorated with an expensive looking necklace.

Yellow petals of asters, loosely strewn over the sculptures, complete the tasteful arrangement.

The chamber on the god Murugan's right hand side (to the south) is the abode of his half-brother, Gaṇeśa. Gaṇapati, 'Lord of [Śiva's] troops,' as he is also called (he was a young lover and playmate of Pārvatī, who kneaded his form out of the remnants of the beauty paste for her body and breathed him to life, as the legend goes), – Piḷḷaiyār, in short (to use his Tamil name, 'Noble Child') has already been extensively discussed in the previous section of the present sketches. So we must not dwell too long on his description. His statue is draped and adorned very much like that of his half-brother Murugan – in white, yellow and red, strewn with asters. He is marked on his forehead with a yellow and red tilaka and wears, in addition, a heavy garland around his shoulders and pot belly.

Gaṇeśa

Lakṣmī

On the other side, to the north, we notice the statue of the Devī. Here it is Lakṣmī, the goddess of fortune. She wears a green dress and performs the same gestures with the two lower hands of her four arms like Murugan, showing freedom from fear (*abhayada*) and granting wishes (*varada*).

When we look behind us, we perceive Murugan's mount, the peacock, also carved out of black granite with the lotus bud (*balipīṭha*) behind it. Both statuettes are adorned with flower petals.

The peacock's head is exquisitely carved in a naturalistic manner. In its beak the bird holds a captivated cobra. Birds and snakes are thought to be enemies in Hindu mythology.

Peacock (detail)

The Nine Planets (Navagraha)

We pass the shrine of the Nine Planets in the north-western corner and then, in front of the north wall of the temple hall, we marvel at the pedestal of the festival statues. They are made of bronze and wait to be carried through the neighbouring streets (like Roonstraße, Feidikstraße, Hohe Straße etc.) once a year during the Great Festival (*mahotsava*) of Murugan's kōvil.

Murugan with consorts
Utsavamūrti

Six-headed Murugan
Ṣaṇmukha, utsavamūrti

The last pavilion we encounter during our half circumambulation, in the north-eastern corner, houses the statue of Bhairava, an incarnation of Śiva in his 'awe-inspiring' attitude, recognisable by his dog, whose muzzle only just peeks out, down below on the right, behind the Terrible One's garments.

Śiva Bhairava

Desk and kiosk

In the opposite corner there is a small kiosk with devotional items – jars, oil lamps, incense, etc. – which also serves as a small office for the temple's initiator and manager, Mr. Krishna Yoganathan. We sincerely thank Mr. Yoganathan for patiently answering all our nosey questions, showing a group of Indology students around his sanctum and generally for his kind cooperation.

Krishna Yoganathan
Initiator and manager of the temple

Times of visit: February 7, 2001 (inauguration); January 26, 2002; September 4, 2007.
Address: Thiru Nallur Sri Arumuka Velalakan Hindu Tempel Hamm e.V. (Europa).
Roonstr. 2a, D-59065 Hamm, Germany.
Tel./Fax: 02381 – 291 03.

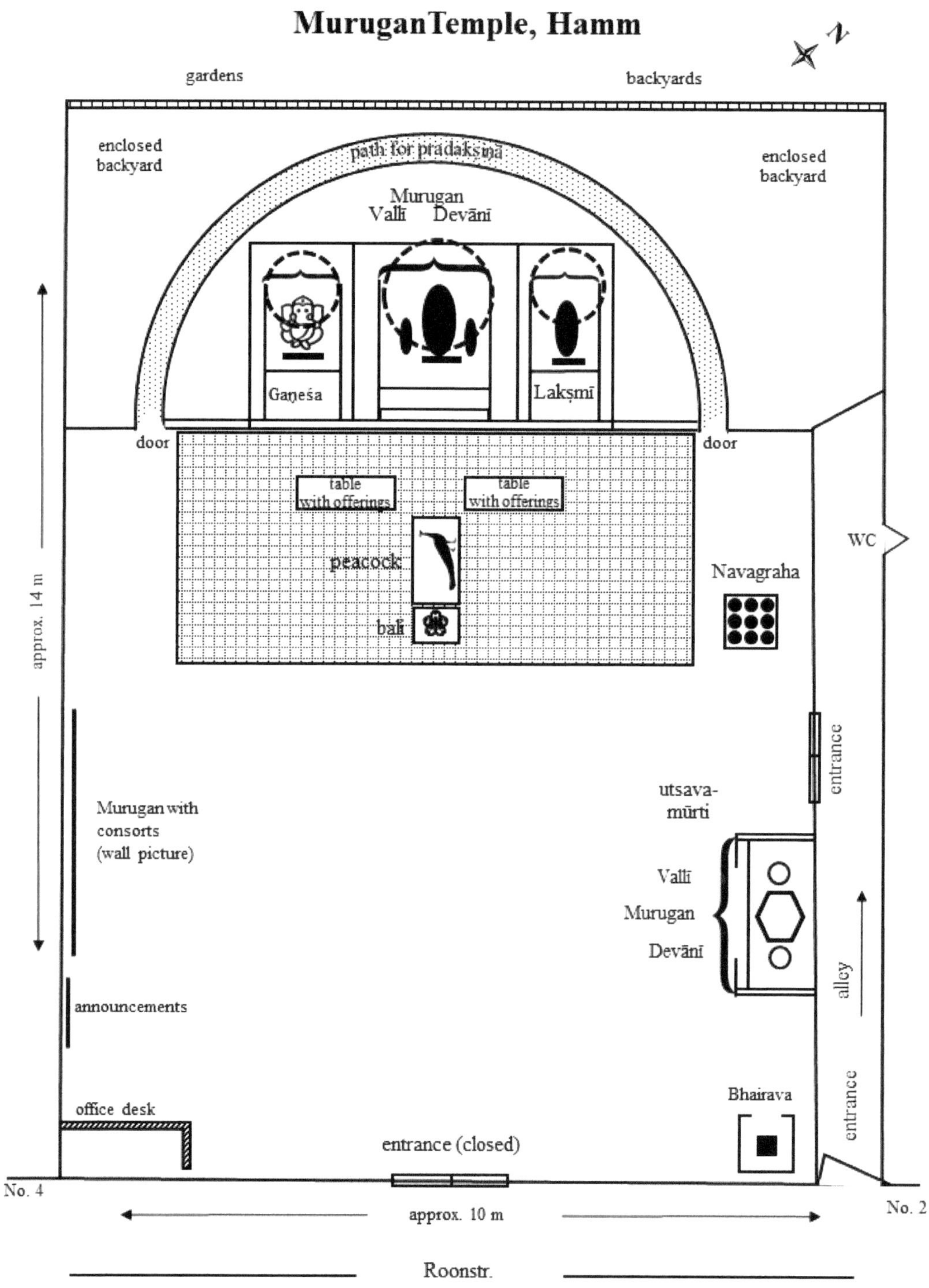
MuruganTemple, Hamm
N
gardens
backyards
enclosed backyard
path for pradakṣinā
enclosed backyard
Murugan
Vallī Devānī
Gaṇeśa
Lakṣmī
door
door
table with offerings
table with offerings
peacock
bali
WC
Navagraha
approx. 14 m
entrance
utsava-mūrti
Murugan with consorts (wall picture)
Vallī
Murugan
Devānī
alley
announcements
entrance
Bhairava
office desk
entrance (closed)
No. 4
No. 2
approx. 10 m
Roonstr.

‘A Temple under Renovation’
The Śrī Subrahmaṇya Svāmī Kōvil in Colombo

Śrī Subrahmaṇya Svāmī Kōvil, Colombo
Interim pavilion during renovation

Before we could say anything, we were told that one of the four brahmins present in the temple had spent two years in Germany, in the city of Hamm. This brahmin gave his name as Padmanābha. He revealed that he had officiated as a brahmin in the Murugan temple in Hamm in Roonstraße. Also, that he had worked in the *Jaffna Stores* (opposite) in Hamm and he knew the small Tamil restaurant and take-away opposite *Jaffna Stores* in Feidikstraße, (formerly the Olze bakery), just beside the house where we had been living ourselves in Feidikstr. 72, for 15 years up to 1995. He had also been working in Dortmund for two years. His wife and daughter who were also present in the temple had been with him in Germany. He asked us to give his greetings to Yoganathan, operator of the Murugan temple in Roonstraße – small world!

The Śrī Subrahmaṇya Svāmī Kōvil (the 'Temple of the Lord, the Noble Subrahmaṇya,' i. e. Murugan) in Colombo is mentioned by S. Arumugam, *Some Ancient Hindu Temples of Sri Lanka* (1982, pp. 72f). According to Arumugam, the present Subrahmaṇya statue was housed, 'as far back as 1822... in a shrine built by one Periyathamby (and others) in his land at Dam Street, Colombo.' In about 1867 the work on the first temple in Kew Road started and finished in 1870 under the name of Kadiresan Kōvil, Slave Island, 'to be remodelled, enlarged and reconstructed... in 1902 with the name of Sri Sivasubrahmaniya Swami Kōvil, Slave Island.' A temple trust was founded in 1942. In 1962, further renovation work began, 'also providing parivara moorthy [*parivāra-mūrti*, statues of the retinue] shrines for Vinayakar [Gaṇeśa], Nadaraja [Śiva Naṭarāja], Maha Vishnu, Saniyasuvarar [Śany-Asura, Saturn], Navakgraham [Navagraha, Nine Planets], etc.'

After this renovation, the Kumbhābhiṣeka is said to have been celebrated in 1975, which is corroborated by donators' plates in the Gaṇeśa-Vināyaka shrine. The gopuram which, according to Arumugam, was only planned in 1975, was erected in the meantime, and completed on March 29, 1993. A plate on the front (south) site of the gopuram reads: 'Raj-Kopuram Construction, Architect 1993.3.29 (March 29, 1993), Visva Sri. MRV Nagalingam Asary [Ācārya], Thiruppullani, Thamilnadu.'

Today, the temple is under renovation again. The beautiful ancient friezes, frescoes and statues are deplorably decayed by the humid climate.

One of the frescoes depicts Subrahmaṇya ('Who is friendly with the brahmins'), a Sanskrit name of Murugan predominantly used in South India. The youthful god stands in front of his mount, the blue and green speckled peacock, which cranes its neck adoringly upwards to its lord. The figure is richly decorated with bracelets, necklaces, a massive sapphire on its chest, jewelled girdles and a heavy mālā (garland) from neck to toes. The god wears a yellow, striped dhotī (hipcloth), his navel naked. The tilaka mark is painted on his forehead. Weighty earrings and the basket crown (*karaṇḍamukuṭa*) complete his head ornaments. The lance (*vēl*) leans against his right armpit, a flag in his left. The deity has four arms; with his lower right hand he holds a missile (*śakti*). Both upper hands point their palms to the observer with upturned fingers and ring fingers bent; the right hand balances a chisel (*ṭaṅka*). The upper left wields the disk (*cakra*). The lower left rests relaxed on the left thigh (*kaṭy-avalambanā*).

The masterly work of art radiates an aura of majestic calm.

Subrahmaṇya

Murugan Ṣaṇmukha with consorts
A withered frieze

Murugan Daṇḍāyudhapāṇi

Provisional arrangement
during renovation

All shrines are emptied of their statues and filled with construction materials and tools. For the statues (both sthalamūrtis and utsavamūrtis), an interim pavilion, made of wood and wire, has been erected immediately west of the main maṇḍapa for the duration of the renovation.

The whole temple is one big construction site but nevertheless, an endless stream of devotees flows into the place of worship for regular services. These services are officiated by four temple brahmins, assisted by two servants (without thread). The temple staff are very cooperative in answering questions.

The temple faces south, as it will in the future too. This irregularity is explained by the temple manager, Mr. S. Kanagalingam, by the position of the surrounding buildings. It was simply not possible to make it face east. He seems resigned to this. According to Arumugam, the old temple was forced to move to its present destination in 1867 and the change was facilitated by the officials through a donation of £500, a considerable sum in those times. But it seems that even then, and even in Ceylon, the new site of the temple structure was not chosen by the temple priests, instead they had to accept what was given to them by external forces. In consequence, the angle of the temple had to be adapted to its surroundings. These are very much the same circumstances that many emigrant temples face today. The problem

Subrahmaṇya (Murugan) as main deity of the temple

with the orientation of a temple is not a new one but one that arises whenever a temple is newly built in established urban surroundings.

According to his position in the interim pavilion, Subrahmaṇya, i. e. Murugan, is undoubtedly the main deity of this temple.

Navagraha and other sthalamūrtis temporarily displaced

He resides in front and in the centre of his entourage – all of them temporarily displaced sthalamūrtis and dislodged utsavamūrtis alike.

Utsavamūrtis
temporary setup

All sorts of devotional equipment are stored in the provisional space too.

Be it a bronze *vēl* decorated with statues and bells,

Vēl, adorned with figures of Murugan and consorts with bells

or ancient gadgets like an electric percussion machine for ritual usage. A similar one is in use in the Varasiddhi-Vināyaka Gaṇeśa Temple in Toronto.

Percussion machine

A sign explains why brahmins must only enter the sanctissimum when stripped to the waist. There is always the danger of evil spirits hiding in the folds of clothes. One does not want to bring them in.

A sighn at the main entrance

Near the main entrance a plan of the future temple setup informs the visitor how the temple of old will look like in the future, after renovation. It is our impression, based on some evidence, that Tamil temples, due to adverse climatic conditions, need renovation about every forty years.

Time of visit: April 15, 2006, Saturday before Easter, one day after Hindu New Year, 9:20-10:35 a.m.

Name as mentioned in the official letter-head of the temple: (English) Arulmihu Sivasubramaniya Swamy Kōvil; (Tamil) Aruḷmiku Civacuvviramaṇiya Cuvāmi Kōvil; (Sinhala) Arulmihu Sivasupparamaṇiya Suvāmi Kōvil. [Sanskrit translation: Śrī Śiva-Subrahmaṇya-Svāmi-Devasthāna, 'Temple of Lord Śiva and the Noble Subrahmaṇya (i.e. Murugan)]

Address: 131, Kew Road, Colombo-2, Sri Lanka. Phone 43222.

Śrī Subrahmaṇya Svāmī Kōvil, Colombo, west side
Main entrance, gopuram with clock-tower (left) and belltower (right)

Śrī Subrahmaṇya Svāmī Kōvil, Colombo

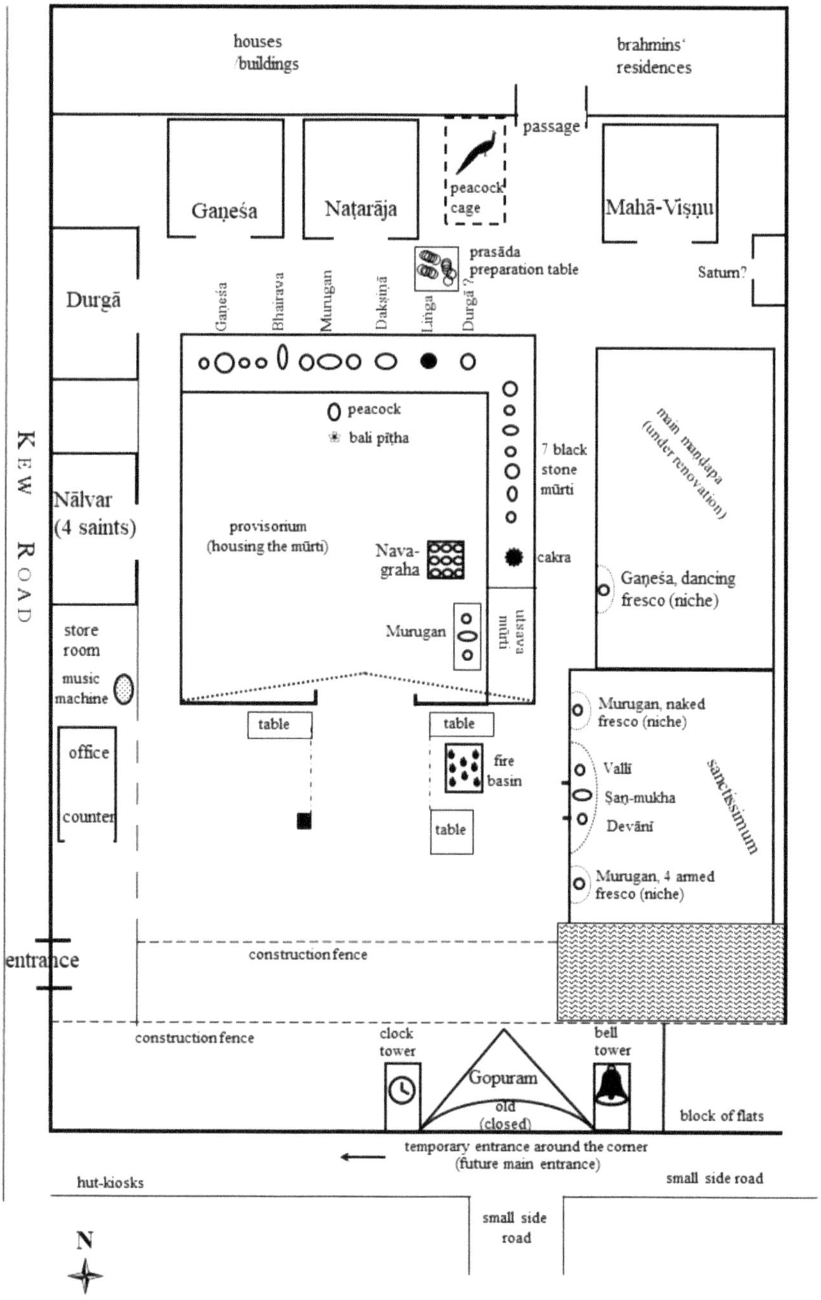

‘Murugan in Canada’
The Canada Kanthaswamy Kōvil in Scarborough

Canada Kanthaswamy Kōvil, Scarborough; south side

Kanthaswamy is an anglicised written form of Tamil *Kantacuvāmi*, derived from Sanskrit *Skandasvāmī*, i. e. Murugan. Skandasvāmī means, ‘The Leaping Lord.’ That might refer to a certain fighting technique as Murugan is, besides other functions, a god of war.

The Skandasvāmī temple was founded in 2000 with an elaborate inauguration ceremony (*kumbhābhiṣeka*). The whole of the temple building encircles approximately 100 x 30 square meters, including the temple hall on the east side which extends over 40 x 30 meters. To the west there is a spacious ‘wedding hall’ for around 600 people with a large stage, a kitchen, changing rooms and sanitary facilities. The temple has cost 1.3 million Canadian Dollars.

Entrance, exit and car park

Interior of the temple hall, view from the south entrance

A hotel was once located on the present temple premises. It is not clear whether the former hotel building was renovated and restructured to become a Hindu temple, or if it was demolished and erected anew.

Precursor of the present, permanent sanctum was a 'temporary place' in Kennedy/Finch Rd, set up by Toronto Hindus as early as 1991.

The temple committee consists of approximately 500 members. It

Wedding hall

Wedding hall stage

permanently employs three brahmins, all of them from Sri Lanka. The eldest of them was educated in Tamil Nadu.

Our visit fell on the day of Sarasvatī pūjā, two days before the end of the Navarātri festival, which was celebrated in 2004 on October, 22.

The orientation of the temple is exactly to the east. Perhaps it should be taken into consideration that this setup corresponds to the whole city of Toronto, where nearly all the main roads and blocks point at right angles from west to east and from south to north.

Murugan Skandasvāmī and his two consorts
Main shrine (*mūlagarbha*)

Murugan with consorts
Painting

Murugan Skandasvāmī with consorts
Utsavamūrti

Pantheon and Iconography

We enter the temple hall through the south entrance and observe (from the side, see picture at top of p. 118) the abodes of, from left to right, Śiva Dakṣiṇāmūrti, Murugan in the main shrine, Śivaliṅga, Gaurī, Murugan Ṣaṇmukha with consorts and the Nine Planets. In between we see Śiva's mount Nandī and Murugan's peacock, behind both the lotus bud (*balipīṭha*) and the flagpole (*stambha*).

We walk into the centre of the temple hall, turn to the left and come to a halt in front of the unusually huge sanctissimum, housing the granite statues of the chief god of this temple, Murugan Skandasvāmī, and his two consorts (picture on p. 119).

Since previously discussing Murugan in two other temples, we need not linger too long now on his description.

We identify him easily by his lance (*vēl*), and recognise his consorts: Vallī, the dark-complexioned daughter of a jungle hunter and fair Devānī, the heavenly maiden, Indra's offspring.

Standing in front of the main shrine, we observe the pavilion of Murugan's half-brother Gaṇeśa right behind it. And there is not only one, but a pair of goddesses in the opposite north-west corner: the deity of fortune, Lakṣmī, and Durgā (the friendly counterpart of the terrible Kālī).

Two minor divine figures must be placed near the sanctissimum in a major temple like this and these are: a representation of Śiva Dakṣiṇāmūrti, always to the south and Caṇḍeśvara, Śiva's general, with Murugan's troops to the north.

Directly in front of the sanctissimum to one side, stands a plentifully decorated Śivaliṅga, complete with garland, cummerbund, mark of three strokes (*tripuṇḍra*), yellow and red tilaka and flowers.

Liṅga – granite statue

It is even equipped with its own watchguard, namely Śiva's mount Nandī, the zebu bull, in an extraordinarily handsome design.

Śiva's bull Nandī
Watching the Liṅga

On the other side, to the north, we find the pavilion of Gaurī who is a manifestation of Śiva's spouse Umā (aka Pārvatī).

Gaurī, the Fair One

Gaurī means literally 'She of white colour,' the 'Fair One.' Accordingly, the brahmin in service was busy painting during our visit, the black granite stone representing Gaurī white, using the vibhūti, i. e. the ashes of a sacrificial fire.

Along the north wall, we pass a shrine with the Six-headed Murugan and his consorts first, then the Vasantamaṇḍapa ('Spring shrine') with the festival statues (*utsavamūrti*), which accommodates, among others, Murugan and his consorts again.

During the Navarātri festivities, a golu arrangement is customary in most Tamil temples. In this obviously popular temple, the temporary collection, brought by devotees, is extraordinarily opulent.

In front of the Spring shrine and the golu table, we find the pavilion of the Nine Planets (Navagraha).

Golu arrangement

In the north-east corner, we finally reach a small shrine for the monkey hero-god Hanumān, known already in the ancient, pre-Christian Sanskrit epic *Rāmāyaṇa*. Hanumān can be encountered in quite a few Tamil temples.

Hanumān

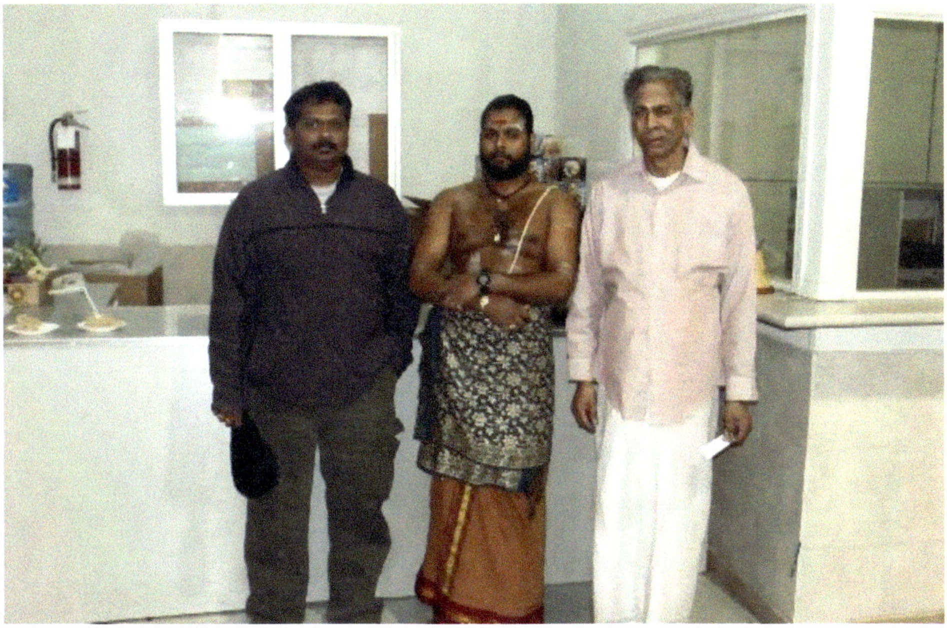

Our interlocutors were the temple custodian, an emigrant from Jaffna, Mr. Thiyagaraja and Mr. Thurai, 'Lincoln' – a member of the temple committee. Lincoln is Managing Director of the 'Great Toronto Truck & Forklift Driving School.' Born in Malaysia, he was educated in Scotland and now lives in Toronto.

One of the temple brahmins was decorating some statues, Gaurī in particular, for the Sarasvatī pūjā, which was scheduled for the same day. In between, he also performed a short Gaṇeśa pūjā for two lady-devotees visiting the temple.

Time of visit: October 20, 2004, approx. 11:00-12:30 hrs.
Address: 733 Birchmount Road, Scarborough, ON M1K 1R5, Canada.
Phone 416-438 1882.
www.canadakanthaswamytemple.com.

Canada Kanthaswamy Temple, Toronto

— Birchmount Rd. —

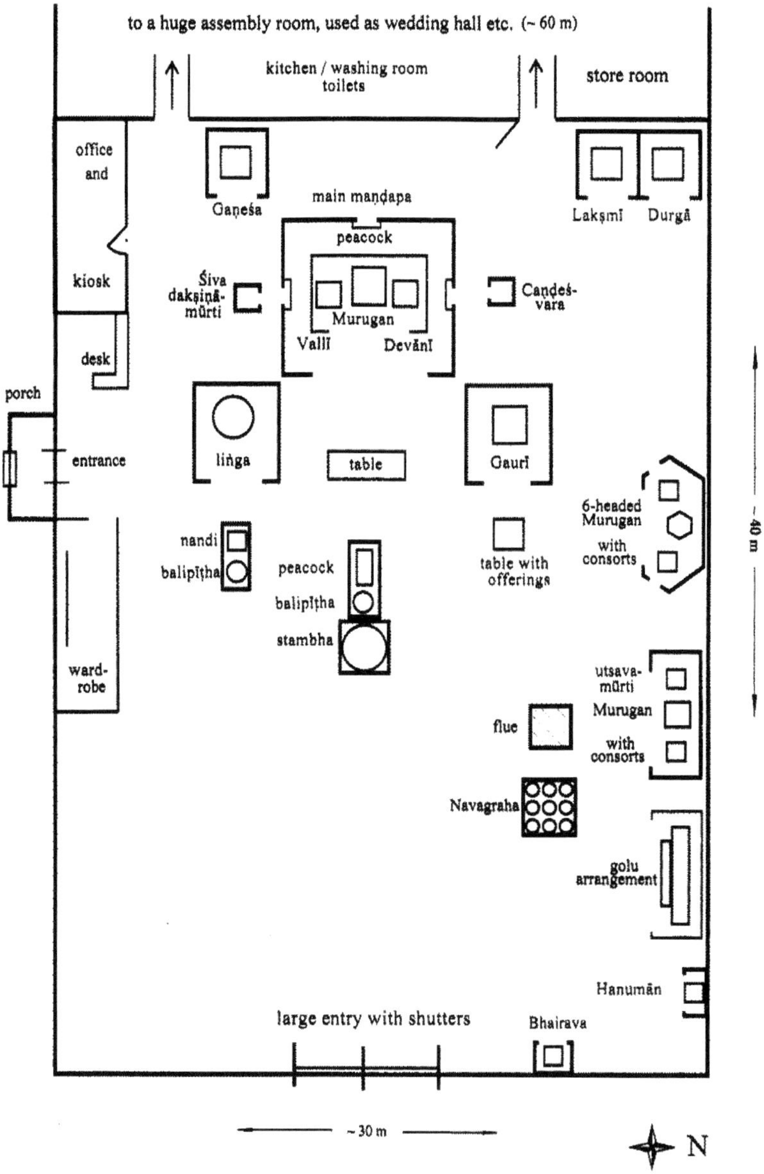

‘The God Lance’
The Nallūr Murugan Kōvil in Scarborough

The god Lance – in the sanctissimum

Temple Priest, Building and Organisation

The home and cognate temple is the famous Murugan sanctum in Nallūr on the Jaffna peninsula in Sri Lanka. Like the model in Nallūr, here too there is no personified depiction of god Murugan standing in the sanctissimum, but only his unmistakable attribute, the lance, in Tamil *vēl*.

On our arrival on a Monday morning, the temple is (and will remain for the next two and half hours) deserted, except for the priest who, having welcomed us, readily shows us around. On his card his name appears as ‘Bala Thiru Kunanantha Kurukkal’ (English

Bāla Thiru Kunānantha Kurukkal
Temple priest

version), in Tamil written as 'Pā. Tirukkuṇānantakkurukkaḷ (Nallūr)' [in Sanskrit 'Bāla Śrī Guṇānanda Kurukkal]. He personally wrote his name down for us as 'Thirukunanatha Sarma' [Śrī Guṇanātha Śarmā].

Bāla was initiated in Nallūr as Kurukkal, 'officiating Brahman priests in Śiva temples' (*Tamil Lexicon*). His card defines his occupation as 'Hindu Chief Priest, Marriage Registrar, Astrologer.' He is thirty years old, married, descendant of a brahmin family of the temple in Nallūr. The family belongs to the Viśvanāgar Kurukkal tradition. His deceased elder brother officiated as chief priest at the rathotsava ('chariot festival') in Nallūr, of which Bāla showed us a photograph.

Photograph of the Chariot Festival in Nallūr

His father's name is Bāla Subrahmaṇyam Kurukkal. He is seventy-five years old and lives in Colombo.

Bāla is proud of the successful healings he has to his credit. Alcoholism, surgical wounds, stomach problems – he treats them all with pūjā and herbs, which he imports from Sri Lanka and stores on shelves in the temple.

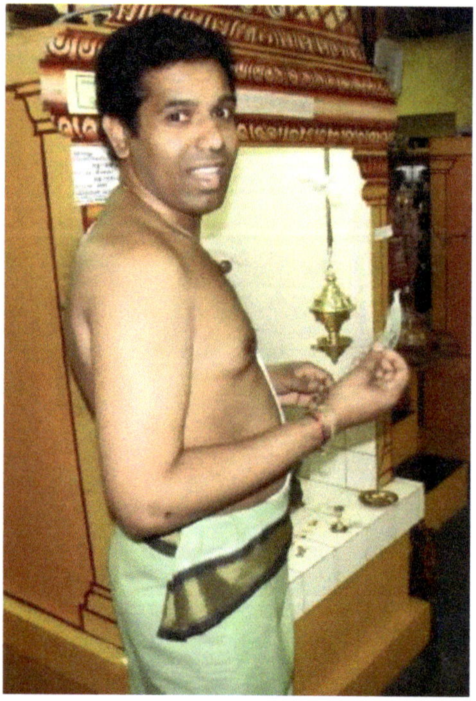

A woman, whose back vertebrae, thanks to his treatment, healed supernaturally fast after an operation, has converted ('changed' in Bāla's words) to Hinduism – a detail that illustrates Bāla's universalistic conception of his religion. The movable electronic screen of the *om* sign above the sanctissimum was installed by students of engineering who afterwards completed their studies in two instead of four years. The former owner of the estate, a Sikh who was still childless aged 56, regularly joined the pūjā in the temple and is now a father of a month old baby.

The temple society is comprised of sixty-eight members. There are close connections with the community in Nallūr. This year, at the same time as in Jaffna, the Great Chariot Festival

Shelves with medicinal herbs and drugs

Wedding hall

Nugget Avenue seen out of a temple window

Temple building: a former warehouse.
Under blue cover: the temple chariot

(*rathotsava*) was celebrated in Scarborough too. It lasted twenty-eight days, from August 21 through to September 16, 2004. There were 7.000 participants. The *Vēl* temple is becoming more and more popular; consequently, the pūjā must begin earlier from day to day.

The temple was founded with a Great Inauguration Ceremony on October 7, 2000. In the neighbourhood of the temple, haulage contractors and warehouses prevail.

The temple itself is set up in a former warehouse. The two-storied unit was purchased for 3.2 million Canadian Dollars. It extends over 35 x 20 square meters.

On the north side along the temple wall is a kitchen, a storeroom and an office. There is a kiosk inside the temple hall. The back exit on the west side leads to a passageway with a door to the street and a staircase to the upper storey, where there are a wedding theatre for 125 persons, a spacious attic, washrooms and lavatories.

Iconography and Pantheon

The granite and bronze statues cost 150.000 Canadian Dollars. They were carved by the late famous artist Devasenāpati and his workshop from Kumbhakonam, India. He had been educated in the artists' (*śilpaśāstrī*) school of Kāñcīpuram.

The lance (*vēl*) venerated in the main shrine (see p. 125) is made of solid silver. It weighs 400 kg and is ornamented with half a kilo of gold.

A guardian deity for the *Vēl* is positioned, viewed from the sanctissimum, on the right side, directly in front. It is the god Śiva in his awe-inspiring manifestation as Bhairava, the Terrible One. Like Murugan himself, Bhairava too does not appear here *in persona* but is represented by his attributes: the trident and a dog, both cast in reddish bronze.

Sanctissimum: *Vēl* with Murugan's consorts
In the foreground: Bhairava's trident, the saint Appar and the Liṅga

Bhairava's trident

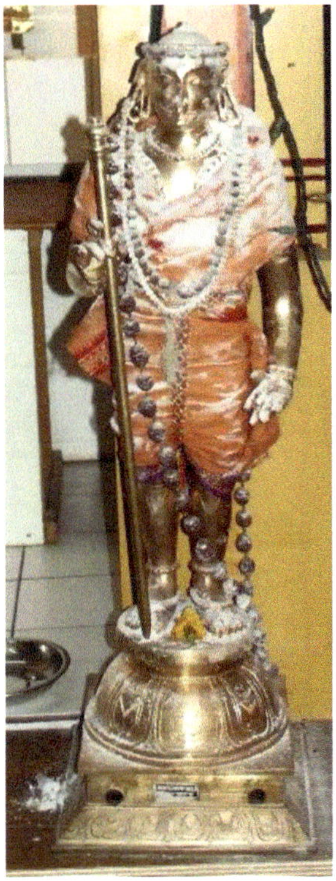

Appar

Bhairava's dog

Murugan's mount (*vahana*), the peacock

One of the four Tamil saints, called Appar, keeps watch in front of the left side of the main shrine.

In their middle, we perceive Murugan's mount, the peacock, carved out of black granite.

Liṅga with bull Nandī and lotus bud (*balipīṭha*). A small liṅga with yoni substitutes the flagpole (*stambha*).

In front of the guardians we see the shrine of the elephant-headed Gaṇeśa on the right side; to the left, the pavilion of the Śiva Liṅga. Gaṇeśa and the Liṅga are also honoured by their respective mounts, the rat and the bull, each with the appropriate lotus bud (*balipīṭha*).

Like so many Tamil emigrant temples, this residence of the *Vēl* is not 'purpose-built,' therefore the roof of the ex-warehouse is rather near to the ground. Consequently, the obligatory flagpole in front of the sanctissimum

Gaṇeśa

is missing. As a substitute, a small granite Liṅga, planted in a yoni (symbolising the vulva), has been set up here, in front of the Śiva Liṅga.

Viṣṇu and his spouses, the goddess Fortune, Lakṣmī and the goddess Earth, Bhūdevī, are situated at a place still further in front of the *Vēl*, facing the rising sun.

Viṣṇu and his spouses, Lakṣmī and Bhūdevī

Ayyappan's eighteen steps

A place of honour – directly beside the main shrine – is given to two local deities, Ayyappan and Aiyaṉār. Ayyappan is believed to be the son of Mohinī, who is the female manifestation of Viṣṇu and of Śiva. Hence one of his epithets, Hariharaputra, 'Son (*putra*) of Viṣṇu (*Hari*) and Śiva (*Hara*).' His cult is centred in the South Indian state of Kerala but has spread far and wide. Eighteen steps lead up to his pedestal, where he is depicted seated in the lotus position, with a meditation band around his knees, showing the gestures of granting fearlessness and wishes.

Ayyappan on top of his eighteen steps

Aiyan̲ār is shown flanked by his consorts, Pūraṇī and Puṣkalā. He is a South Indian 'guardian deity of the village' (*Tamil Lexicon*) and is petitioned for rich harvests and fertility.

Aiyan̲ār with two consorts

When we now proceed to the east, along the northern wall, we see a special feature of this sanctum, namely an altar with six assisting deities. According to the signs on top of the single figures, the first is Sūrya, the sun god, here appearing not in the centre of the Nine Planets, but separately. The next is Gaṇeśa in his manifestation as Śrī Siddhi-Vināyaka. Then Pārvatī, Śiva's spouse, under the name of Śrī Kamala-ambikā ('Mom Lotus'). In the fourth place, the goddess who heals smallpox, Mārī-Ambā (Māriyamman), venerated in South India. She is next to the monkey hero-god Hanumān under the name of Āñjaneya who helps out as 'devotee Hanumān' (*bhakta Hanumān*) during the morning pūjā for Śiva. The final statue is a cobra (Nāga) with six hoods, regarded as a god, who winds around a Liṅga.

The six assisting deities
Detail: six-headed cobra

<

Sūrya, Gaṇeśa, Pārvatī, Mārī-ambā, Hanumān and a divine cobra with six hoods. Granite statuettes

Splendid indeed is the altar with the golu arrangement, which is set up during the Navarātri festival celebrated in the honour of Śiva. Here the golu figures are presented together with the bronze festival statues (*utsavamūrti*) with a six-headed Skanda (=Murugan Ṣaṇmukha), a 'solid' bronze cast, whose head, hands and mount (*vāhana*) were created by the abovementioned artist Devasenāpati, a short time before his death, weighing 275 kilograms and costing 7.000 CAD.

Another extraordinary piece is a bronze statuette showing Murugan as a baby (Bāla-Murugan), sucking his toe, while he is sitting on the coils of a five-headed cobra.

Murugan Ṣaṇmukha, riding the peacock

Bāla Murugan

Gajavallīmahāvallī

Bāla, the temple priest, directs our attention to a very rare bronze statue, of which another copy exists, as he points out, otherwise only in Nallūr: It is a *Gajavallīmahāvallī*, a depiction of both of Murugan's consorts, Vallī and Devānī, in a sole figure. The right side of the statue, 'Mahāvallī,' represents Vallī and the left, 'Gajavallī,' shows Devānī. The idea of 'Two in One' can be seen in sculptures of Ardhanārīśvara, the 'Lord who is half woman,' i.e. Śiva in his male and female manifestations or Harihara, i.e. Viṣṇu (Hari) and Śiva (Hara) combined.

Here, the Siamese twin stands on a lotus pedestal, which is positioned on the right side of the six-headed and twelve-armed Murugan. She holds a lotus flower in each of her hands. The separate Vallī and Devānī always seize lotus flowers too. Her legs are clad in different garments; the right leg in a rustic fabric, the left in a rich, elaborate style. Her right breast is partly covered by a band or ribbon, the indigenous covering of a forest girl as the dark-complexioned Vallī is believed to be a hunter's daughter. Her left breast is naked, according to a certain dress code for high-caste women (the Sri Lankan Sīgiri Rock Ladies spring to mind) as the divine Devānī is the god Indra's daughter. If we take a close look, we discern different patterns in the ornaments on both sides of her basket-crown (*karaṇḍamukuṭa*) and in the styles of her necklaces.

To come across such an exceptional piece of Sri Lankan artistry in an industrial quarter of Toronto is certainly unexpected.

Bāla Śrī Guṇānanda Kurukkal has created, through his temple, a remarkable microcosm, like an air bubble, in which he and his devotees can survive in the surrounding alien macrocosm.

Time of visit: October 24, 2004, 10:00-12:30 hrs.
Address: 20 Nugget Avenue, Unit #1, Scarborough, ON M1S 3A7, Canada.

Ōm
The movable electronic screen above the sanctissimum

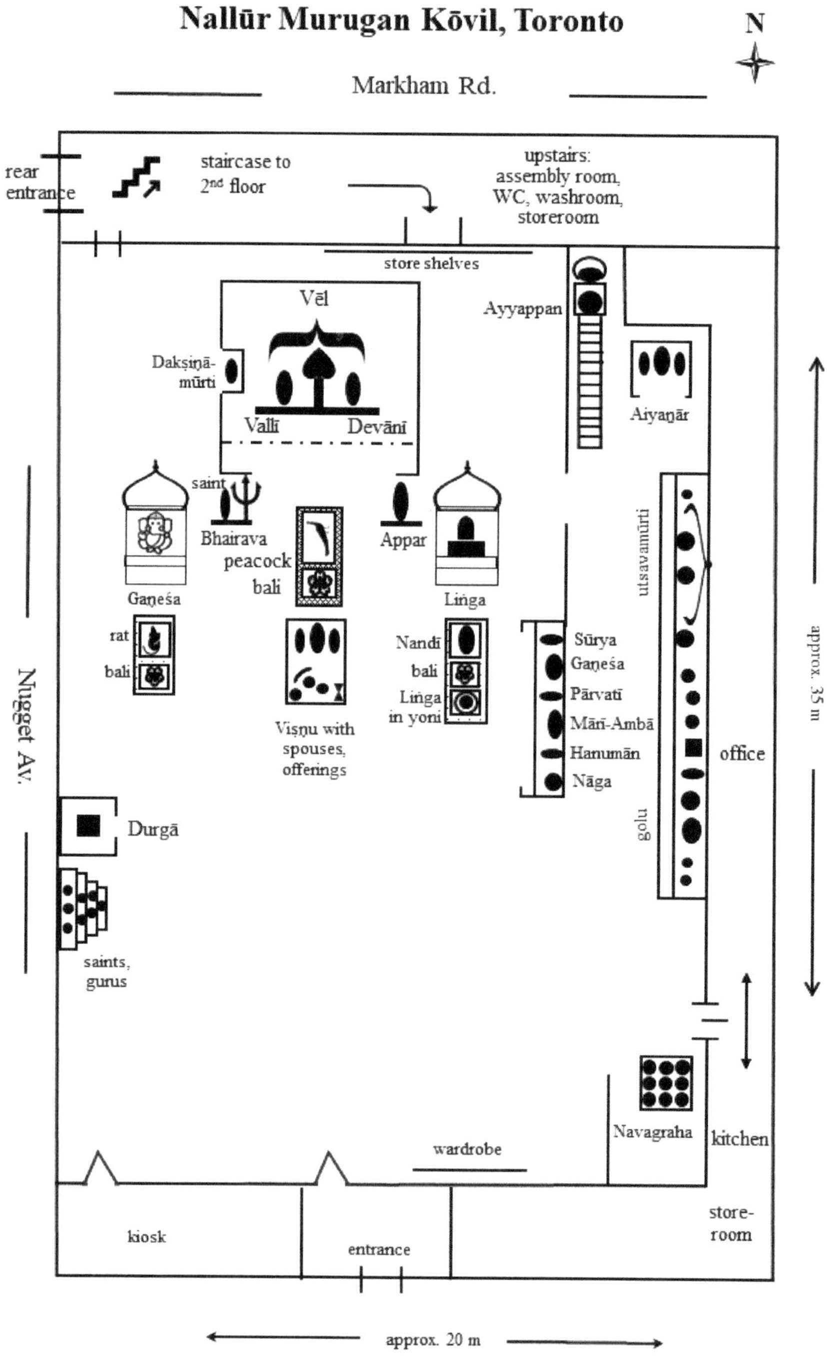
Nallūr Murugan Kōvil, Toronto
N
Markham Rd.
rear entrance
staircase to 2nd floor
upstairs: assembly room, WC, washroom, storeroom
store shelves
Vēl
Dakṣiṇā-mūrti
Vallī
Devānī
Ayyappan
Aiyaṉār
saint
Bhairava
peacock
bali
Appar
Gaṇeśa
Liṅga
utsavamūrti
rat
bali
Viṣṇu with spouses, offerings
Nandī
bali
Liṅga in yoni
Sūrya
Gaṇeśa
Pārvatī
Mārī-Ambā
Hanumān
Nāga
office
golu
Nugget Av.
approx. 35 m
Durgā
saints, gurus
Navagraha
kitchen
wardrobe
kiosk
entrance
store-room
approx. 20 m

‘Murugan in the Coconut Grove’ The Kārttikeya Kōvil in Mādampē

Name as mentioned on the entrance gate in Tamil and Sinhala script:
Tamil: *Śrī Kaliyakavarata Murugan Kōvil, Mātampai.*
Sinhala: *Puṃci Kataragama Dēvasthānaya, Mādampē.*

Śiva, who has just copulated with his spouse, Pārvatī, lets his semen fall onto the God of Fire, Agni. The semen, heated by the ascetic fieriness of the divine celibate, Śiva, is too hot even for Agni, who hurls Śiva’s seed into the holy Gaṅgā. The divine river begins to boil and throws the semen out as well, from which emanates a handsome lad. ‘Six (!) princesses (the Pleiades) who came to the river to take a bath saw the baby and each called him her son. And as they offered him their breasts, the boy took on six heads with six mouths, and he was suckled by each of them. Therefore, his name is Kārttikeya, “Who is descended from the Kṛttikās (the Pleiades).” However, he did not have a mother, for Kārttikeya (aka Murugan) was begot by his father alone.’

This is the aetiology, explaining why Murugan has six heads and is therefore also called Ṣaṇmukha, the 'Six-headed One.' It is told in the *Śivapurāṇa* for example but also in many other South Indian collections of Śaiva myths. It must be added that in India and Sri Lanka they only count six Pleiades instead of the western 'Siebengestirn.' The Pleiades are called Kṛttikās in Sanskrit – Kārttikeya is its metronymic.

The Kārttikeya Kōvil in Mādampē displays particularly beautiful frescoes which illustrate the nature of the six-headed god. The temple is located directly on the east side of the highway no. 3 from Negombo to Chilaw/Puttalam near the provincial town of Mādampē.

What we learn about the temple is common knowledge, such as our

three-wheeler driver Susantha can provide. (Susantha was born in the neighbouring town of Chilaw and works in Negombo. He still has many relatives, friends and business acquaintances in Chilaw.) According to Susantha, the temple was built and financed by a rich Tamil business man from Jaffna. A uniformed youth who keeps watch over the premises gives the name of the temple owner as K. P. Rasaiya. Mr. Rasaiya evaded the civil war and bought a large coconut palm estate.

He decided to build a Murugan temple on this ground, where a very small and neglected Murugan shrine was already situated. (The Gaṇeśa temple we presented first in this volume, in T. Nagar, Chennai, has a similar genesis). The work on the temple was finished by its inauguration approximately two years ago (in 2004).

Mr Rasaiya hired artisans from South India who created the elaborate frescoes, hence the temple's richness of statues and friezes, combined with outstanding artisanship. An abundance of scenes on the roofs of the seven pavilions vividly evokes the many myths and legends around Kārttikeya.

Pantheon and Iconography

We enter the temple premises not through the main gate directly opposite the road but through the (smaller) east gate, according to the traditional custom. To our right rises a tall bell tower. At its side we pass the shrine of Bhairava (the god Śiva in his awe-inspiring manifestation), who keeps watch at the entrance. His usual watch dog, one of his symbols, peeps out behind his right knee and two more hounds lie at his feet.

Bhairava
Fresco on the roof of his shrine, north side

The artisans treated the traditional features of iconography freely and they made themselves independent from the fetters of standard clichés. A fine example awaits us at the next shrine on the north side, where the Nine Planets (Navagraha) use to have their regular place: Mercury, Venus, Mars, Jupiter, Saturn, Sun and Moon, Rāhu (demon of eclipses) and Ketu (demon of comets and meteors).

Here these mighty, highly respected astrological bodies are housed in the sun god's chariot and Sūrya himself, the central figure of the Nine Planets, functions as charioteer, steering five eager-looking, lively, if not unruly, stallions in front of his solar carriage.

The sun god Sūrya as charioteer.
In the pavilion behind him are the 'planets.'

Roof of the central shrine
Kārttikeya (Murugan Ṣaṇmukha) with consorts Vallī and Devānī

Murugan with consorts in the sanctissimum, nearly invisible in the dark background.
In the foreground: middle – lotus bud (*balipīṭha*), left – lance; far left – a guardian

Entrance to sanctissimum, east side.
Foreground: coconut grate, bell tower, the sun god's pavilion
Background left: Gaṇeśa and Aiyaṉār

Only temple brahmins are allowed to enter the sanctissimum. We remain standing in front, trying to recognise the large black granite statues, the sthalamūrtis of Murugan Kārttikeya and his two consorts, which regrettably are nearly completely hidden by the dark shade inside the main shrine. Before them we perceive the lotus bud (*balipīṭha*) and Murugan's mount, the peacock, also his lance and the huge figures of two guardians on both sides of the entrance.

We commence our walk around the main shrine (*mūlagarbha*), always keeping it to our right side, thus performing a pradakṣiṇā. At the inner fence at the back of the sanctissimum (west) we come across the figures of four star-maidens, sporting a star on top of their diadems, sitting at a water basin containing proliferous lotus plants.

One of the four star-maidens

Shrines of Gaṇeśa (right) and Aiyaṉār

Turning round and looking to the south-west, we observe two shrines, already from a distance. The larger one accommodates Gaṇeśa, Murugan's half-brother, whose place is suitably behind the main god, on his right side. In the smaller one resides Aiyaṉār, a popular local village guardian.

We pass the shrine of Viṣṇu and his two spouses, Lakṣmī and Bhūdevī, the goddesses Fortune and Earth respectively.

Here, at the north-west corner of the temple compound, we turn to the right and take our time to thoroughly study the abundance of figurines and friezes on the roof of the main shrine. The north side is where the expensive bronze statues – the utsavamūrtis – are placed, which are carried around the temple during eminent festivities. At present they are hidden inside the temple structure but the plaster figurines on the roof outside give a representative impression of their imposing opulence.

We want to concentrate on two groups of deities here, on the north side, both dealing with central figures of the Śaiva pantheon. The first is the 'holy family,' depicting Śiva as *pater familiās*, quite contrary in his peacefulness and dignity, to other manifestations of his, like the terrible Bhairava or the naked ascetic.

The holy family – Śiva as *pater familiās*

Śiva sits relaxed, his left lower leg bent upwards (*lalitāsana*), amongst his family, on top of his home mountain Kailāsa in the Himālayas. His shimmering body is smeared with white ashes of the sacrificial fire, the vibhūti, – as has become the custom of naked, often hemp smoking Śaiva sādhus ('saints'). His necklace is a cobra that has curled itself around his throat. In his matted hair wriggles another snake.

Śiva always carries the crescent of the moon and the holy river Gaṅgā, personified as a beautiful nymph, upon his head. His left upper hand holds an antelope (*mṛga*), the right one an axe (*paraśu*). The right lower hand is the 'half-moon hand' (*ardha-candra-hasta*), which urges the devotee to put some fire in it and the left lower hand rests comfortably on his leg (*kaṭy-avalambita*).

Śiva's spouse Pārvatī holds a lotus bud, her left rests on her knee. Her elephant-headed, pot-bellied son, Gaṇeśa, his trunk curled, seizes an elephant goad (*aṅkuśa*) in his upper left hand, an axe in his upper right and both his lower hands show the half-moon (*ardha-candra-hasta*) gesture. Gaṇeśa's mount, the rat, stands up straight in front of his left foot, as if begging for a laḍḍū (of which Gaṇeśa, fond of sweet-meats, always carries a supply).

Brahmā, Viṣṇu, Śiva and Murugan

But this is a Murugan temple, so Murugan is the main person. Still a boy, he stands opposite Gaṇeśa. He also urges the observer to put some fire in his right hand while his left hand holds the lance and at the same time embraces his peacock. A heavenly maiden (Apsaras), holding a lute (*vīṇā*) and a parrot (*śuka*), entertains the family with music and dance.

The second party we would like to focus on here is just beside the first one. It is a pretty modification of the well-known divine triad: the Trimūrti, consisting of Brahmā, Viṣṇu and Śiva, but appropriately enlarged by Murugan, the favourite deity (*iṣṭadevatā*) of this sanctum.

Brahmā, the *creator*, has four heads and the observer can perceive only two of them on this temple roof frieze, the other two being situated on the invisible back side. Brahmā, the ancient priest deity from Vedic times, holds a rosary (*akṣamālā*) in his upper right hand and balances a kamaṇḍalu – a vessel filled with holy water – in his upper left. His right lower hand grants freedom from fear (*abhayada*) and the lower left begs for fire. Brahmā, first of all brahmins, wears the sacred thread over his left shoulder.

Viṣṇu, the *preserver*, blue-complexioned, is crowned with a diadem (*kirīṭamukuṭa*). The mace in his lower left hand symbolises authority and power. The spiralled conch in his upper left connects him with fertility-granting water, hinting at his creative might. When blown by a warrior, the shell will give a martial sound. The wheel (*cakra*) that he balances upon the fingers of his upper right hand symbolises the power of a universal monarch, a cakravartī: he rules not only over the whole of the earth but also over the wheel of reincarnation. Viṣṇu's typical gesture as the preserver of the universe is the abhayadamudrā, conducted by his right lower hand, granting freedom from fear and assuring shelter with open palm, fingers pointed upwards.

Śiva, the *destroyer*, once more with antelope and axe, grants freedom from fear too. With his fourth hand he hugs his son, Murugan the adolescent, who enjoys the place of honour on Śiva's upwards bended knee.

In sharp contrast appears Murugan, the war god, under his epithet Daṇḍāyudhapāṇi, 'He with his weapon the stick in his hand.'

Murugan Daṇḍāyudhapāṇi

Left: Pārvatī with six-headed Kārttikeya
Right: six Kṛttikās

Pārvatī and the six-headed Kārttikeya on her knee, sitting peacefully side by side with the six Pleiades, the foster-mothers, each with a Bāla-Skanda shall conclude our visit to this exceptional 'place of god' (*devasthāna*) in the coconut grove and the section on Murugan temples too.

Time of visit: April 6, 2006, about 10:00-11:30 a.m.

Kārttikeya Kōvil, Mādampē

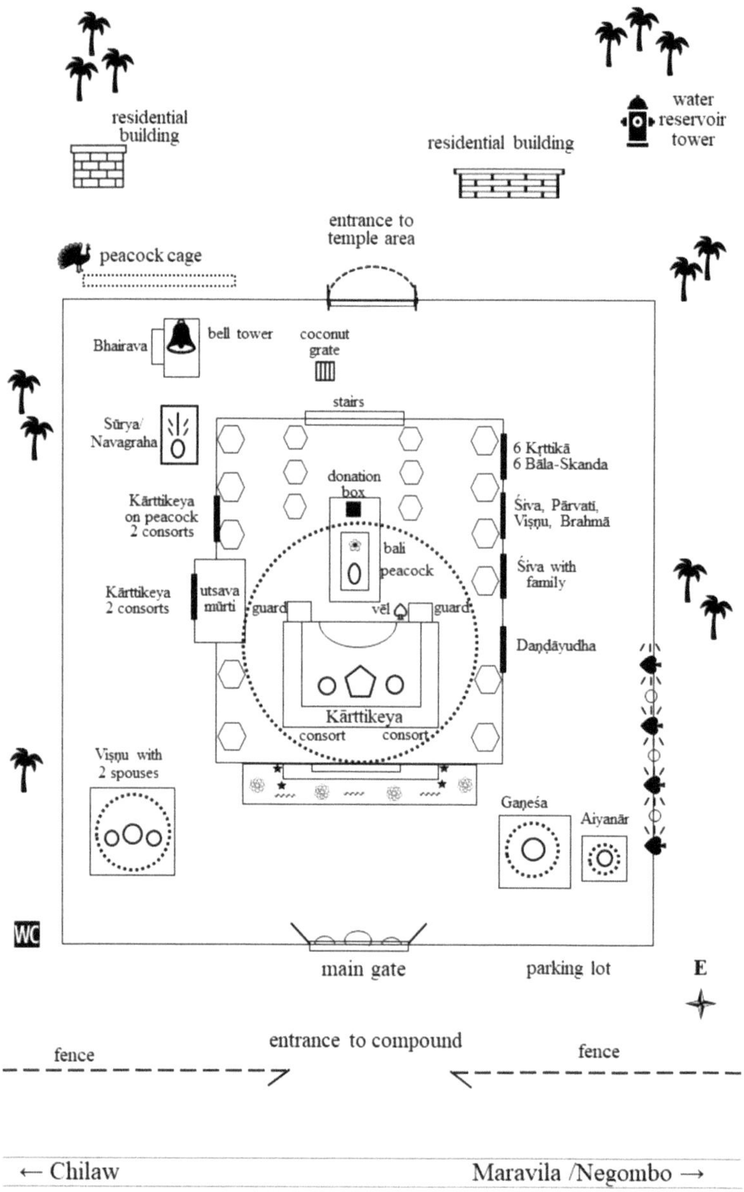

Devī Temples

‘Mīnākṣī in the Cottage’
The Mīnākṣī -Ambā Temple in Scarborough

Entrance to the Scarborough Mīnākṣī temple, south side

The Worship of Female Deities in Tamil Temples: A Short Introduction

The veneration of female deities is rooted in age old magical beliefs and cults. Popular goddesses, not only in India, but all over the world, originated from local vegetation genii and fertility divinities. Rituals soon emerged which were centred around many different mother goddesses. In India, such divine females are called Śakti, literally ‘Power,’ the ‘Powerful One,’ or Devī (cf. Latin *deus*), ‘Goddess.’ Since ancient times, these Śaktis have belonged to the archaic religious-historical level we call the *substratum*. This substratum is formed into a unifying larger conglomerate, which we like to term the *mainstream*, or mainstream Hinduism. Many phenomena in the dynamics of Hinduism in general, can be better understood if we bear this interaction between substratum and mainstream in mind.

Some call the different layers of substratum and mainstream Hinduism the 'Small Tradition' versus the 'Great Tradition'. This terminology might be misleading since the so-called Small Tradition, lying at the basis of all Hindu phenomena – as the substratum – does not remain strictly separated and secluded in local niches. It influences the 'Great Tradition' – the mainstream – always and everywhere, inducing fresh, original influences. This simplified conception only describes a part of the picture, ignoring the intellectual philosophy – the *superstratum*, the third, overlaid level. We therefore suggest the following threefold stratification of contemporary Hinduism:

- *superstratum*
- *mainstream* ↑
- *substratum*

The goddesses who are worshipped in Tamil Hindu temples do all originally belong to the substratum. This becomes clear by their very names and functions which point to elementary, rural, local levels: Nāgabhūṣaṇī-Ambā, 'The Mother bejewelled with cobras' stems from snake cults; Kālī, the 'Black One,' and Durgā, 'She who is difficult to approach,' are clearly an antagonistic pair of local goddesses from Bengal; Śītalā, 'The Cool One,' and Mārī-Ambā are implored to heal smallpox and Kāmākṣī, who holds a sugarcane in her hand, is a goddess of vegetation. Draupadī, mutual spouse of the five Pāṇḍava brothers is known from the grand Sanskrit epic *Mahābhārata*, which points back to ancient times when one's family lineage was determined by the mothers's line.

Only at the mainstream level could all these different local goddesses be declared to be one and the same main goddess – in Śivaïsm she is Umā or Pārvatī – and is considered the spouse of the high god Śiva. Śiva himself must be seen as an amalgamation of several diverse deities: Vedic and autochthonous, like Rudra (god of the wilderness), Agni (the God Fire) and, amongst others, several virile fertility gods. As, for example, Kālī (belonging to the substratum) has been melded with Pārvatī (in the mainstream), the native independent gods Gaṇeśa and Murugan are worshipped as Kālī's sons, and can be assigned in Kālī temples (like in Beau Vallon, Mauritius; see pp. 233ff) to a position beside their 'mother' Pārvatī alias Kālī. On the substratum level, the original Kālī has nothing to do with Gaṇeśa or Murugan at all.

'Ousting the Devī.' The dynamics of mainstream Hinduism are to a large degree influenced and even dominated by a nearly omnipresent *rivalry between deities*. Since gods are man-made, and not the other way around, it is human rivalry, personal preferences or competition between higher and lower social strata that is reflected in the divine struggles. A devotee has the chance to elect for himself a personal 'favourite deity,' an iṣṭadevatā. The believer will then desire to provide a prominent place in mythology, or if possible, in a temple for his iṣṭadevatā. It will not always be necessary to build a new temple for one's favourite. Existing temples use to be renovated

every forty years or so (at least in our experience), which may be due to the hot and humid climate in Sri Lanka or Mauritius. Here is an opportunity for a rich layman to donate money for the renovation but under one condition: he will demand that his favourite god or goddess will be enthroned as the main deity of the temple. This will often result in the residing god being superseded by the new favourite. Consequently, the vanquisher will take his place in the sanctissimum, and the previously venerated deity will not be ousted completely from the temple premises but will receive a minor place beside, behind or in the background of the successful conqueror. Typically, a mainstream Devī will oust another, weaker one or the mighty high god Śiva will assert himself against a former goddess who has lost her support in the local community, like in the Śiva-Mīnākṣī temple in Port Louis in Mauritius (see pp. 283ff).

These are examples of what we call *Ousting the Devī*. Informally, one might even speak of 'Devī mobbing.'

The reverse can happen too, such as in the Vināyaka-Śītalā temple in Beau Vallon (see pp. 181ff). Here an obvious iṣṭadevatā, the smallpox goddess Mārī-Ambā, has ousted the powerful mainstream god Gaṇeśa – a clear case of 'Deva mobbing.'

The Superstratum. However, Hinduism is not restricted to the two levels of *substratum* and *mainstream* only. There is still a 'higher,' an intellectual level, which we recognise as the *superstratum*. This superstratum is of minor importance to most of the devotees who worship Devīs in Tamil temples. The pious believers desire health, children, affluence and many other celebrated advantages of everyday life. All this can already be achieved on the levels of substratum and mainstream prayers. The superstratum is reserved for spiritual concerns of intellectually advanced *homines religiosi*.

The superstratum is characterised by magical constructions on an upgraded level. It features spiritual inventions which are rooted in magical practices of the substratum but have become much more refined over the centuries. Let us take as an example the Śrī Cakra, a magical cultic object, which we can observe for instance in the Kāmākṣī temple in Māṅgāḍu (see p. 248) and also in the expats' Mīnākṣī temple in Scarborough. This Śrī Cakra is called a yantra in Tantrism – it is a magical diagram into which a deity, a goddess, can be banished by spells, a mysterious syllable or a mantra. Another example of the presence of the superstratum is the use of sacrificial ashes, called vibhūti, not only for decoration but also manipulation, to manipulate through its magical power a goddess like Mīnākṣī for ones's own benefit. The ritual temple flagpoles (*dhvaja-stambha*) and their identification with spiritual veins in the human body are another example, as are certain meditative techniques, which are apt to achieve unity with the deity by Vedāntic philosophical theorems.

Temple interior

Śaktism and Tantrism (which would be the conventional terms for superstratum) must be strictly kept apart: Śāktism belongs to the substratum, Tantrism (or rather Āgamism, in Śaiva philosophy) to the superstratum.

Let us return at the end of this short introduction to the level of the substratum: Śāktism is often brought in connection with what is called 'left hand' (*vāma*) practices, as opposed to 'right hand' rituals in orthodox Hindu movements. Such 'left hand' practices may include the ritual consuming of meat or alcohol which are atrocities in 'right hand' Hindu performances, or even ritual promiscuity as part of orgiastic cults. (See M. Meisig: *Der Kult der Großen Mutter in Indien*, 1994, p. 97.) We want to make it very clear from the outset that the Tamil temple cult in Devī temples is a phenomenon of mainstream Hinduism and has nothing whatsoever to do with such Bacchanalian binges.

The Mīnākṣī Temple in Scarborough: History and Organisation

Our sketches of Tamil Devī temples shall begin with the Mīnākṣī temple in Scarborough, Toronto.

The temple is managed by the *Sri Meenatchy Amman Society*. Its traditional model is the *Mīnākṣī-Sundareśvara temple* in Madurai, Tamil Nadu.

Mr Selvakumar Rajaratnam
in his temple office

A picture of the Madurai Mīnākṣī is posted beside the entrance door.

The temple's opening hours are 10:30-13:00.

The preceding outlay of the present temple was a provisional arrangement, too. It had been located, until recently, in a busy immigrants' quarter, among small, bazar-like shops, between the subway stations Dufferin and Lansdowne, in 1279 Bloor Street West, Toronto.

Our interviewee is the temple initiator and manager, Mr Selvakumar Rajaratnam.

After his emigration, Mr Rajaratnam ('Raja') settled in Paris for twelve years then relocated to Toronto where has has lived for 15 years. He managed a jeweller's boutique in Bloor Street, where his former temple had slowly become bigger over the years. Raja has, in his own words, changed his life and is now retired. He has leased the estate for 2.500 Canadian Dollars (CAD) a month, where the temple has been set up in a charming cottage. Raja has an option for purchasing the whole site for 1.1 million CAD, where he plans to build the future temple beside the present site.

A building plan for the details of the planned temple is posted in today's cottage. However, due to lack of money, the planned building of the new construction will still take some time.

The temple brahmin
S. Jegatheeswara Kurukkal

The temple brahmin, S. Jegatheeswara Kurukkal, comes from Colombo-15, Sri Lanka (Jegatheeswara for Sanskrit Jagadīśvara). His home temple is in Nallūr on the Jaffna peninsula in Sri Lanka. He has been engaged for four years and will be returning to Nallūr in one year.

Brahmin on duty

The Mahākumbhābhiṣeka (inauguration) ritual of the present temple building took place on November 3, 2003. This year the temple will celebrate its first anniversary. For this occasion, the statue of Mīnākṣī has been presented with a golden crown.

Temple manager assisting the brahmin

The Mahotsava, the Great Temple Festival, is celebrated annually at the end of August/beginning of September.

Whereas the future building shall be facing the east, the present temple set up is orientated to the north. When asked for the reason, the brahmin answered, 'North is second best.' This means that the present orientation was dictated by the already existing building conditions. The eastern (or, as would also be appropriate for a Devī temple, the southern direction) was impossible, so they chose the north (like for example the Varasiddhi-Vināyaka temple in Toronto, which faces north, too; see pp. 35ff).

The temple statues were basically set up according to Raja's ideas.

Iconography and Pantheon

The granite statues or sthalamūrtis were carved in Mahābalipuram, one of the most important places for Tamil temple artisans.

After entering the temple from the south, we stand right in front of the Nine Planets (Navagraha) at the eastern side of the temple. We notice that the statue wearing a pink cummerbund, depicting Sūrya, the sun god, correctly faces the east, as prescribed in the ritual handbooks.

The Nine Planets (Navagraha)

Commencing our tour of the kōvil from here – clockwise, performing a pradakṣiṇā (circumambulation) – we first come across the shrines of Gaṇeśa and Lakṣmī in the south east corner.

Gaṇeśa and Lakṣmī

Gaṇeśa

An important function of the god Gaṇeśa is to make the believers happy by removing obstacles. That is why he should be saluted first when visiting a temple. And that is also why the goddess of fortune, Lakṣmī, is placed by his side.

Lakṣmī

We walk along the southern wall, behind the main maṇḍapa and notice Śiva Dakṣiṇāmūrti (on the outer back side of the sanctissimum) who correctly faces the south.

In the south east corner of the temple reside Murugan and Ayyappan.

Murugan and Ayyappan

The statues and paintings on the western wall (depicting Kṛṣṇa, a golu arrangement, Hanumān and Sai Baba) are of minor importance, so we turn directly to the centre of the temple.

Here we find the main shrine for the goddess Mīnākṣī, and, on its left side (to the west), one holding Śiva's symbol, the Śivaliṅga. Both pavilions are set up side by side, like in the model temple of Mīnākṣī in Madurai.

Śivaliṅga

The Liṅga, representing the male organ (Śiva's phallus), rests in a longish bowl of black marble, placed at a right angle, which symbolises the Yoni, the female organ. The Yoni is draped with a red and yellow shawl. In its centre, beneath the Liṅga, we see a round, yellow and red mark, a tilaka. The edges of the Yoni are adorned with white flowers. The Liṅga is enveloped by a metal cobra in three coils; behind the Liṅga rises the snake's body, ending up on top with five heads in the form of lion heads, each of which bears a pointed lance. Śiva's symbol is also painted with the same tilaka as on the Yoni: a round yellow and red mark. Above the tilaka we notice three horizontal lines, the Śaiva emblem (*tripuṇḍra*). Two large flower petals, red and white, complete the adornments. A rosary made of fruit kernels festoons the object of veneration. We did not count the beads, but usually such a rosary consists of 108 beads, which – like 18 or 1.008 – is a holy number in Hindu tradition.

Mīnākṣī with her parrot

The granite statue (*sthalamūrti*) of Mīnākṣī, measuring about 1.20 metres, is taller than its model in the Madurai *Mīnākṣī-Sundareśvara* temple. On the other hand, the statue in Madurai is said by many to be astonishingly small.

Mīnākṣī's sign of identification is a parrot, sitting on a budding flower in her right hand. Since the parrot is also the sign of the love god Kāma, much has been speculated about the parrot's significance particularly for Mīnākṣī.

The goddess's left hand hangs loosely down, showing the lolahasta gesture. The figure's body is covered with a yellow-orange cloth. The goddess stands relaxed in the tribhaṅga position, her left hip slightly pushed outwards.

Frieze of Mīnākṣī on top of her shrine

The two main shrines
Mīnākṣī and the Śivaliṅga

Both main shrines are equipped with their own insignia, placed in front respectively: the lotus bud (*balipīṭha*) and Śiva's mount, the zebu bull Nandī (also for Mīnākṣī).

A ritual flagpole (*dhvajastambha*) would also normally belong here. The temple precedent in Bloor Street did have such a flagpole, but it would not fit into the present cottage as the roof was too low.

During important ceremonies, the temple bell is sounded. Its ritualistic function seems to be to make the deity aware of the event and to heighten the edifying effect.

Veneration Rituals

Upacāra rites. During the first part of our visit, a regular pūjā was being performed. The brahmin enacted several upacāra rites, i. e. such feats as a host would execute in honour of an distinguished guest. Here the host is the brahmin's patron, called *yajamāna* in Sanskrit, 'a person who performs a regular sacrifice and pays its expenses,' or 'a person who employs a priest or priests to sacrifice for him' (Apte). The guest is the deity.

Part of these guest rites are, for example: welcoming the guest (who, as we are visiting a Mīnākṣī temple, is of course the main goddess);

– offering her water for washing her face and rinsing the mouth;

– feeding her with curd;

– quenching her thirst with milk;

– anointing her with a mixture of honey, milk and curd;

– refreshing her with coconut water;

– offering her water again to cleanse herself after the meal;

– honouring her with lights and incense;

and delighting her with flattering praise.

All these rites are permanently accompanied and underlined by incessant prayers and gestures.

Golu arrangement. During these guest rites, devotees carried their own statuettes and paintings, which had been part of the golu arrangement in the temple during the Navarātri festivities, around the shrines, before bringing them back into their homes.

Golu arrangement

The *Tamil Lexicon* explains under the lemma *kolu* கொலு (pronounced *golu*): 'decorations in a Hindu house at the time of the Navarātri-festival; decorations [of gods, goddesses, mounts, saints, musicians and other celestial beings] in a Hindu house [and temple, like in all the temples we visited in Toronto] at the time of the Navarātri-festival; set up in a *kolu-maṇṭapam*, கொலுமண்டபம், (*golu-maṇḍapa*).'

The golu arrangement is very often established and mixed up with the regular utsavamūrtis, the bronze festival statues, which are normally housed in the 'spring shrine' (*vasantamaṇḍapa*) along the northern wall of a Śaiva temple.

Śrī Cakra. The temple brahmin, Jegatheeswara Kurukkal, has greatest respect of the Śrī Cakra in front of the main statue, which ends in a bindu at its top. This bindu ('drop'), he assures us, is the seat of the goddess, which is why it is believed to be extraordinarily powerful. Jegatheeswara wears such a Cakra as an amulet on his chest, too.

Śrī Cakra
Included in the ritual

Śrī Cakra
Bathed in milk

Śrī Cakra
And smeared with Sandal paste

Granite statue (*sthalamūrti*) of Mīnākṣī with vibhūti make up

Abhiṣeka ceremony. This morning, the regular pūjā was followed by an opulent consecration ceremony, an abhiṣeka. The host (*yajamāna*) – in other words, the client – was Mr. S. Sarvananthan, accompanied by his wife.

Mr. S. Sarvananthan and his wife

Mr Sarvananthan left Sri Lanka twenty-one years ago, living at first in Detmold (Germany) for nine years, then in the Netherlands for ten years. Now he has been living in Canada for three years. He forgot how to speak German in the meantime but he still understands it.

The abhiṣeka ceremony costs 108 CAD (108 being a holy number in Hinduism).

During this abhiṣeka ritual, the statue of Mīnākṣī was made up with white vibhūti ashes (ashes left over of a sacrificial fire) *for the first time ever*.

Mīnākṣī
Getting transformed
into Ardhanārīśvara

Part of the ritual is the painting of the statue's face with a yellow and red liquid. This procedure shall indicate the impersonation of the Mīnākṣī statue as Śiva Ardhanārīśvara, 'the Lord (Śiva) who is half (*ardha*) woman (*nārī*).' Śiva Ardhanārīśvara is frequently depicted already in ancient South Indian bronze statues.

During the abhiṣeka ceremony, the right half of the face was painted yellow (representing the male aspect), the left half rendered red (female).

Mīnākṣī
as Ardhanārīśvara

Cleansing the statue with water

The abhiṣeka ceremony was concluded by cleansing the statue with water one more time.

The whole procedure lasted approximately one and a half hours.

Time of visit: Saturday, October 30, 2004, 10:15-13:30 hrs.
Address: 3354 Kingston Road (/Markham), Scarborough, ON, M1M 1R2, Canada.

www.srimeenakshiammantemple.com
email: info@ srimeenakshiammantemple.com
Phone 416-535 6560 and 416-358 2441.

Site for the future Mīnākṣī temple
Directly beside the present cottage

Sri Meenatchy Amman Temple, Toronto

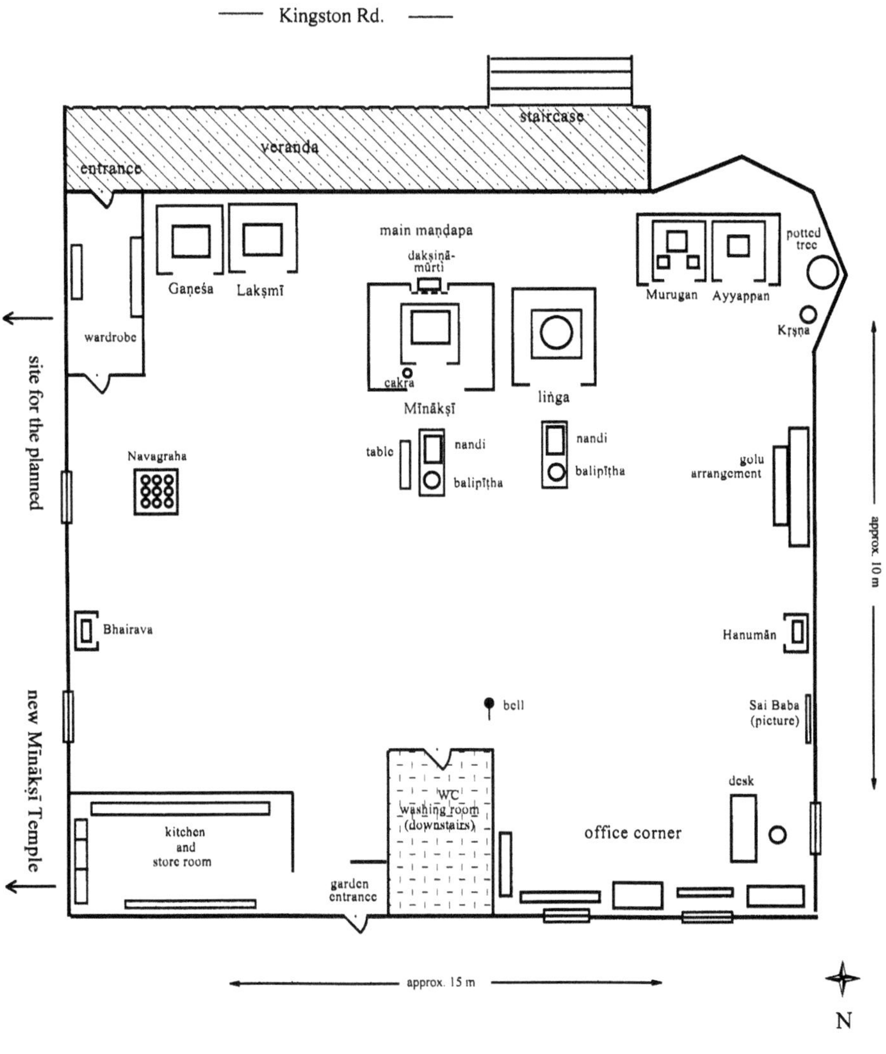

‘The Goddess in the Neighbourhood’
The Muṭṭu-Mārī-Ambā Temple in Negombo

Entrance to the Devī temple in Negombo, west side, Sea Street

Temple Staff, History and Organisation

The ‘Temple of the Illustrious Mother Who [Removes] the Obstacle of Smallpox and the Lord Kārttikeya Whose Weapon Is the Lance’ (*Sri Muthu-mari-amman Kathir-vel-ayutha Swamy Temple*) was inaugurated on June 11, 1952, so the visitor is informed by the foundation memorial board directly on the left of the entrance. The main deity whose granite statue is venerated in the sanctissimum is Mārī-Ambā (in Tamil *Māri-y-Amma<u>n</u>* or *Muṭṭu-Māri-y-Amma<u>n</u>*; anglicised as *Muthu-Mariamman*), the goddess of smallpox. The male god Kārttikeya (aka Murugan), whose name appears in the second place, only occupies a subordinate position in the temple hierarchy.

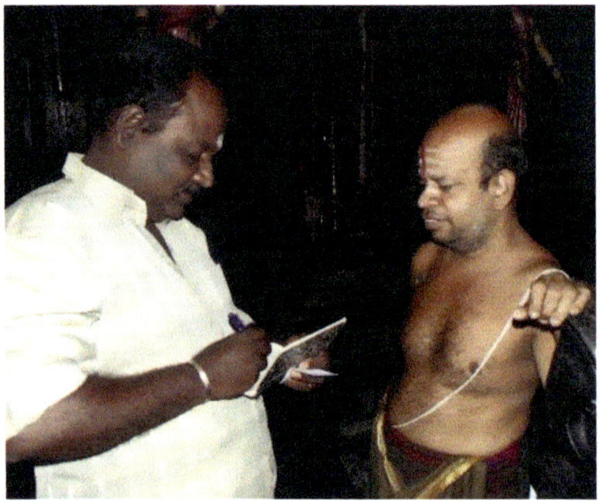

Mr. P. Thiyagarajan, temple trustee, and Jagadeeshwara Sharma

Vamathevan Sharma

His symbol, the lance, is accommodated in a minor pavilion, in line with his half-brother Gaṇeśa, behind the main shrine (*mūlagarbha* or *mūlasthāna*). Also, a Bāla-Murugan, i. e. Murugan's manifestation as a baby, turns up in the south-north annex of this temple. (NB The Mārī-Ambā temple is situated nearly opposite the Siddhi-Vināyaka temple on the other side of Sea Street in Negombo).

Our interviewees are Mr. P. Thiyagarajan, temple trustee, Mr. R. Jagadeeshwara Sharma, temple brahmin and chief priest and Mr. S. Vamathevan Sharma (Jagadeeshwara Sharma's cousin), brahmin and temple priest. He is much younger than both the others.

Two brahmins are on service together with two members, probably father and son, of the wreath-binder's family, who live in an adjacent hut to the east and are busy weaving reeds.

The foundation memorial board refers to the most recent Kumbhābhiṣeka ceremony which was celebrated after an earlier, smaller structure of the temple had been enlarged and renovated. The ancient temple building was erected around 1880 and the 1952 edifice was then founded by Mr.

Wreath binder

Nattukottai Nagarathar (Chettiar), from Negombo.

The main statue of Mārī-Ambā, so we are told, is around '500 years old.' It should be much older than today's temple building.

Sanctissimum
Granite statue of Mārī-Ambā, and bronze statues

The image in the sanctissimum of the kōvil does not face east, but west (more precisely north-west). Jagadeeswara Sharma, the chief priest, explains that the outline of the temple compound made this irregularity necessary. We would add that like many other temples, this one also had to be orientated to the busy Sea Street, fitting the temple smoothly into the immediate surroundings. Pūjā items, for example, can be bought in the *Murugan Pooja Centre* opposite the temple on Sea Street. Devotional paraphernalia can also be purchased for the main temple festival during Navarātri in October every year, when there is a big temple car procession (*rathayātrā*) through Negombo town.

Negombo has a population of 122.000, most of them Roman Catholic Christians, also many Muslims. There are at least two big churches (San Sebastian and St. Mary), two mosques, one large Buddhist temple and four Hindu temples.

Mr. Thiyagarajan reckons that about 200 devotees visit the temple per day with about 500 on Fridays. For the main temple festival in October, he estimates their number to be 5.000.

The temple society's members do not plan to erect a gopuram or to install a flagpole (*dhvajastambha*). The temple is a typical little city temple, comparable to its neighbour, the Siddhi-Vināyaka temple, or to the Āśvattha-Vṛkṣa-Vināyaka Temple in T. Nagar in Chennai. It is similar to Tamil emigrants' temples like the Siddhi-Vināyaka and the Murugan kōvils in the city of Hamm, Germany.

Temple Layout

When the visitor enters the temple from Sea Street (from the west), he will immediately face the main shrine with the granite statue (*sthalamūrti*) of Mārī-Ambā, which is hard to make out in the deep shade of her domicile. Two bronze statuettes of Kālī are positioned right in front of her. Mārī-Ambā has a head-dress of snakes, Kālī a halo of fire. Two female guardians keep watch over the garbhagṛha on both sides of the wooden door.

Behind the main shrine of the goddess, we find the pavilions of both her sons. Here again, Mārī-Ambā, a deity of the substratum, is, on the level of the mainstream, identified with Śiva's spouse Pārvatī. The elephant-headed Gaṇeśa resides in the north-east corner.

Parallel to him, in the south-east corner, Murugan is represented by his prominent symbol, the lance.

Gaṇeśa

Murugan
represented by his symbol, the lance (*vēl*)

The space between both divine brothers, along the eastern wall behind the main shrine, is occupied first by the Nine Planets.

The Nine Planets (Navagraha)

Kālī and a hero

Between the Nine Planets and Murugan's lance stand two figures. They are carved out of wood, quite erratically, among all those granite statues. One represents a hero (*vīra*), thus functioning as a guardian and the other depicts the fearsome goddess Kālī who – as we shall see (pp. 239ff) – has her own sanctum in the immediate neighbourhood across the street.

Having circled the main hall of the temple in a pradakṣiṇā, we step into an annex that stretches from south to north. At the end of this hallway lies the Spring Pavilion (*vasantamaṇḍapa*) that normally contains the utsavamūrtis. Today the open front of that pavilion is covered by a curtain with a portrayal of Murugan.

Annex leading to the
Spring Pavilion (*vasantamaṇḍapa*)

On the left wall of this hallway we pass, among others, a shrine for Bāla-Murugan, i.e. Murugan as a baby.

Bāla-Murugan, temple frieze

Bhairava (*sthalamūrti*)

On our way back, we see the maṇḍapa for Śiva Bhairava, i.e. Śiva in his awe-inspiring manifestation. As always, he can be recognised by the trident and the dog behind him.

Bhairava in the frieze of his maṇḍapa
In his missing hands there is
an axe and an antelope

Vamathevan Sharma likens the line from the main maṇḍapa of a temple up to its gopuram to the male human body:

The maṇḍapa is the head, the vāhana (deity's mount) the heart, the balipīṭha (lotus bud) the naval, the dhvaja-stambha (flagpole) the genital organ, the gopuram the feet. (Cf. J. Cartman: *Hinduism in Ceylon*, 1957, p. 96.)

Mount (*vāhana*) and lotus bud (*balipīṭha*) in front of Māri-ambā's shrine

Adjacent to the Muthu-Mariamman temple, on the same compound, lies a small and apparently very old, independent shrine for the goddess Durgā, on the north-side of the temple, facing south.

Sanctum for Durgā

Practically all devotees also perform their pūjā inside the Durgā shrine. The entrance is not restricted to brahmins – instead, the devotees decorate the Durgā idol themselves. The oil-lamps there are not made of terracotta, as usual but of half pieces of lemon. The flesh is scratched out by three women in front of the Durgā sanctuary, and the lemon peels are filled with coconut oil.

Inside her shrine, there is no Durgā image but the goddess is represented by a trident (*triśūla*).

Having completed their pūjā in front of Durgā, all devotees also pay homage to the picture of the god Ayyappan in the inner compound between the Durgā shrine and the main temple.

The well in this compound must be used only for consecration (*abhiṣeka*) purposes but is free for use by the temple brahmins.

Well in the inner compound

Behind the small Durgā shrine there is a huge three-storey building under construction which is going to become the wedding hall. It is also designed for functions and cultural events like Bhāratanāṭya (Indian dance). It is planned to be completed 'in one month', i.e. by the beginning of October, just in time for the annual chariot festival (*rathayātrā*).

Entrance from the inside

Times of visit: April 18, 2006, Tuesday, 8:45-10:30 a.m. – August 31, 2008, Sunday, 9:10-10:10 a.m.
Address: No 101, Sea Street (corner Asarappā Road), Negombo, Sri Lanka.

A bird's eye view of the Muthu-Mari-amman Temple in Negombo From the north

Muttu-Māri-Ambā Temple, Negombo

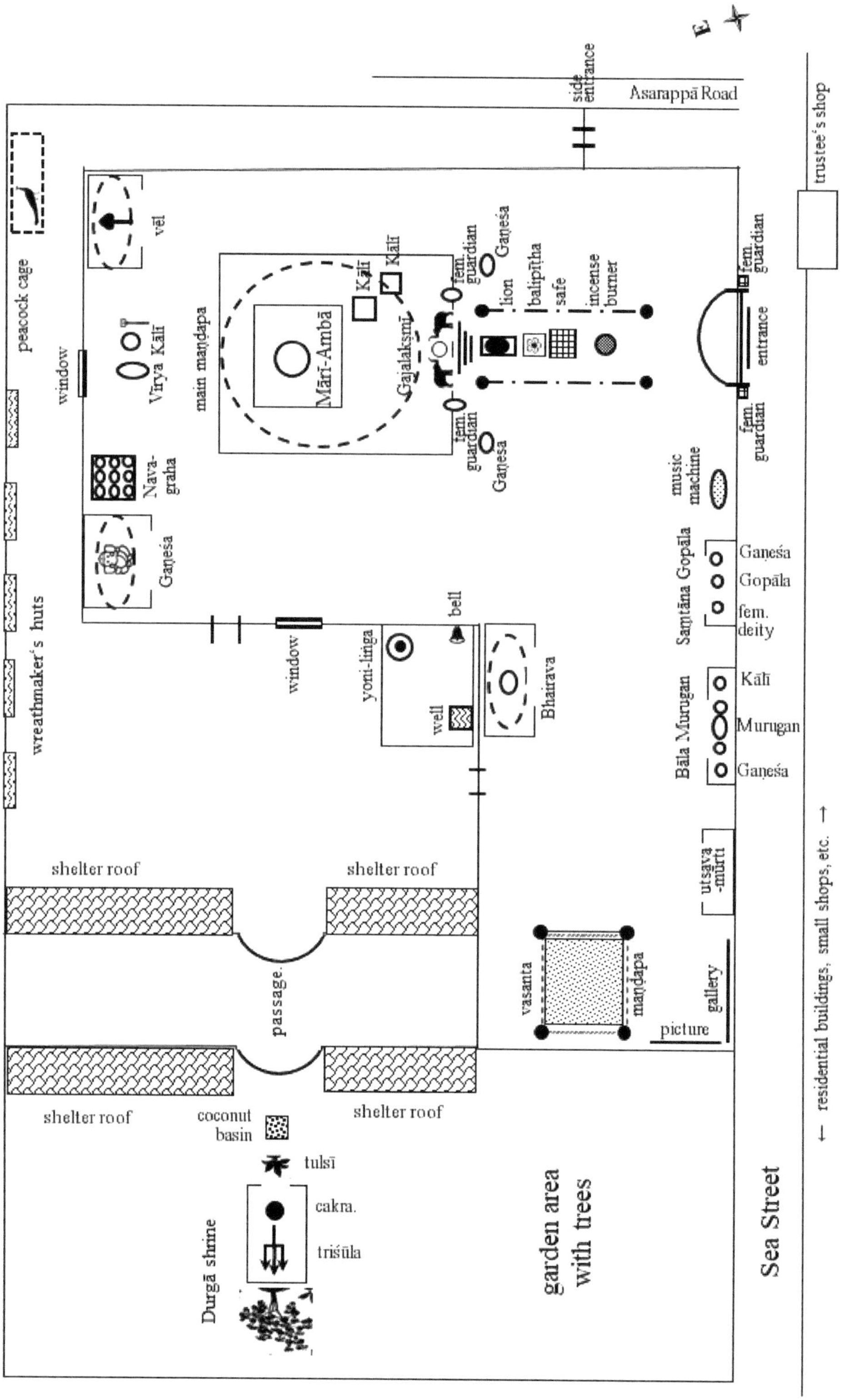

'Mārī-Ambā in Mauritius'
The Goddess of Smallpox in l'Escalier

Front view of the shrine of Mārī-Ambā in l'Escalier

The modest shrine of Mārī-Ambā, the goddess of smallpox, is located in the immediate neighbourhood of an overpowering Veṅkaṭeśvara temple. Both kōvils are not quite finished yet, for example, some service rooms – kitchen and toilets, are still under construction.

The slightly weather-beaten entrance gate is shut but not locked. Having passed beyond this, one walks over the lawn of the open temple compound to the temple building proper. In front of the entrance to the temple hall, on a roofless but paved front-yard, stands a pedestal with a small flagpole (*dhvaja-stambha*), granite lotus bud (*balipīṭha*) and lion, the goddess's mount.

Entrance gate

Female guardians at the temple hall door

There are statues of female guardians at both sides of the door of the temple hall. They are armed with a club and a short sword or dagger and crowned with the usual basket-helmet (*karaṇḍa-mukuṭa*), the appropriate headwear for assistant demigoddesses. Each commands a maned lion that bares its teeth against any offender, the lion being the mainstream Great Goddess's mount (*vāhana*) and transferred to the Devī from the substratum.

The ornamented door itself is locked. The reason for this precaution seems to be that the whole site is situated rather remotely and has a deserted, scarcely visited atmosphere.

Flagpole (*dhvajastambha*) in front of the temple door

The temple of the goddess of smallpox in l'Escalier

The three domes above the sanctissimum are decorated with friezes of the deities residing below.

On the round southern dome, to the right of the goddess, there is a figure of Gaṇeśa, looking south. To her left, at the round northern dome, a depiction of Murugan with his peacock, facing north.

The longish, barrel-like, larger top structure belongs to the goddess Mārī-Ambā herself, who gracefully looks down eastwards over her devotees. She sits relaxed in the half-lotus position (*ardha-paryaṅka* or *lalitāsana*). In the hands of her four arms, she holds: in the lower right a pitcher (*kalaśa*), in the upper right a noose (*pāśa*), in the upper left 'a small drum (*ḍamaru*) shaped like an hour-glass' (Apte) and in the lower left a sword (*khaḍga*) or sacrificial knife.

Murugan

Mārī-Ambā in the frieze of her dome

Gazing through a window and checking the inside of the temple hall, we find the outward constellation corroborated: in the middle there is the statue of Mārī-Ambā, to her right Gaṇeśa and to her left Murugan.

Beside the temple, on the south side, we stand in front of another shrine, dedicated to Kṛṣṇa. He plays the flute, standing upon a red lotus flower. A rare feature is the protective seven-headed cobra towering above his head.

Above the entrance gate an inscription on a banner reads 'La Baraque Shri Mariammen Kōvil Sangam, 1er Novembre 1998.'

La Baraque is a district of L'Escalier, albeit – as its name suggests – not exactly the richest. The meaning of the inscription is not clear. It could refer to the founders' meeting of the temple society or perhaps to the inauguration date of the temple itself.

Time of visit: April 12, 2001, 14:15 hrs.

Kṛṣṇa

‘Śītalā and Gaṇeśa’
The Vinayagur Seedalamen Temple in Beau Vallon

The Śītalā-Ambā temple in Beau Vallon
Main entrance, flanked by Gaṇeśa and Murugan

Prologue

Śītalā, ‘The Cool One’, is the North Indian equal of Mārī-Ambā, the goddess of smallpox. Quite a few citizens of Mauritius have North Indian ancestors who were brought to the island as indentured labourers. Many still cultivate their traditional roots, the language and legends of their home country. The following legend is translated from a collection of semi-religious folktales in Hindi, narrated by the women in Avadh (Uttar Pradesh) themselves on their vigils of fasting in the hot North Indian summer nights during Śītalā-Aṣṭamī. This is the week dedicated to the dreaded goddess of smallpox, who appears naked, riding a donkey. It is highly probable that this or similar legends are still told today by the descendants of those early Indian inhabitants in Mauritius.

Once upon a time there was a king and a queen. Although they bore the title of 'king' and 'queen,' they were so poor that they could hardly afford one meal a day. To make things worse, they had seven daughters.

The tale continues with an introductory sequence – very much like the German folktale of 'Hänsel und Gretel' – that due to extreme poverty, the king leaves his seven daughters alone in the woods. Looking for a means for survival, the girls make the decision to become the mighty goddess of smallpox called 'Śītalā Devī', the 'Cool Goddess.'

What should become of them? One day they found out that there was no Śītalā Devī in the next township. So, they decided: 'We shall become Śītalā Devī!'

But that was easier said than done. To be a goddess, one of course needed supernatural powers!

They tore out some small bushes and spoke: 'If we have divine powers, water shall gush up here!' They formed seven little donkeys out of soil and spoke: 'If we have divine powers, they shall become genuine donkeys!' The same moment, water began to gush up and the donkeys intoned a deafening 'hee-haw! hee-haw!'

The seven sisters mounted the donkeys and began their way into the town.

They went to the king's palace, and to the house of a minstrel. Before long, the king's son and all the minstrel's children were ill with smallpox.

The seven sisters, now being transformed into the goddess of smallpox, have the power not only to heal from the disease, they can also infect people with it.

The seven sisters wished to visit the king. He had already received the message: 'Your majesty, here are visitors for you!' The king asked: 'How many men are there on foot and how many on horseback?' – 'There is no one on foot, and no one on horseback. They are riding donkeys!'

The king gave order to receive these visitors with boiling oil and bamboo clubs. Burned by the boiling oil, the sisters ran away screaming. At the base of a well they fell to the ground, writhing with pain.

The minstrel's wife was just fetching water from the well. She removed the full jar from the rope and beat the loose end of the rope to make it dry. Cool water drops fell upon the seven sisters. At once their pain disappeared and their wrath cooled down. With gratitude, they intoned a blessing for the minstrel's wife: 'As you made us cool, in the same way shall coolness be imparted onto your children!'

The minstrel's wife thought: 'If they know of my children's illness, they must be goddesses!' She broke a jar and started to pour water on the seven sisters with the shards. The more they cooled down, the better the children's condition at home became. When they were completely recovered, they demanded food. The minstrel's mother came running to the well and griped: 'At last the children want to eat again, but you are stuck here to the well!' But her daughter-in-law responded: 'Please don't gripe, mother! Thanks to the seven sisters the children have recovered!'

Now that the illness was over, a feast was celebrated in the minstrel's house. The sound of music reached up to the king's palace. The king ordered his men to find out who dared to make music while the prince was truly suffering with sickness. When he came to know that it was the minstrel from whose house the music came, the king arrested, bound and locked him in a dark dungeon. But Śītalā Devī cut the minstrel's bonds and set him free. Thereupon the king arrested and bound the minstrel again. But Śītalā Devī cut his bonds again. Every time the king had the minstrel arrested again, his bonds were severed by Śītalā Devī.

Finally, the king admitted defeat and stooped before Śītalā Devī. He performed a great sacrifice and made a vow to induce Śītalā Devī to let his son recover. But Śītalā Devī remained adamant. 'Your wife shall strip off all her clothes and build an altar for me,' she demanded. 'Then you shall offer me food. If you do that, you can keep your son, but he will remain blind on one eye and disfigured by pockmarks. If you don't follow my orders, he will die!'

Desperately, the king and queen did as they were told. Their son recovered but due to the goddess's wrath he remained scarred by pockmarks and blind in one eye.

The *Vinayagur Seedalamen Temple*

'The Temple of Vināyaka and Śītalā-Ambā' in Beau Vallon, Mauritius, lies slantwise to the Kālī-Ambā temple we had just left on the opposite side of the road. We entered the premises at about one p.m. on April 2, 2001. The festivities of the Durgā Pūjā had just come to an end. The estate measures about 30 x 50 square metres. To the right of the temple stands a hall of the same size, used for teaching purposes, temple dancing lessons, sundry festivities and a temple school. To the left is a building with kitchen, toilets and a bathroom.

Our interviewee is the brahmin Kārttikeya Kurukkal from Chennai, the capital of Tamil Nadu, India. He was educated in Bangalore and has now been working in Mauritius for one year. He has an employment contract with the temple society, lasting for five years. Income and working conditions are better here than in India but he did say he was homesick, adding that it was not too bad because he was not completely alone on the island; some relatives live here too.

Kārttikeya Kurukkal
Temple brahmin

On our arrival, Kārttikeya Kurukkal is busy making horoscopes for two young Indian-Mauritian ladies. He proclaims his results in Hindi. Before he turns to his next clients, another two young Indian-Mauritian ladies, he takes a short break to tell us a lengthy legend that is supposed to explain the difference between the goddesses Śītalā and Mārī-Ambā. The bottom line is that Mārī-Ambā is only the relevant authority for smallpox, whereas Śītalā oversees all sorts of illnesses and epidemics. Therefore Śītalā-Ambā is also prophylactically invoked for support.

Kārttikeya Kurukkal still performs a short pūjā for us. We receive the prasāda, i.e. the left-overs of Śītalā's meal, coming in the shape of four bananas.

At about two o'clock the brahmin has finished his horoscopes. He locks his temple with a grid and is ready for his lunch break. He is already dining on the rest of the prasāda – two bananas.

Temple Setup, Iconography and Pantheon

The temple is orientated to the south (with a twist to the south-east).

The visitor descends a few stairs from the road. The main entrance to the temple is made of two large, carved wooden door-wings and there are additional simple entrance doors on both sides.

Above the main entrance, on the outside, there is a stucco relief of Śītalā-Ambā. The goddess is clad in red garments, holding ears of grain in her right hand. Beside the right door-wing, on the wall outside, there is a mural of Gaṇeśa; on the opposite side Murugan with his peacock and lance. The artist has placed Murugan in the middle of the letter *ōm* in Tamil script:

ௐ

The insides of the open door-wings are decorated with the same character. A foundation stone beside Gaṇeśa's mural informs the visitor that this temple was founded in 1856 but this cannot be the date of the present building; it must refer to the very first, the original version of this temple.

'This stone has been laid by Hon. Sir Veerasamy Ringadeo to commemorate the 121st anniversary of the Shri Vinayagur Seedalamen Tamil temple Beau-Vallon Mahebourg founded 1856.'

In the centre of the entrance hall rises a three-armed flagpole (*dhvajastambha*), wrapped in long sugarcane fibres. We must not forget the large bell hanging from the ceiling in front of it.

Bell, flagpole, lotus bud and bull
in front of Śītalā's sanctissimum

Śītalā's mount, the bull,
with Śivaïtic tilaka (yellow and red point)
inside a tripuṇḍra (three horizontal streaks)

Between the flagpole and the sanctissimum lie the lotus bud (*balipīṭha*) and the mount of the Devi. It is Śiva's bull Nandī (Nāgabhūṣaṇī-Ambā rides the same vāhana, in Toronto and in Frankfurt). The animal's horns are painted a silver colour while the lotus and mount are made of black granite.

A mural of Śiva and Pārvatī as 'lover couple' decorates the right wall beside the side door.

Śiva and Pārvatī

Murugan's peacock

At the left wall of the entrance hall, we notice a peacock, painted in blue. It is flanked by two female figures: Murugan's consorts, Vallī and Devānī. The three of them are adorned with pink garments. The peacock will serve as a kind of chariot to carry Murugan's utsavamūrti during processions.

To the left in front of the sanctissimum we perceive a side altar for Durgā. The popular goddess rides a roaring tiger, his jaws wide open. With the hands of her six arms, she clutches (from right to left) a (1) mace and a (2) short sword or knife. The next (3) signals freedom from fear, (4) urges the devotee to put some fire in her 'half-moon hand' (*ardha-candra-hasta*), (5) holds a bow and (6) wields a trident.

She has received a lime fruit as an offering, stuck on the point of her sword. Limes are Durgā's favourite donation. The statue is decorated with an auburn dress and veil with a simple crown (*karaṇḍamukuṭa*) of female deities. She has put on lipstick and her fingernails are painted red too.

Durgā, Kṛṣṇa and Mahāviṣṇu

To her right stands Kṛṣṇa, playing the flute and to her left, the blue complexioned Mahaviṣṇu, wearing his diadem (*kirīṭamukuṭa*), holding his usual attributes: the mace (lower right hand), disk (upper right) and conch (upper left). His lower left hand is covered by a yellow scarf – signalling freedom from fear.

The space between entrance hall and sanctissimum is separated by a wall with a small passageway in the middle. In this ante-room, the pūjā utensils are stored but nothing else. Only the brahmin is allowed to enter this area and the sanctissimum.

The garbhagṛha contains a red-clad granite statue of Śītalā-Ambā. Due to the adverse visibility conditions, it cannot be confirmed whether the main goddess is accompanied here by any subsidiary deities. On our inquiry the brahmin's answer is no, the goddess stands alone in her mūlagṛha.

Kṛṣṇa in a pool

Shrines with snake stones

Ancient dome with a frieze of Gaṇeśa

Outside, west of the temple hall we come across a small empty pool with blueish tiles. On a platform inside the pool stands a figurine of Kṛṣṇa-Gopāla, playing the flute, in front of a white cow.

At the rear, in the north of the compound, there are three connected shrines with a larger one in the middle. They are formed like hoods of a cobra and each contains a snake stone (nāgakkal) and a Śaiva trident. The floor is littered with the leftovers of incense and earthen oil lamps.

Śītalā or Gaṇeśa?

Finally, there remains the question of why this sanctum is called 'The temple of Vināyaka and Śītalā-Ambā,' as in the sanctissimum, there is only Śītalā? We think it is because it was originally a Gaṇeśa temple and was only re-dedicated to Śītalā later.

We can bring forward four arguments in favour of this contention.

Firstly, there is no statue or painting of Gaṇeśa whatsoever inside the temple. The elephant-headed god is represented only by the mural outside the main entrance which could have been set up after a renovation.

Secondly, according to the foundation stone, there must have been a re-inauguration of the temple in 1977, 121 years after the original consecration in 1856.

Thirdly, Gaṇeśa is only represented irremovably outside the temple, namely in a frieze in the dome above the sanctissimum. The architecture of this dome is obviously more ancient than the interior setup of the temple hall.

Fourthly, it is a traditional custom to place statues or busts of *that* deity in the frieze on top of a shrine which is housed underneath and Gaṇeśa's figure decorates the dome above the sanctissimum, which – probably since 1977 – accommodates Śītalā.

In summary, the temple must have been re-dedicated, re-named and re-inaugurated 121 years after its foundation in 1856. A donor who financed the renovation was possibly a fervent devotee of Śītalā, the goddess of smallpox. The usual story would be that this donor had made a vow to contribute to the temple when he or a near and dear one had been cured of the disease (comparable to the events which led to the renovation of the Śiva-Mīnākṣī temple in Port Louis, also in

Mauritius; see pp. 283ff). In this process, all evidence, at least as far as possible, of the former favourite deity (*iṣṭadevatā*), Gaṇeśa, had been removed from the sanctum. Gaṇeśa is only portrayed as a mural beside the temple entrance, representing the one-tusked god, being a subsidiary figure.

We face the rare and extraordinary, (in our experience, singular) case, not that the Devī from the substratum was ousted by a more powerful, mainstream, male deity, but, quite the contrary, that the maverick North Indian outsider, Śītalā, has superseded the long-established potentate, Gaṇeśa.

Time of visit: April 2, 2001, about 13:00-14:30 hrs.

The Hindi tale in the prologue is translated from: *Die Pockengöttin. Fastenmärchen der Frauen von Avadh.* Gesammelt von Indu Prakash Pandey. Aus dem Hindi übersetzt von Indu Prakash Pandey und Heidemarie Pandey. Mit einem märchentypologischen Anhang von Konrad Meisig (Beiträge zur Indologie, 36), Wiesbaden 2002. As to recent, especially South Indian, forms of Śītalā, cf. F.W. Bunce: *An Encyclopaedia of Hindu Deities…*, 2000, vol. 1, p. 514, article Shitala; her yantra on p. 939, ill. 210. Cf. also N. N. Bhattacharyya: *The Indian Mother Goddess*, ²1977, pp. 53-57.

Sītalā-Ambā-Temple, Beau Vallon

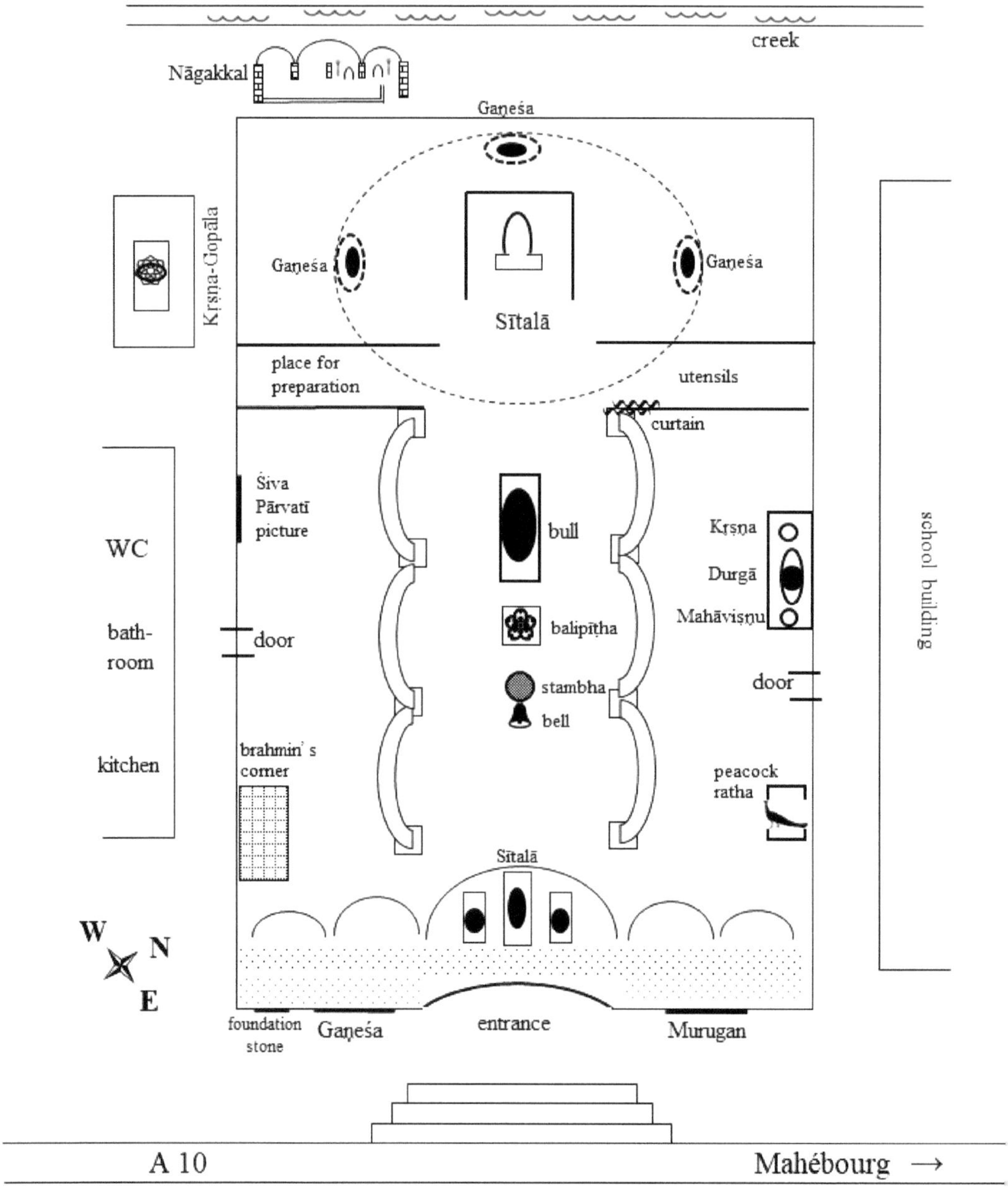

‘Bejewelled with Cobras’ The Nāgabhūṣaṇī-Ambā Kōvil in Scarborough

Nāgabhūṣaṇī-Ambā in Scarborough – bronze statue

Nāgabhūṣaṇī-Ambā kōvil means the ‘Temple of the Mother Who Is Bejewelled with Cobras.’ This mother is a wrathful snake-goddess with fangs. Her home temple stands in Nainativu, an island off the shore of Jaffna in the very north of Sri Lanka.

Mr. Somadatta helps out in the temple during the absence of the main priest. The following survey of the temple background is based on his kind and much appreciated information.

Temple Background

Nāgabhūṣaṇī-Ambā’s temple here in Scarborough, a suburb of Toronto, measures about 30x15 square metres. It is located in a former shopping street or mall. The forefront is made of large shop-windows. On the opposite side, beyond the temple hall, there is a spacious assembly room. The sanctum is said to be four years old, so it was inaugurated around the year 2000.

This is obviously an interim temple. There are no maṇḍapas (pavilions) for the granite statues to make them sthalamūrtis ('immovable statues'), no tiles, as needed for protection when coconuts are smashed as offerings. The rent for the unit is 7.000 CAD per month.

The main priest, called 'Aiyyar' ('Iyar'), is absent on account of the flu. He is rumoured to be a charismatic saint with the ability to mind-read. He certainly dominates the temple and the temple organisation. A skilful provider of donations, he bought a five acre estate for 1.5 million CAD, where he founded the *Gurukul Learning Centre* (610 Coronation Drive, Scarborough). According to the relevant brochure, it seems to be some sort of Hindu-commercial cultural institute. The present interim temple will be relocated there as soon as the official bureaucratic permit is granted. This permit is still being refused because of the residents' fear of noise and disturbances.

Learn how to read and write

In addition to the main priest, the temple employs two more brahmins. During our visit they were busy with a pūjā for infant pre-school candidates to facilitate their learning to read and write. As far as we could see, they did not confine themselves to spiritual services, they tried hard to teach the youngsters some Tamil characters.

Like in all the other Toronto Tamil temples, a golu arrangement was installed, to be terminated on the same day, the last of the Navarātri festival in Śiva's honour.

Pantheon and Iconography

The temple must be proud of its large variety and diversity of divine images. The following description cannot encompass all of them, but we will try to give an adequate impression.

The temple hall is divided into three lines (from east to west): the *Frontline* with three bodies keeping watch, namely Bhairava, Nandī and the Nine Planets. Then the *Interim sanctissimum*, a broad pedestal presenting the granite statues of seven different deities, including the principal goddess, Nāgabhūṣaṇī-Ambā and, at the back, the *Viṣṇu Corner*, a collection of heterogeneous sculptures, mostly Vaiṣṇava deities surrounded by cobras.

The Frontline. The first, easternmost line, is occupied by three guardians, watching over the deities in front of them. In their centre, on a table between diverse pūjā utensils – among other things fruits, incense, chandeliers, oil-lamps, bells, jars filled with ghee (melted butter), sacrificial ladles and so on – we perceive Śiva's zebu bull, Nandī.

Bhairava with Nāga

On his south side stands Bhairava, the terrifying manifestation of Śiva, always clutching his trident. Traditionally, his place would be in the north-east corner but the temple layout made this impossible. Here, Bhairava is accompanied by a Nāga, a cobra guardian, as seems fit in a temple of the snake goddess.

The main row or *interim sanctissimum*

North of Nandī reside the Nine Planets, believed to be extremely powerful and therefore dangerous because of their magical influence.

The 'Interim Sanctissimum.' On a chess board, we would now leave the row of pawns and proceed to the queen with her knights and rooks, only she is flanked here by her sons and the knights and rooks are transferred to a third row at the back.

This main line consists of eight statues (Gaṇeśa represented twice).

Seen from the perspective of the main goddess, to her extreme right, we are surprised to find an ekamukhaliṅga, i.e. Śiva's phallus (*Liṅga*), into which the carver has incorporated one (*eka*) face (*mukha*) with Śiva's features. The granite stone is decorated with aster flowers and a tilaka is painted on the forehead.

(1) Ekamukhaliṅga

Next to the symbol of the Devī's spouse comes her favourite son, the elephant-faced Gaṇeśa, a sweet-tooth, always fond of a treat, and for that reason, is decorated with bananas and mangos.

(2) Gaṇeśa
Decorated with bananas and mangos

(3) Durgā decorated with limes

(4) Nāgabhūṣaṇī-Ambā

(5) Murugan

(6) Śiva Dakṣiṇāmūrti

(7) Ayyappan

Durgā, on the other hand, often receives limes as offerings, as we have already observed in some other temples.

The place in the centre is inhabited by the main goddess, the 'Mother bejewelled with cobras.' Here, she is decorated with genuine jewels galore. The brahmins have draped an oversized garland of red and yellow flowers around her shoulders, reaching down to her feet. She wears yellow make up with red and yellow tilakas adorning her forehead and palms. These point at the observer in the gestures of providing shelter (*abhayada*) and granting wishes (*varada*). Above the gilded basket-helmet five golden cobra-heads serve as her hood.

The place to her left side befits Murugan.

The next place is taken by a manifestation of Śiva, albeit Śiva Dakṣiṇāmūrti would normally face south (Sanskrit *dakṣiṇa*), standing outside the southern wall of the devī's main shrine (*mūlagarbha*). This was not possible here in the interim sanctuary.

Ayyappan, the popular South Indian village-god, forms, on the extreme left, the counterpart to Śiva's ekamukhaliṅga in the south. His bronze statue concludes the line of the seven protagonists.

The 'Viṣṇu Corner.' We walk behind this Row of Seven, pass a depiction of the popular guru Sai Baba and stand in front of the granite nāgakkals. The cult of snake stones leads back to the very origins, the substratum of Śaiva spiritualism. It has its proper place here in the temple of the cobra goddess.

Nāgakkal

An additional bronze statue of her stands in the middle of this third row. It is accompanied by a statuette of the snake goddess in her benevolent, beautiful aspect.

Under the very eyes of Nāgabhūṣaṇī-Ambā the devotees have created a veritable snake pit, containing dozens and hundreds of tiny bronze statuettes of wriggling hooded cobras.

We reach the Viṣṇu corner of the snake temple. In Vaiṣṇava mythology, it is the universal five-headed cobra named Śeṣa, upon whose coils Viṣṇu rests from his work as preserver of our Brahma Egg (*brahmāṇḍa*), our world system, which had been created by Brahmā and destroyed by Śiva. It will then be created anew by Brahmā, to continue the never ending saṃsāra ('cycle'). These three gods, Brahmā, Viṣṇu and Śiva form the triad (*Trimūrti*) of Hindu high gods.

The Vaiṣṇava pantheon is represented next by the celebrated couple of Kṛṣṇa and Rādhā. Kṛṣṇa (playing the flute) is Viṣṇu's eighth incarnation (Avatāra). He has descended (Sanskrit *avatarati*) to proclaim the famous 'Song of God' (*Bhagavadgītā*), considered by many the principal book in the canon of Vaiṣṇava Hinduism.

Śeṣa

Kṛṣṇa

Two different depictions of Nāgabhūṣaṇī

Snake pit in front of Nāgabhūṣaṇī

Finally, we stand in front of a Vaiṣṇava altar. The shrine accommodates Viṣṇu, together with his spouse, the goddess of fortune, Lakṣmī. They are flanked by Viṣṇu's fourth Avatāra, the man-lion Narasiṃha, and the Śivaïtic goddess Kālī (on Lakṣmī's left hand side). These deities conclude the Viṣṇu corner and our visit to the sanctum of Nāgabhūṣaṇī-Ambā.

Time of visit: October 22, 2004, about 10:00-12:00 hrs. Last day of the Navarātri festival.
Address: Nagapoosani Amman Kōvil Toronto, 5637 Finch Avenue East, Unit 5 A, Scarborough, ON M1B 5K9, Canada.
tel. 416-412 1289
www.gurukul.ca
gurukul@anjaliinternational.com
Communication Centre: ✆ 416-208 3060.

(From left:) Narasiṃha, Viṣṇu with Lakṣmī, and Kālī

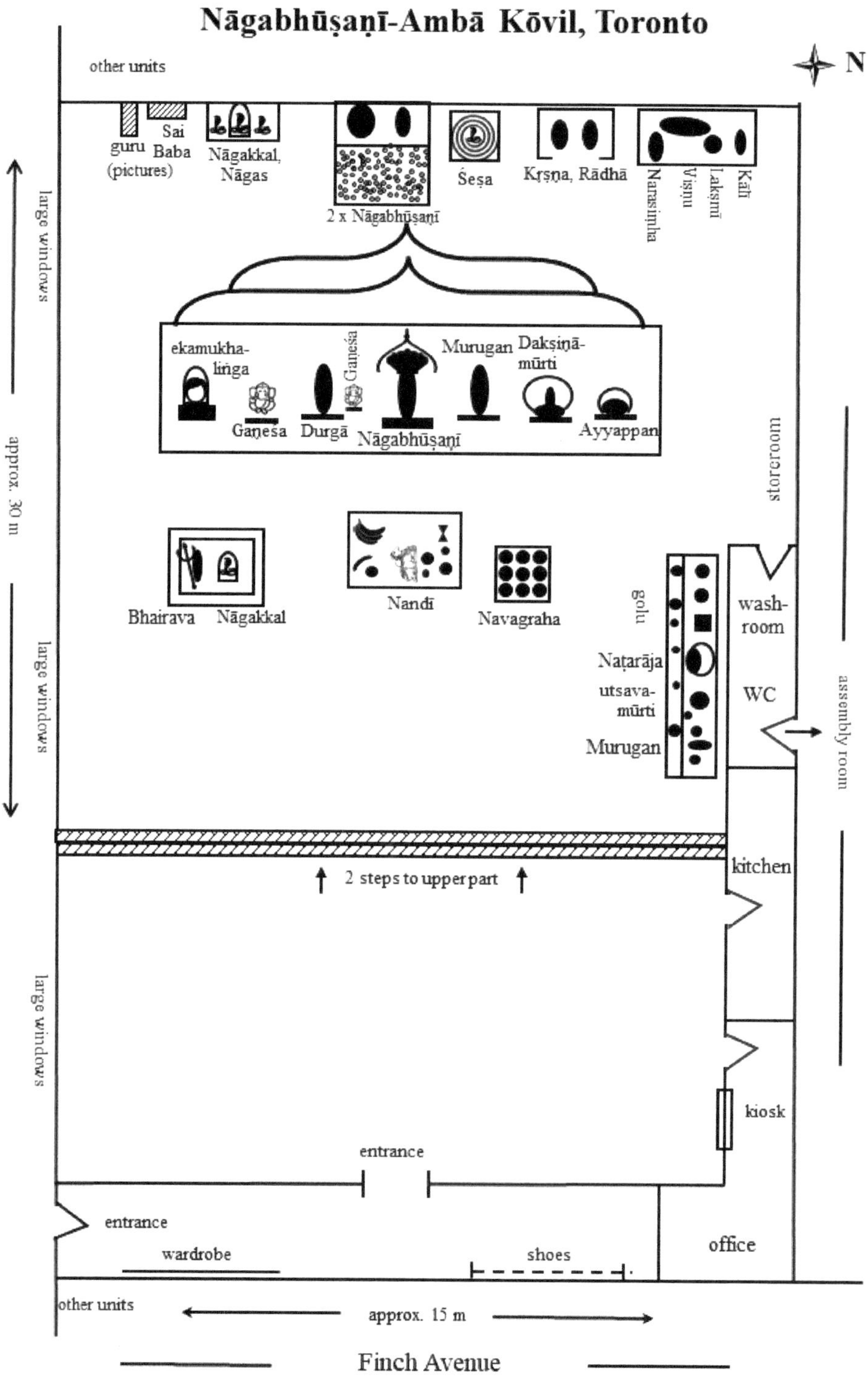
Nāgabhūṣaṇī-Ambā Kōvil, Toronto
N
other units
guru (pictures)
Sai Baba
Nāgakkal, Nāgas
2 x Nāgabhūṣaṇī
Śeṣa
Kṛṣṇa, Rādhā
Narasiṃha
Viṣṇu
Lakṣmī
Kālī
large windows
approx. 30 m
large windows
large windows
ekamukha-liṅga
Gaṇesa
Gaṇeśa
Durgā
Nāgabhūṣaṇī
Murugan
Dakṣiṇā-mūrti
Ayyappan
storeroom
Bhairava
Nāgakkal
Nandī
Navagraha
golu
Naṭarāja
utsava-mūrti
Murugan
wash-room
WC
assembly room
2 steps to upper part
kitchen
kiosk
entrance
entrance
wardrobe
shoes
office
other units
approx. 15 m
Finch Avenue

'The Snake Goddess in the Metropolis'
The Nāgabhūṣaṇī-Ambā Temple in Frankfurt

Nāgabhūṣaṇī-Ambā in Frankfurt

Śrī Cakra

The snake cult is one of the deepest and strongest roots in the *substratum* of Śivaïsm. Also in the *mainstream* Śaiva sanctuaries cobra goddesses could keep her position. And even on the level of the *superstratum* the snake Devī named Nāgabhūṣaṇī-Ambā is

Nāgabhūṣaṇī Devī (Frankfurt)
The Śrī Cakra at her feet

represented in her Frankfurt temple, namely in the shape of a Śrī Cakra, a miniature model of her temple, a microcosmic symbol of her magical power.

Her granite statue in the sanctissimum (*mūlagarbha*) sits in a relaxed pose. The palm of the lower right hand of her four arms has fingers upright, pointing at the observer, reassuring the devotee of her willingness to provide shelter (*abhayada*). Her lower left hand, fingers pointing downwards, promises to fulfil wishes (*varada*). The upper right holds a noose (*pāśa*), the upper left wields a stylised axe (*paraśu*). A keen observer will perceive the cobra fangs in the corners of her mouth. The eyes are half-closed, as if in meditation. Five cobra heads combine their hoods into one above her head.

The goddess is fully dressed and made up, she wears a rich yellow robe, an embroidered purple scarf and a heavy mālā (garland) of white and yellow aster flowers reaching down to her feet. Her neck and breast are adorned with shining necklaces and brooches. She is crowned with a basket helmet (*karaṇḍamukuṭa*), the usual headgear of a female deity. Red and yellow tilakas adorn her forehead, palms, the weapons in her hands and the five cobra heads.

Nāgabhūṣaṇī-Ambā, bronze festival statue

Nāgabhūṣaṇī-Ambā, murals on the temple walls in Frankfurt

The temple murals of the goddess present a lighter, friendlier deity. On one of these paintings, she sits on the coils of her five-headed cobra, offshore from her home temple in Nainativu, near Jaffna.

Temple Staff and Organisation

We visit the *Sri Nagapooshani Amman Tempel* in Frankfurt on the day before the Taipoṅkal festival, which in 2007 falls on 14th January. *Tai-p-poṅkal* is the name of the first day of *Tai* (the ninth Tamil month, about January/February). It is celebrated with *poṅkal*, sweetened and seasoned rice. In the temple, the preparations for the festival are in full swing.

Our interview partner is Jensi, a nineteen-year-old student, born in Lahnstein, Germany. (She has been sent as a stand-in for Mr. Kugaraja, her uncle, whom we had called for an appointment.) Her family moved from Lahnstein to Frankfurt in 1998/1999. Each Saturday between 11am-5pm she accompanies her mother and grandmother to the temple. They go there for the pūjā and help in the kitchen. Although her mother is a stout believer, it is her father, from whom Jensi regularly receives instructions about Tamil Hinduism and religious questions. She explains her scepticism of religion in general and Tamil Hinduism in particular, by the fact that she has grown up in a different culture where she wasn't confronted daily and from all sides by Tamil spirituality.

The brahmin on duty, Mr. Sivasri Siva Kumarathasa Kurukal (S. K. Kurukal), deputises for one month, until the end of January, as the regular brahmin, Mr. Mohan Sharma, who is on holiday. Kumarathasa Kurukal comes from Scarborough, Toronto, in Canada. He is employed there as chief priest of the Ayyappan temple.

Mr. Kumarathasa Kurukal
Brahmin on duty

He is thirty years old and has been living in Canada for six years. Mohan Sharma was present too but he kept himself in the background.

The temple brahmins, casual and on duty
Mohan Sharma (left), Kumarathasa Kurukal

During the pūjā, the hall is foggy
with smoke from the incense

The temple brahmin is employed by the temple society and he earns a monthly salary of 500-600 Euro. In addition, he receives 20% of what is donated during the pūjā on the plate with the offerings. The priest lives in a small flat opposite to the temple entrance in the same street.

The temple finances itself through donations (standing orders are welcome) or by selling saris, which have been purchased for a reasonable price in India or Sri Lanka. The devotees donate these saris to the goddess and after the Devı has donned them, they are again re-bought by the donator. After this procedure, the saris aren't ordinary textiles any more. Now they are prasāda, an object – like, for example food which the goddess has tasted – that had tangibly contact with the deity and is therefore magically charged with her superhuman power. This is why these robes are sometimes considered as taboo and must be burnt directly after the re-buy in the temple. This praxis is reported to be originally from a temple in Manhattan, for instance. Normally such saris are no longer worn – they are mostly used to sew clothes for little children. The most pragmatic explanation is the fact that those saris are stained and greasy by the leftovers of offerings like coconut oil or milk.

Once the delays and setbacks following the inauguration of the temple have been overcome, the present chairperson of the temple committee is enormously devoted to his task and oversees the disciplined, well-ordered and buoyant life of his community. He also appears to be quite successful in acquiring donations.

The pūjā on Friday nights (7p.m.) is frequented by an especially large number of devotees. Particularly for the young people, these get-togethers facilitate their making friends. Still today (and in Germany too), most marriages – as Jensi remarks – are arranged by the parents.

Today, the regular pūjā at midday is attended by about fifteen people, among them some children too.

A young man has ordered a special commemoration pūjā, a rite that is performed for his father who has died one year ago. The client (called in Sanskrit yajamāna, the 'offering one') is accompanied by two friends who take pictures and seem to be unsure as to the ritual procedure. The offerings for the goddess consist of a packet of Basmati rice, a banana, two oranges and some fresh vegetables, like leek, celeries, carrot and parsley to make soup.

Devotee's offering to the goddess

For two years, the temple has celebrated an annual festival, the mahotsava (Great Festival) in June/July. The bronze festival statue (*utsavamūrti*) of the goddess is carried around the block upon a temple chariot. This procession would last about two hours. Unlike in Sri Lanka, where these excursions of the goddess always take place at night (for it is much too hot during the day), the event is celebrated in Germany in the light of day. The rally is guarded by the police who block the road, and prevent exhausted participants or onlookers from sitting on the hoods of parked cars. The residents watch the procession from open windows, passing buckets with water to moisten the pavement on which some devotees, fulfilling a vow, roll themselves along lengthwise in front of the temple chariot.

Pantheon and Iconography

Three features must be part of the setup of any Tamil Śaiva temple. Firstly, the flagpole (*dhvajastambha*) which, in certain speculations, is identified with imaginary veins (*nāḍī*) in the human body that play an indispensable role in Āgamic and Tāntrik meditation techniques.

Secondly, a granite lotus bud, called balipīṭha, which means 'bench for offerings,' because the bud usually rests upon a pedestal which can be used for offerings to the chief deity. And thirdly, the deity's mount, an attributive or symbolic animal, like the rat (Gaṇeśa), the peacock (Murugan), the lion (Pārvatī), the goose (Brahmā), or the vulture (Viṣṇu), etc. A special honour has been imparted upon the cobra goddess, in-as-much as she rides a bull, like Śiva himself.

Flagpole, lotus bud and bull

On the frieze of the sanctissimum, the goddess is crowned by a Liṅga with Yoni, the spiritual versions of the male and female organs.

Liṅga with Yoni
on the frieze of the sanctissimum

During our visit, the brahmin on duty is busy preparing the shrines for the pūjā. The sanctissimum must of course be cleaned before the goddess' darśana ('audience') for the devotees.

Brahmin on duty, rinsing the sanctissimum

The sthalamūrtis (locally fixed granite statues) are still naked inside their pavilions, waiting to be dressed, made up and decorated.

The goddess at 12:25 hrs

Half an hour later, they are unrecognisable, splendidly rigged out for the solemn occasion.

The goddess at 12:45 hrs

To the right and left of the Devī's main shrine, there are pedestals for her entourage; one for a magnificently adorned Śivaliṅga.

On the left we see an altar for Lakṣmī (goddess of fortune)), a meditating Śiva and Sarasvatī (the goddess of science and fine arts).

Liṅga

Lakṣmī, Śiva and Sarasvatī

Behind the sanctissimum, in the south-west and north-west corners of the temple hall, stand the pavilions of the two 'sons' of the Great Goddess, Gaṇeśa and Murugan.

Gaṇeśa
Before… (at 12:14 hrs)

Murugan
Before… (at 12:16 hrs)

…and after (at 13:29 hrs)

And after… (at 13:16 hrs)

Gaṇeśa in the frieze of his pavilion
Notice his rats

Murugan in the frieze of his pavilion
Notice his peacocks

In the middle between the two half-brothers stands the shrine for Veṅkaṭeśvara. This god does not exactly belong in the Śaiva pantheon but is considered by some as the son of Śiva and Viṣṇu's female manifestation, Mohinī and should therefore be entitled to a place in Śaiva temples as well.

Veṅkaṭeśvara

The northern area of a Śaiva Tamil temple is traditionally reserved for the pavilion of the Nine Planets (Navagraha). Some visitors are in a hurry and mainly come to venerate these magically powerful deities and demigods, hoping for speedy results of their *do ut des*.

Brahmin dousing the Nine Planets

Near to the Nine Planets, we find the vasantamaṇḍapa, the Spring Pavilion. It is the abode of the utsavamūrtis of the temple deities, which may be removed from their places and carried through the streets around the temple during the mahotsava, the Great Festival.

Utsavamūrtis

The last shrine which we reach at the end of our circumambulation is that of Śiva Bhairava, Śiva in his awe-inspiring manifestation. Armed with his trident and accompanied by his dog, he stands guard in the east, where traditionally the main entrance ought to be.

Śiva Bhairava

Trimūrti
Brahmā – Viṣṇu – Śiva

The four Tamil saints
Tirujñānasaṃbandha, Appar
Sundaramūrti and Mānikkavacagar

The walls of the temple hall are decorated with an abundance of murals. A selection shall conclude our sketch of the temple of the snake goddess in the metropolis.

Śiva Ardhanārīśvara

Harihara

Name of the temple: *Sri Nagapooshani Amman Temple*, anglicised for Tamil *Śrī Nākapūṣaṇī Ammāṉ Ālayam* (Sanskrit: Śrī Nāgabhūṣaṇī-Ambā Ālaya, 'Place of the Illustrious Mother Who is Bejewelled with Cobras').

Time of visit: Januar 13, 2007, about 11:00-13:30.

Address: Hinduistischer Kultur- und Traditions-Verein e.V. (Vereinsregister Nr. 13446), Adalbertstr. 61-63, D-60486 Frankfurt.

Tel.: 069-979 456 18. Fax: 069-979 456 25.

View along the temple hall from the east

Main entrance, viewed from the north

Nāgabhūṣaṇī-Ambā Temple, Frankfurt

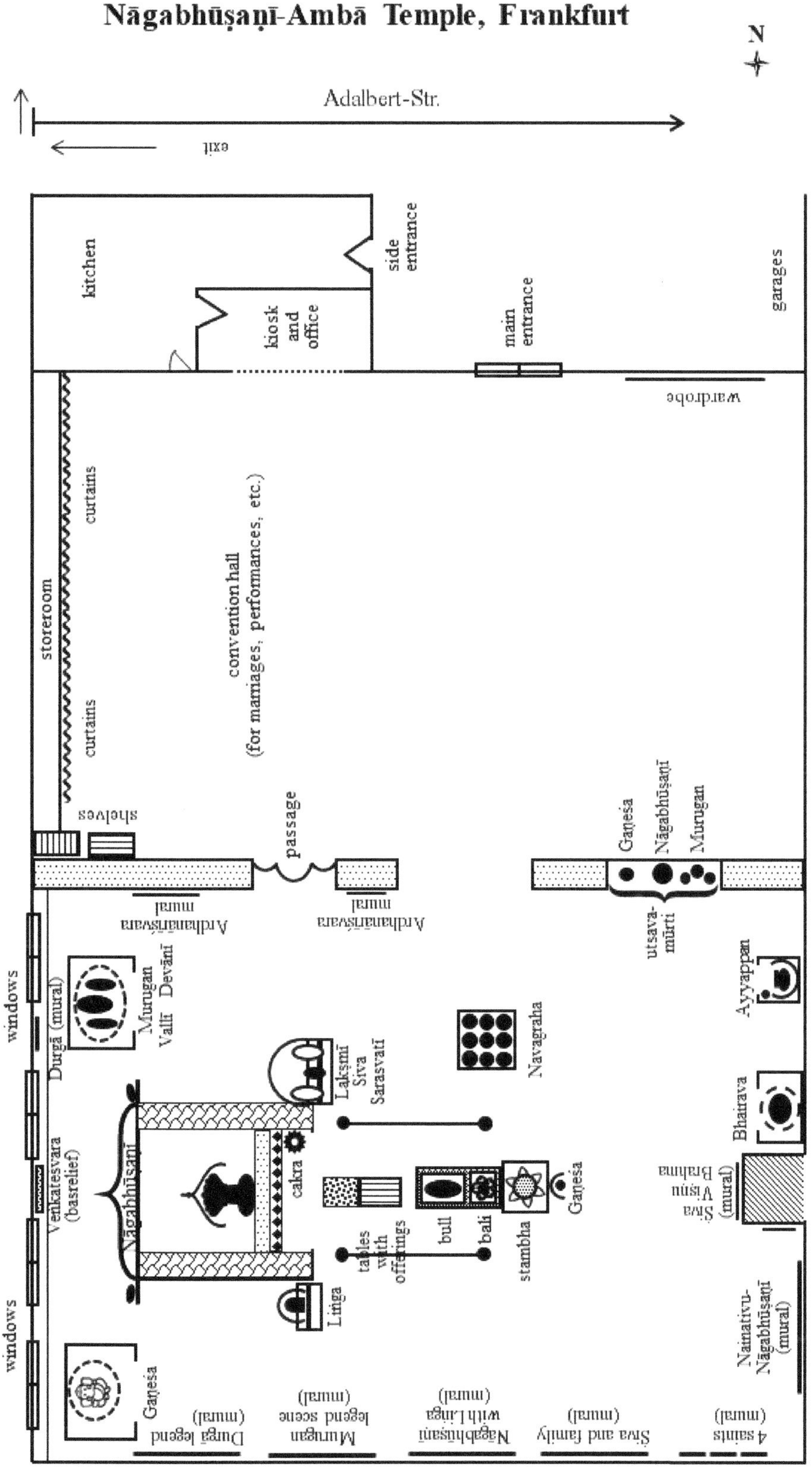

'No Shoe · No Jacket · No Photo · No Video · No Cell Phone'
The Durgā-Devī-Ambā Devasthānam in Toronto

Durgā, the mother-goddess

Our interviewee is the 'Chief Priest, Founder, Director, President, Astrologer and Hindu Registrar of Marriage.' This is how Mr Sivasri K. Thiagarajahkurukkal describes his functions in the official brochure of the *Durka Devi Ambal Thevasthanam* (in anglicised Tamil writing; also called: Toronto Sri Durka Hindu Temple), apparently the most affluent Tamil temple in Toronto. He and his wife Meena Rani Thiagarajahkurukkal are the driving force behind the devasthāna ('place of the divinity'). The chief priest explains that he has devised the set-up and iconography of his sanctum all by himself. There is no model temple in Sri Lanka or India.

The sanctum has found rich sponsors. The site alone had cost 800.000 CAD and the temple as a whole amounted to two million. Each of the three chariots for the great Chariot Festival (*rathotsava*) cost 200.000 CAD, which were also donated by wealthy businessmen.

Sivasri K. Thiagarajahkurukkal

The temple hall measures approximately 70 x 30 square metres. There are simple but nevertheless lavish interior furnishings. The granite statues, also contributed by donors, came from India, partly (if not all) from Kumbhakonam. A specialty of the temple are the sixty-four sculptures of Śaiva saints along the long walls of the temple hall.

A call for donations in the entrance hall asks for money for the completion of the tiling of the temple floor with granite. About two thirds of the floor remains untiled. The estimated costs are twenty-five CAD for each square foot. One reason for donating is subtly suggested in the call: if you are generous yourself, the goddess will be generous to you – *do ut des*.

There is also a building plan of the projected gopuram (temple tower). The height will be sixty-two feet, the costs will be approximately one million CAD. An architect from Chennai is commissioned with the construction: Padmasri Muthiah Sthapati [a traditional architect], Svarnam Architect and Svarnam Exports, Chennai 90. A Canadian building contractor attends to the shells.

An antecedent of today's Durgā temple existed in a small unit from 1991 onwards. The present building was inaugurated on July 2, 2001. An extensive documentation of the kumbhābhiṣeka ceremony has been produced on DVD, also a brochure containing photos, speeches and greeting addresses by politicians. Forty brahmins from all over the globe attended to the rites.

The temple seems to permanently employ five brahmins, including Mr Thiagarajah. Every Tuesday, a special pūjā is conducted, which is attended today by about forty devotees. Interrupted by the pūjā ceremonies is a Navakoṭi ('Ninety Million') ritual, which has been going on for three years yet. A certain mantra must be repeated ninety million times by four brahmins in the sanctissimum.

85% of the visitors are Jaffna Tamils, the remaining 15% being North Indians and astonishingly, some Chinese Durgā bhaktas.

All Tamil temples finance themselves by donations and pūjā fees; no such temple has a sharply defined 'parish,' whose members would have to contribute church taxes to their temple. The Toronto Durgā temple is a huge venture with a far-reaching catchment area. This year, the great Temple Festival (*mahotsava*), one of the most lucrative income sources of a Tamil temple, concluded on July 27, 2004, and was proud to have three temple chariots (cf. above, p. 216).

Temple Layout and Iconography

The temple is orientated southward; Durgā faces the midday sun, with a slight turn to the east. The visitor enters the sanctum from Carnforth Road through a huge door and finds himself in a spacious anteroom of about 5 x 30 square metres.

To the right and left of the entrance there are wardrobes and a place to leave shoes. To the west, there are doors opening to the porter's kiosk, the manager's office, toilets, washrooms and a storeroom. A broad door, directly opposite the main entrance, leads to the temple hall proper.

We start our tour of the Toronto Durgā temple with a pradakṣiṇā, a clockwise circumambulation. We concentrate on the shrines and devotional objects on the periphery, those that are near to the walls. Above the entrance door hangs a big poster of Durgā herself – the Devī gazes at her own picture. We turn to the west and come across the maṇḍapa of the Tamil hero-saint Vīrabhadra first. Along the western wall of the temple, we pass the doors to the kitchen, the employees' office (i.e. the brahmins' room for relaxing) and a wash basin for cleansing the pūjā utensils. Near the end of this aisle stands a table, on which the devotees arrange the donations they brought: bananas, mangos, coconuts, flowers, etc. In the south-north direction, on both sides, seven pillars each divide the exterior area near the wall from the interior space near the sanctissimum. In the niches along the outer walls, to the west and east, small busts of the sixty-four Śaiva saints stand behind glass-panes.

Now we turn to the sons of the goddess whose shrines are situated behind the sanctissimum on the north wall. Gaṇeśa has his appropriate place to the right of the Devī, Murugan with his two consorts to the left. On the roof of Murugan's maṇḍapa there are friezes of the god, depicting him sitting (west), standing (south) and half-naked, as Daṇḍāyudhapāṇi, 'the One with a stick in his hand.'

Behind the sanctissimum, between the helpful god with the trunk and the war-god with the lance, hangs a painting of the main goddess, the four-armed Durgā, holding the conch (*śaṅkha*) in her upper right hand, disk (*cakra*) and trident (*triśūla*) in the left and showing the gesture of granting shelter (*abhayada*) with the lower right.

விநாயகர் சன்னிதியும் அங்கு அமர்ந்த விநாயகரும்

முருகன் சன்னிதியும் அங்கு அமர்ந்த வள்ளி தெய்வானை சமேத முருகப்பெருமானும்

The 'Spring Pavilion' housing the bronze utsavamūrtis

Walking alongside the eastern wall, we first reach the maṇḍapa of the Nine Planets. In front of it stands a large basin for the oil-lamps lit by the devotees.

To the right the grand altar with the utsavamūrtis awaits. The festival statuettes there are made of bronze. We discern (the order is slightly different from that of the picture in the brochure, reprinted here): a not very tall six-headed Murugan Ṣaṇmukha with consorts, Śiva with Pārvatī, a one-headed Murugan with consorts, a five-headed Gaṇeśa Pañcamukha on an elevated throne and a saint sitting in the yoga pose. Two female guardians stand to the right and left of the altar, holding disk and conch, leaning on their clubs (*gadā*).

Above this Spring Pavilion (*vasantamaṇḍapa*) there are friezes of five deities: The one in the centre is a blue-complexioned goddess, balancing disk and conch upon her upright outstretched fingertips – she undoubtedly represents the chief divinity of the temple, Durgā. To her right sits the goddess Lakṣmī, with two lotuses in her hands. Next, to her right, enthrones Gaṇeśa. To Durgā's left we perceive Sarasvatī with the Indian lute (*vīṇā*), to her left Gaṇeśa's counterpart, here depicted as a child, Bāla-Murugan, with the lance (*vēl*) in his left.

In the south-east corner, there is a comparably small maṇḍapa for Śiva Bhairava. We take a half turn and walk to the central area of the temple hall. Here, we find, as expected, the three insignia of the main deity: flagpole (*dhvajastambha*), lotus bud (*balipīṭha*) and the goddess's mount (*vāhana*), a lion (*siṃha*). Mount and lotus are carved out of black granite stone with the tall flagpole shimmering in bronze.

The goddess's mount, a lion
Behind, the lotus bud

In front of the sanctissimum, the Devī looks upon a pedestal with a small Liṅga of granite and a relatively tall bronze statue of Durgā at its side.

Part of the traditional layout of a Devī temple is having different companions in front of the sanctissimum. The goddess of fortune, Lakṣmī has her entourage here, where they belong. She is represented by a sthalamūrti of black granite and sits cross-legged in the lotus position (*padmāsana*) holding fully blown lotuses in both hands. The friezes in the dome of her maṇḍapa reveal her as a Gajalakṣmī, because she is flanked to her right and left by elephants with raised trunks. The niches in the outside walls of her pavilion contain Śiva, the Lord of Dance (Naṭarāja) in the east, a naked preaching Śiva Dakṣiṇāmūrti (in the south, *dakṣiṇa*) and Pārvatī in the west.

Beside Lakṣmī's pavilion is parked a cart with potted plants: tulasī, 'the holy basil held in veneration by the Hindus, especially by the worshippers of Viṣṇu' (Apte) and kuśa, 'a kind of grass considered holy and forming an essential requisite of several religious ceremonies' (Apte). It is used here for the Gaṇeśa pūjā in addition to a plantain and some flowering plants.

The door of the sanctissimum is watched over by two female guardians. In the dome above we perceive, in the west, a sitting Śivānī (Śiva in his female manifestation), colourfully painted. Below her is a black statuette of Śiva. To the north stands Mohinī, the female manifestation of Viṣṇu, who himself has his place below her. In the east there is a Brāhmaṇī with four heads, the fourth – backwards – is invisible, because it is impossible to create it in three dimensions in a frieze. Below her, the god Brahmā, is also four-headed.

The counterpart to Lakṣmī's pavilion forms a large shrine housing both Kālī and Sarasvatī, with separate open fronts. Mahākālī, nearest to the sanctissimum, looks from her shrine to the west, i.e. on the eastern wall of the sanctissimum. Sarasvatī, however, faces south, like Durgā herself. The plaster figurine in the dome of this maṇḍapa only represents Sarasvatī, with her vīṇā.

We finally stop in front of the sanctissimum and study the main statue, a granite sthalamūrti of Durgā. The iconographical attributes of this chief goddess are unusual. She holds Viṣṇu's attributes, the disk (*cakra*) in the upper right and the conch (*śaṅkha*) in the upper left. Her lower right hand shows the gesture of providing shelter (*abhayada-mudrā*), her left lower hand loosely touches her hip (*kaṭyava-lambita-hasta*). She stands on a buffalo's head; it is that of the buffalo demon (*asura*) named Mahiṣa, hence her epithet Durgā Mahiṣāsura-mardinī ('Maimer of the demon Asura'). This appearance of Durgā originated in portrayals shown in South Indian temples. Durgā was depicted like that during the reign of the Pallava dynasty. „In der Pallava-Kunst trägt Durgā nur die Attribute Viṣṇus. Sie... setzt den Fuß auf den von ihr erschlagenen Asura Mahiṣa." (V. Moeller, *Mythologie*, p. 64) The Pallava kings of the 6th century were devoted worshippers of Viṣṇu. (Cf. J. Gonda, *Die Religionen Indiens: II Der jüngere Hinduismus*, 1963, vol. II, p. 126). Mr Thiagarajah claims that the statues, too, were manufactured according to his ideas and conceptions.

In the dome of the main maṇḍapa, the light-blue plaster figurine of Durgā sits relaxed in the 'half-lotus position' (*ardha-paryaṅka* or *lalitāsana*), her left lower leg bent upwards. Female guardian-demons with fangs and two lions, Durgā's mounts, their jaws wide open, crouch by her sides.

Interview with Mr Krishna Shivapragasam

Mr Krishna Shivapragasam is manager and organiser of the Durgā temple in Toronto. The Chief priest Thiagarajah and his wife have urged us to meet him. They have proposed an appointment the same evening and arranged that one of the younger brahmins picks us up at our hotel.

The young brahmin, after his emigration, had spent two years in Munich before he joined his relatives in Toronto. He is still enthusing about Munich and Bayern München.

The interview initiated by Mr Thiagarajah and his wife, took place in the managerial office inside the temple. Mr Shivapragasam objected to being photographed. His picture appears in the official brochure of the inauguration ceremony (mahābhiṣeka) on the first page. The moustache has been shorn off in the meantime. After his emigration he spent two months in Saarbrücken, Germany, then two years in Paris, until he finally reached Toronto. He has been working here for eighteen years now, in the fields of computer engineering and accountancy. He is married with two children.

Mr Shivapragasam manages the website <www.durka.com> from which we learned the addresses of the Canadian Tamil temples in the first place. At the very beginning of this website, Mr Shivapragasam contends three ideals: equality, i.e. refusal of the caste system, religious awareness, but no misuse of Hindu beliefs, i.e. refusal of Hindu fundamentalism; and refusal of commercialising temples – a temple must not be 'used as a money-making venture.'

250.000 Sri Lankan Tamils live in Toronto alone, another 50.000 elsewhere in Canada, mostly in Montreal. Our interview focused on the possibilities and chances for these immigrants to be integrated and the function of the Hindu temples involved. In the USA, 80% of the immigrants become rapidly and completely amalgamated. The situation in Toronto is quite different. Most of the immigrants live in separated groups, dependent on their home countries and apart from the locals. They learn very little American English and continue to speak Anglo-Indian, heavily influenced by Tamil ways of expression. Mr Shivapragasam warns against two dangers: On the one hand he fears US American conditioning, which would mean a complete absorption into westernised culture; on the other he mentions the example of Guyana (north-eastern part of South America), where immigrants from South Asia have forgotten their roots for over one hundred years and have no correct conception of Hinduism. Hindu temples must fight against this loss of tradition, focussing on the 'kids,' the second generation. Their English, by the way, is getting more and more American, because they learn it in school and have more, albeit not many more, contact with non-immigrants. But the young folks too, with their Tamil background, stay secluded and are prone to inter-Tamil marriages. Alliances with whites are extremely rare. He gave a shocking example: a Sikh had his daughter shot, because she wished to marry a white Canadian.

Mr Shivapragasam did not contradict our opinion that it is one of the functions of the temples to hold the balance between the conservative traditionalism of the temple brahmins and a too rapid adjustment of the second generation, the 'kids.'

Mr Shivapragasam is in favour of Tamil temples progressing in a grand and stately manner. He is against what he calls 'templising,' the setting up of many tiny 'mushroom temples' in miserable shacks, where the deities do not have dignified surroundings. In this respect, we are of quite a different opinion (of course without contradicting him), for in smaller temples the statues (often the whole set-up) is much more original, inventive, created with much more devotion and expertise, than that in ostentatious mass-temples. Bounteous donations by affluent sponsors are not necessarily conducive to a time-honoured temple tradition.

Mr Shivapragasam's iṣṭadeva (favourite god) is Gaṇeśa. Most of the visitors of the Durgā temple do have different iṣṭadevatās, other than Durgā, whose temples they prefer. Nevertheless, they do not dare to refuse the goddess 'Who is hard to approach' (i.e. Durgā) their veneration.

'No Shoe · No Jacket · No Photo · No Video · No Cell Phone,' reads the admonition of the temple management to the visitors. That is why the pictures in this chapter are all scanned from the brochure *Canada Toronto Sri Durka Hindu Temple. Maha Kumbabisekam Consecration Ceremony Souvenir.* Toronto, July 2, 2001 (DHT). – The ground plan is ours.

Time of visit: Tuesday, October 25, 2004, 11:00-12:30 a.m., and October 26, 2004, 7-8:30 p.m.
Address: 30 Carnforth Road, Toronto, ON M4A 2K7.
tel. 416-759 9648 or 751 5151.
fax 416-751 7939.
www.durka.com.

Sri Durka Hindu Temple, Toronto

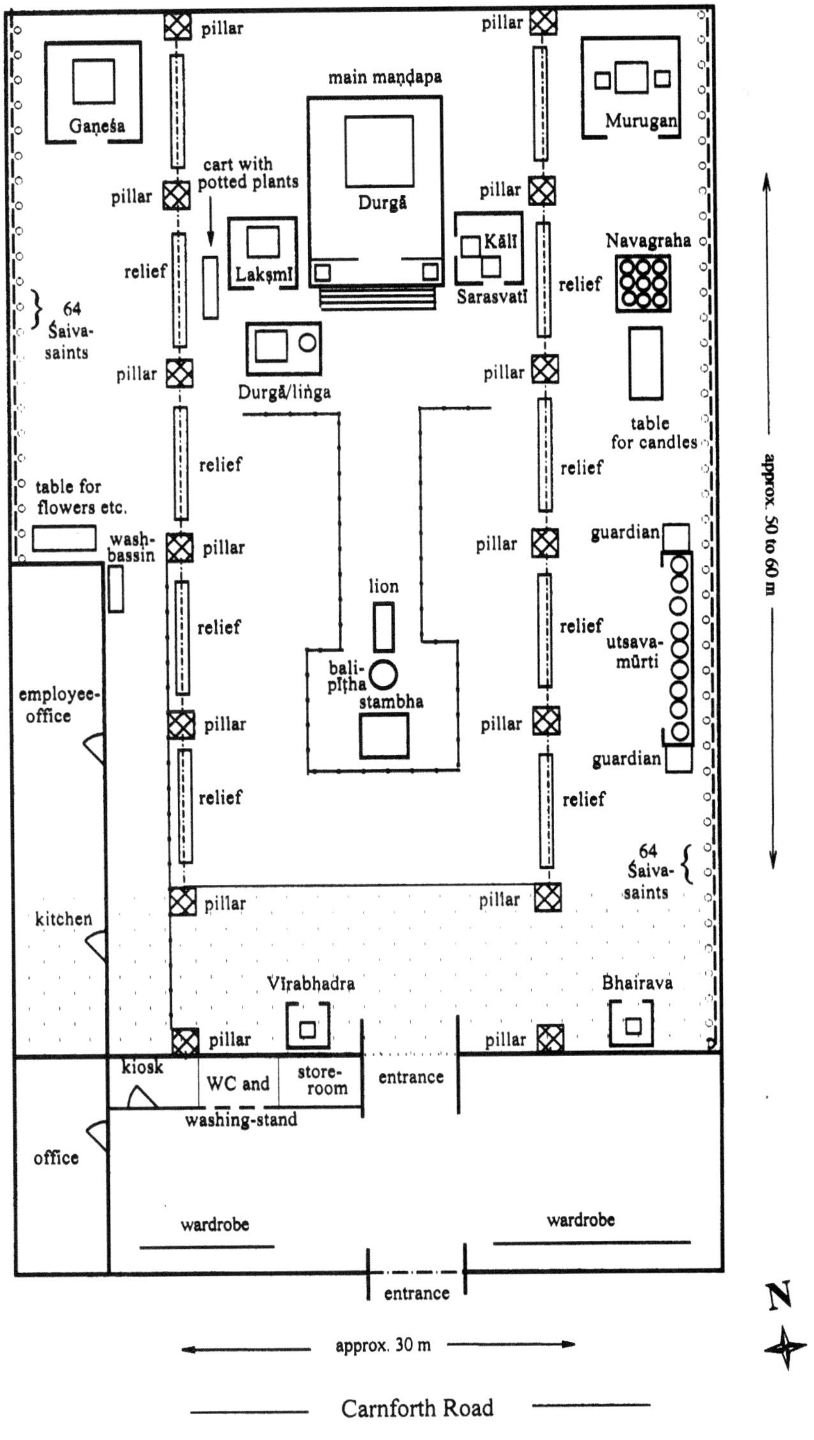

‘The Polyandric Goddess’
The Draupadī-Ambā Temple in Riambel

Draupadī above the main shrine, east front

The hamlet of Riambel is situated on the south coast of Mauritius, near Point aux Roches. The *Drawbadhee Ammen Kovil* (‘Draupadī-Ambā Temple’) has its place directly alongside the little frequented coast road between Point aux Roches and Souillac. The temple building and compound appear to be recently inaugurated and maintained with loving care. Sugarcane plantations and some minor fields with vegetables and herbs dominate the rural countryside. The temple building proper measures about 15 x 8 square metres.

Draupadī is a prominent character in the great Sanskrit epic *Mahābhārata*, the origins of which reach back to the sixth century B.C.- Its framework story deals with the war between the Kauravas and the Pāṇḍavas, descendants of their mutual forefather Bharata. Draupadī is the shared spouse of the five Pāṇḍava brothers. One of them, called Arjuna, is told the famous didactic poem *Bhagavadgītā*, the 'Song of God,' by his charioteer, the god Kṛṣṇa. The polyandric Draupadī, thus representing an age-old matrilinear (not matriarchal!) tradition of Indian culture, enjoys the highest respect all over the Indian subcontinent and – as can be seen out here in Mauritius – far beyond.

The inside of the temple is open to the public. The statues in the sanctissimum are separated from the devotees' hall only by a hip-high banister.

The temple is orientated to the east. In front of the entrance, on a pedestal, we observe four clearly distinguished features, to be found in nearly every Tamil temple: Śiva's trident, the flagpole, the lotus bud and the Devī's mount (borrowed from Śiva), the white zebu bull Nandī.

Inside of the temple with sanctissimum

Temple hall, view to the east

Trident, flagpole, lotus and Nandī

Lotus bud (*balipīṭha*)

The goddess's mount, a white zebu bull

When the devotee has entered the temple hall, he knells a bell hanging from the ceiling, to announce his presence to the deities. There are benches, pushed together on both sides of the entrance door, serving as seating for the visitors.

The sanctissimum is separated by pillars into niches. In the centre the main goddess Draupadī is enthroned, a black granite sthalamūrti placed a little bit to the back.

Draupadī, black granite

Gaṇeśa

To her right, somewhat nearer to the wooden banister, is the altar of Gaṇeśa.

In the corner behind Gaṇeśa stands a small statue of the blue-complexioned god Viṣṇu, beneath a hood of five cobra heads.

Gaṇeśa, and Viṣṇu behind

Viṣṇu beneath a hood of five cobra heads

To the left of the Devī resides Murugan, holding his lance and flanked by two additional golden lances.

The statues of Gaṇeśa and Murugan are smaller than that of the goddess, but also made of granite. A bronze utsavamūrti of Murugan has its place behind his granite figure. The wall to the left (north) of Murugan's shrine is decorated by two paintings of the god. The artist has signed with his name, 'D. Mohun,' and gives the date as '10·1·98.'

Murugan, sthalamūrti

Murugan, painting

Outside the temple building, in the south-east corner, stands a bare pavilion, housing a bearded guardian deity, holding a trident.

Guardian deity

Some steps further along the south side, between the outer wall and the temple building, we come across a pavilion with a locked glass door. It accommodates a female (?) granite figure, clad in green net lace. It is decorated with a comparably plain garland or necklace, the eyes painted white, with a tilaka on the forehead. The head seems to be crowned by a snake hood, reaching downwards to her ears, where there is also a tilaka on each side. Because of the heavily weathered granite, it is not clear if she has fangs. Were this the case, it could be a cobra goddess, a Nāgabhūṣaṇī (?).

On the backside of the wall around the temple compound, in the west, are a kitchen, bathroom and toilets. At the northern wall, outside in the corner between the sanctissimum and the meeting hall, hides a snake stone (nāgakkal), – opposite the shrine of the possibly female goddess in the south.

Snake stone

In the three-storied dome above the sanctissimum, friezes of Draupadī, Gaṇeśa and Murugan keep a lookout in all four directions.

Female (?) deity

Temple tower

Draupadī above entrance

Date of visit: April 10, 2001, 10:00 hrs

Draupadī-Ambā Temple, Riambel

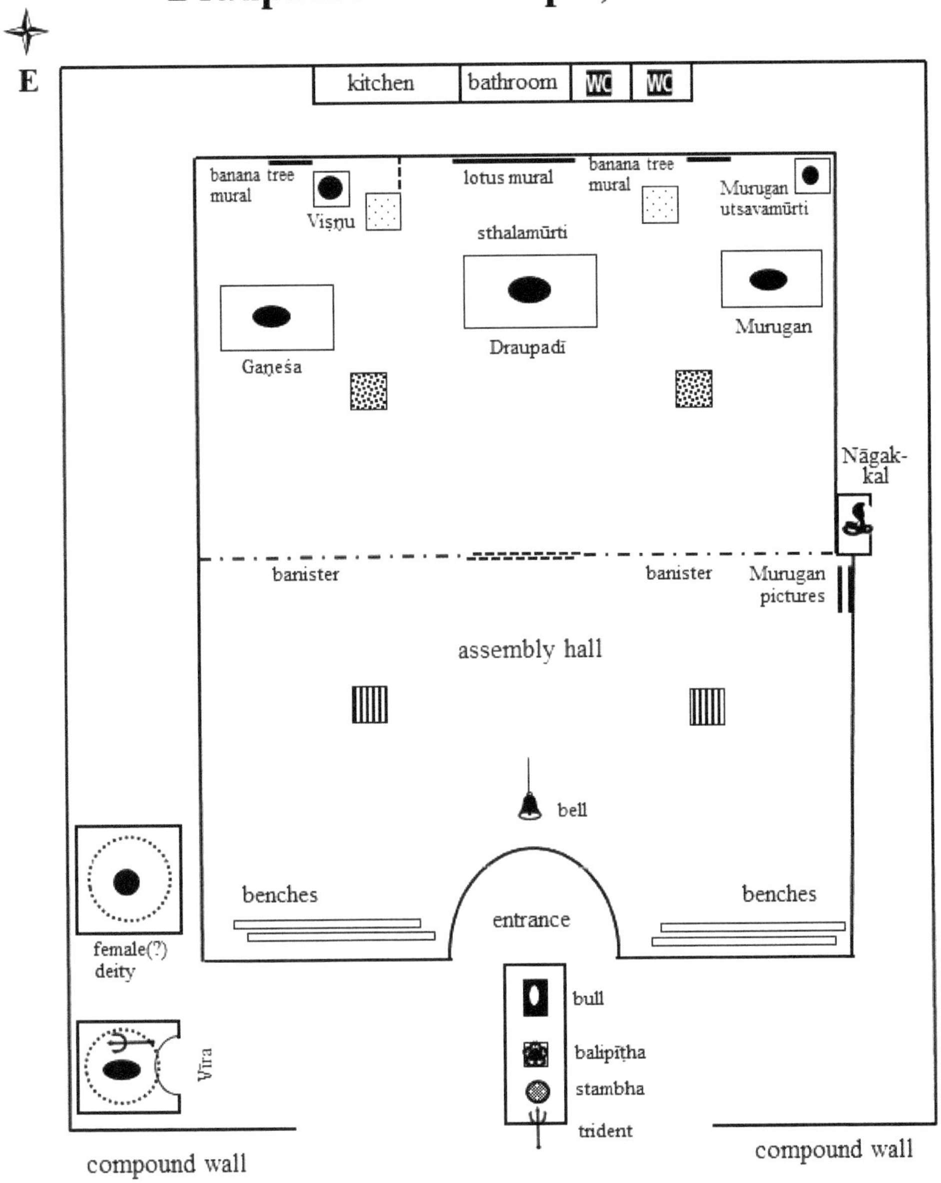

‘Kālī in Mauritius’
The Kālī-Ambā Temple in Beau Vallon

Granite statue of Kālī
Main goddess in the sanctissimum
Accompanied by the elephant-headed Gaṇeśa

Leaving the city of Mahébourg westwards on the local bus service, along the A 10, we pass the suburb of Beau Vallon. Here we catch sight of the rather small, recently built *Kaliammen Kōvil* (Kālī-Ambā temple) on the left side of the road.

Kālī Ambā means ‘Mother Kālī’ (Kālī, the ‘Black One’). Kālī’s famous home temple is situated at the Kālī Ghāṭ in Calcutta (today Kolkata), the capital of West Bengal, India, from where many Indian labourers came to Mauritius.

Alighting from the bus, we do not meet anybody on the temple premises, so we must confine ourselves to a few observations, illustrated by some pictures.

A staircase with six or eight steps leads up to a kind of forecourt. Here, on the right, western side, we perceive two pavilions. The bigger one, laid out

Kālī vanquishes Śiva
In front seven adoring Śivaliṅgas

with blue tiles, houses the stucco figure of a blue-complexioned Kālī.

The goddess stands on her left leg: her right foot is placed on Śiva's breast, as he lies on his back. The sculpture is reminiscent of the well-known dancing Śiva (Naṭarāja) who tramples down Apasmāra, the demon of ignorance; or of Durgā, crushing the bull demon (Mahiṣāsuramardinī). Here, Kālī conquers Śiva, thus claiming her

Kālī conquering Śiva

Kālī in a red sari

predominance as a goddess (who has her roots in the local Bengal substratum) above the mainstream high god.

Kālī is adored by a row of seven stone Liṅgas, set in the floor. A somewhat larger Liṅga is in the middle and three smaller ones on each side.

In the left and narrower of the two shrines, a black marble sculpture of Kālī stands up straight. Kālī is wrapped in a red sari, wearing a quite expensive looking heavy necklace. Her ghastly, long red tongue hangs out of her mouth. On each of the three points of the trident in her lower right hand, limes are impaled as fruit offerings.

Durgā in an open shrine

Turning round and facing the eastern side of the forecourt, we find a statue of Durgā in an open shrine.

The sculpture of white marble, approximately 80 cm tall, stands on a lotus pedestal, wears make up, has donned a sari and is adorned with a luxuriant garland (*mālā*).

In a kind of frontroom to the temple hall proper, we see a Gaṇeśa relief on

Durgā

Entrance to the temple hall

each side of the entrance to the main hall. Above the entrance door there are niches with frescoes of three goddesses. Durgā, the biggest in the middle, wears a blue sari. To her left, in white garments, stands Sarasvatī with a vīṇā, the Indian lute, in two of her hands, while the right upper hand shows the gesture (*mudrā*) of providing freedom from fear (*abhayada*) by pointing the palm with upright fingers to the spectator. Her left hand, with fingers hanging loosely downwards, palm to the front, indicates her willingness to grant wishes (*varada*). Sarasvatī is the patron of science and fine arts. The figure to Durgā's right, in the red sari, is probably Gāyatrī, the god Brahmā's second spouse.

A plaque in the temple wall informs us that the foundation stone of the 'Maha Kaliammen Kōvil' was laid on the 19th April 1993 by Mr Anand Seedheeyan.

Kālī's mount, the tiger

Kālī in the sanctissimum

The entrance door is kept watch over by Kālī's mount, the tiger, gazing at his mistress. Behind him, as an insignia of Kālī's rule, bulges the granite lotus bud (*balipīṭha*) – as usual in Śaiva temples – in front of the sanctissimum (*garbhagṛha*).

Inside the garbhagṛha, behind a locked grid, the black granite statue of the temple's main goddess is enthroned in the middle, clad in green garments.

Kālī's impressive eyes are gilded with gold leaves. On both sides of the nose shimmer nose stickers, painted in yellow and red. The goddess's forehead is marked with three horizontal strokes (*tripuṇḍra*); her helmet adorned with yellow petals. The figure wears various valuable necklaces of gold and jewels, donated by Kālī devotees. A wreath of tagetes flowers lies upon the crest of flames around her.

Kālī shrine behind the temple
Seven Liṅgas in front

Gaṇeśa, white marble

A relatively small white marble statuette is put up to the right side of the goddess. It is the elephant-headed Gaṇeśa who is considered the son of the Great Goddess in mainstream Śaivism. To her left we find bronze figurines of Murugan, the god of war and Śiva's son, with his two consorts.

White Liṅga

Behind the temple we enter a kind of festival court by a separate entrance from the street. The open compound is surrounded on three sides by walls which are approximately two metres high. Beside the entrance a statue of the leader of the monkey army, the god and monkey hero Hanumān, is put up behind glass.

A white Liṅga is set up in the left corner of the back wall, adorned with a garland of flowers and sprinkled with coconut water from recent oblations.

Time of visit: April 2, 2001, 12:30-13:00 hrs.

Kālī-Ambā Temple, Beau Vallon

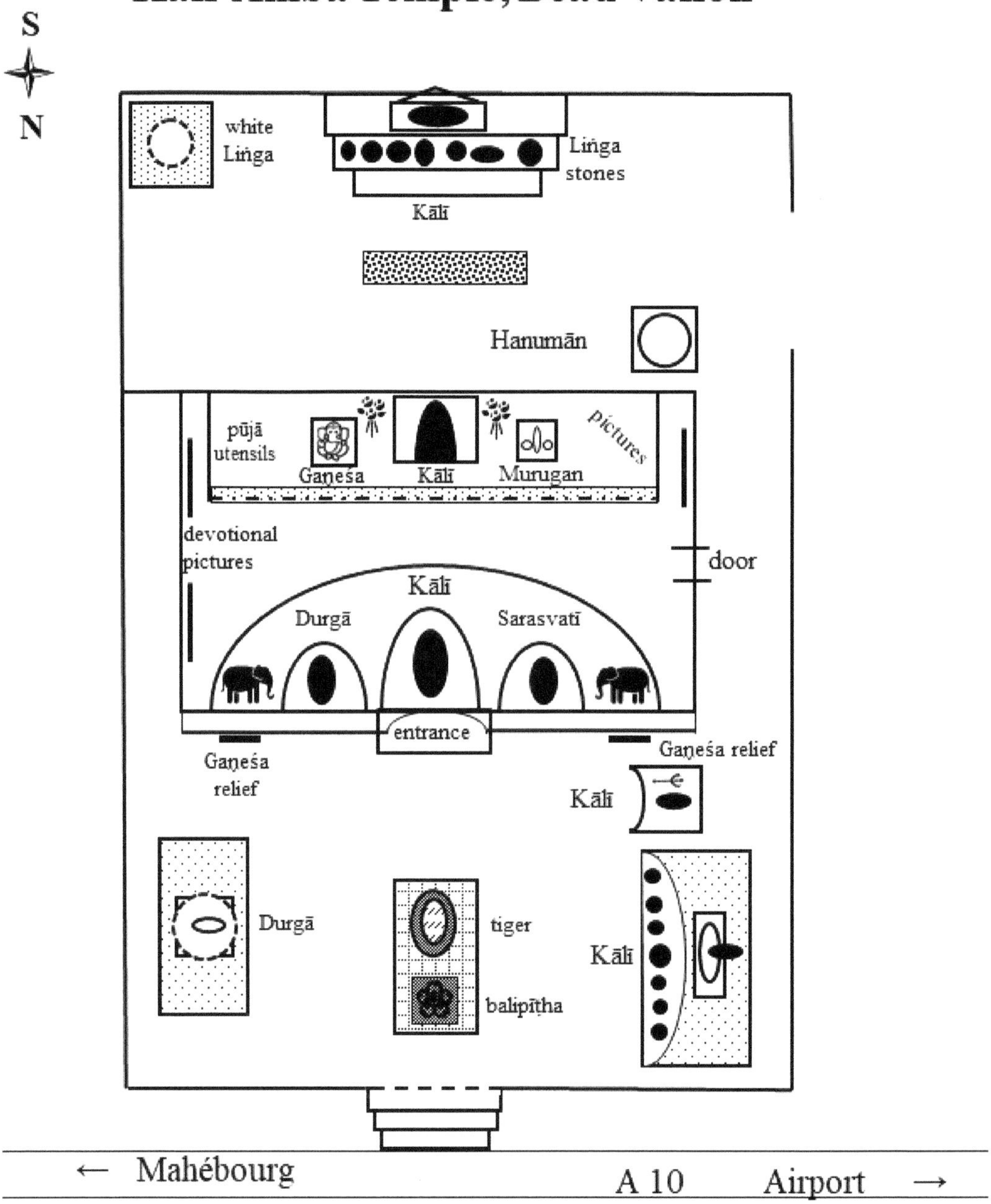

‘A Temple Under Construction’
The Kālī Kōvil in Negombo, Sri Lanka

Temple entrance from the east (Sea Street)

The temple is presently under construction. The remnants of a small shrine, about 150 years old, still exist on the same spot. During reconstruction, all statues have been transferred into a small hut, at the entrance of the temple premises. The statues face east, to the busy Sea Street. To the south, at the entrance, there is a huge tree, with an empty shrine beneath it, possibly the

The empty shrine – above, in the middle, the scratched Liṅga. The original place of worship.

original abode of the main goddess of the sanctum, Kālī. On the front wall of this empty shrine, someone has crudely engraved, or rather scratched, a Liṅga. The original place of worship had undoubtedly been under this tree.

Granite statue of Kālī in the temporary sanctissimum

Further south of the tree is a basin for ritually smashing coconuts, behind it are the brahmin's quarters and the temple manager's office.

The future temple is going to be a huge structure on a large compound, perhaps somewhat bigger even than the neighbouring Siddhi-Vināyaka Ālayam (Gaṇeśa temple). The inauguration ceremony (*kumbhābhiṣeka*) is planned for the end of this year (2006). But from the state of the construction work, this date appears rather improbable.

The main maṇḍapa however, is nearly completed. Kālī will be facing east, like her fresco on the front side of the main maṇḍapa. The raw structures of the parivāra ('retinue' – the subordinate deities) shrines are already finished too. On the west side, from south to north, we see the future pavilions for Gaṇeśa, Viṣṇu and Murugan, in the north-east corner of the Navagrahas.

Bronze Śivaliṅga and bronze statue of Kālī with trident (*triśūla*) and fire halo in the interim sanctissimum

The temple trust manager
Mr. M. Sivapragasam

Further north will be the place of the vasantamaṇḍapa, in which the utsavamūrtis (bronze festival statues) will be kept and at the east side, to the north, the maṇḍapa for Bhairava.

Bell tower

The future pavilions

Near the main shrine, there is a small maṇḍapa for Caṇḍeśvara to the north, a niche for Durgā and, to the south, for Śiva Dakṣiṇāmūrti.

Two tall bell towers have already been finished.

In the provisional temporary hut, we see the granite statue of the main goddess, Kālī. In front of her are lion and granite lotus (*balipīṭha*). At her sides wait the figures of Gaṇeśa and Murugan. Also, inside the interim sanctissimum, on the north side, stands a bronze Śivaliṅga, moreover a bronze statue of Kālī with trident (*triśūla*) and a halo of flames. Opposite the main statue and facing it, we come across the granite statues of the Navagrahas.

Temple brahmin
and trust manager

Outside the provisional temple, on the south side, there is a picture of Ayyappan; on the north side, an image of Hanumān. Opposite the Devī, above the entrance, hangs a large mirror.

During our visit, a brahmin is in service, performing the pūjā for a small crowd of pious followers.

The mahotsava celebrations will begin on Māci-makam, 'the full-moon day in Māci [Sanskrit *māgha*],… the 11th solar month = February-March' (*Tamil Lexicon*) at 6 p.m. Then the procession with the huge temple chariot, which is housed in the barn on the north side of the temple, will be drawn the whole night long until 6 a.m., through the entire city of Negombo.

Our interviewee is the temple trust manager, Mr M. Sivapragasam. His grandfather immigrated from Tamil Nadu to Sri Lanka and his family has managed this holy place for Kālī since then.

The temple trust consists of five trustees, as Mr Sivapragasam further informs us. On a normal Friday, about 500 devotees visit the temple. During festival times, about 2.000 people will join the ceremonies.

Time of visit: Friday, April 28, 2006, about 9:30-10:30 a.m.
Address: No. 153, Sea Street, Negombo, Sri Lanka.

The temple brahmin
performing the Pūjā
in front of the main statue of Kālī

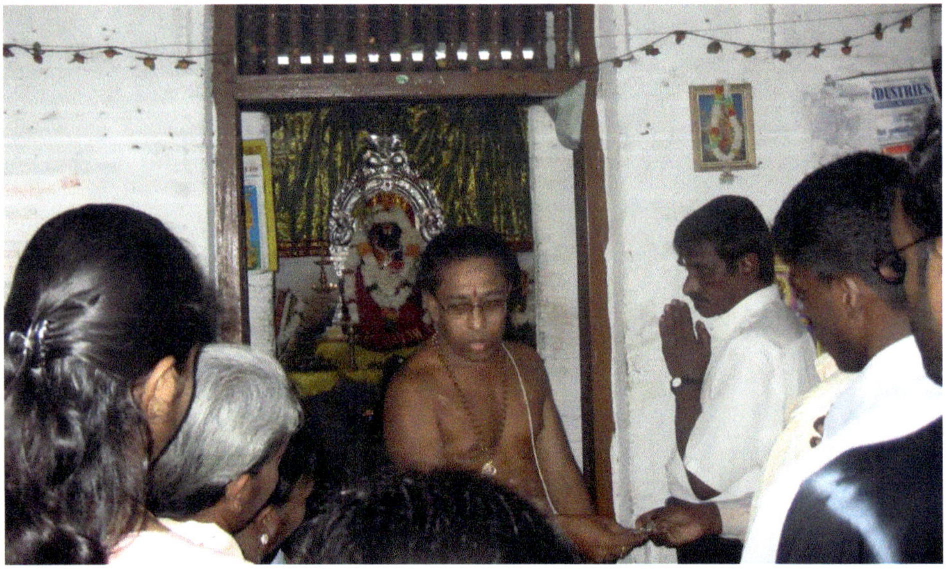

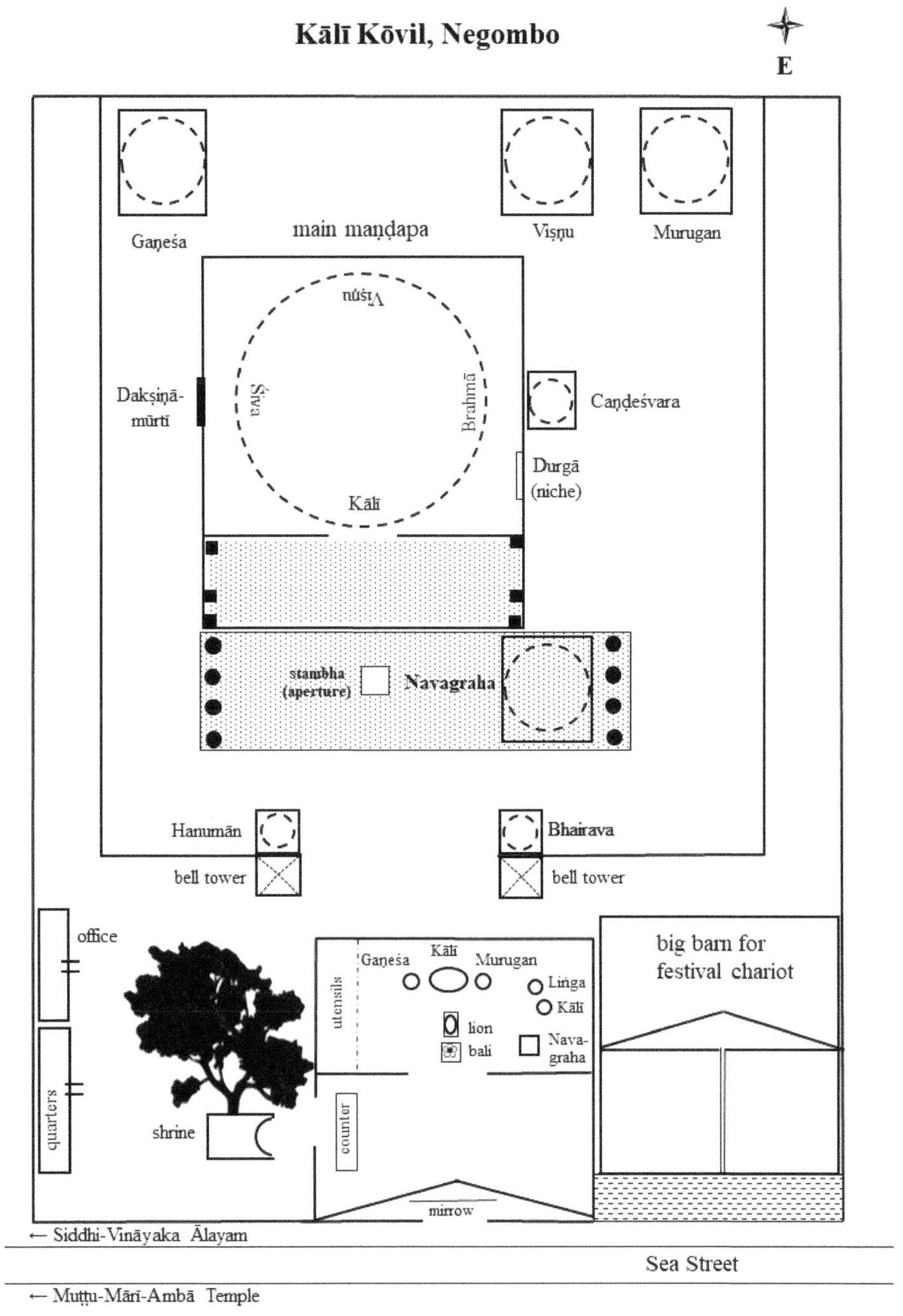
Kālī Kōvil, Negombo
E
Gaṇeśa
main maṇḍapa
Viṣṇu
Murugan
Viṣṇu
Śiva
Brahmā
Kālī
Dakṣiṇā-
mūrtī
Caṇḍeśvara
Durgā
(niche)
stambha
(aperture)
Navagraha
Hanumān
Bhairava
bell tower
bell tower
office
quarters
shrine
utensils
Gaṇeśa
Kālī
Murugan
Liṅga
Kālī
lion
bali
Nava-
graha
counter
mirrow
big barn for
festival chariot
← Siddhi-Vināyaka Ālayam
Sea Street
← Muttu-Mārī-Ambā Temple

‘Ousting the Devī, Part I’ The Kāmākṣī Temple in Māṅgāḍu

Śrī Cakra, Kāmākṣī Temple, Māṅgāḍu

In this mangadu (mango grove) Sri Kamakshi is said to have performed severe penance in the midst of pancagni [‘five fires’]. – *The image (idol) of Sri Thapas Kamakshi* [‘Kāmākṣī performing penance’] [stands] *in Vamapadangustha pose* [‘on the big toe of the left foot’] *in the midst of pancagni and* [is] *folding the right leg. Her left hand points* [to] *the hridayastana* [‘place of her heart’] *and the right hand is raised above her head holding a japamala* [‘rosary’]. *It is said that Sri Kamakshi performed her tapas* [‘penance’] *and got married* [to] *Sri Ekambareswar* [Śiva] *at Kanchi. Therefore if any unmarried girl, who comes and offer vows to Sri Kamakshi, the worshipper will also get married. This is a known fact in this area. – Sri Adi Sankara came here and installed Ardhameru (Sri Chakra)*

which is rare of its kind in India. ... One should see and worship [the temple].
Manali Ramakrishna Mudaliar, B.A.
Hereditary Trustee

Thus reads a sign near the entrance, informing the visitor about the self-image of the Māṅgāḍu Kāmākṣī temple.

A lasting impression, which imposes itself on the visitor today, is that the Kāmākṣī temple in Māṅgāḍu is indeed frequented by many young couples. The pūjā in this temple promises not only health, success, happiness, affluence, etc., but aims primarily to bring forth a marriage partner and children.

It shall be mentioned that Māṅgāḍu (Tamil *Māṅkāṭu*) is located about twenty kilometres to the west of Chennai (former Madras, the capital of Tamil Nadu) on the highway to Bangalore.

In the present chapter, we start the description of a legend that is reflected in the pantheon, iconography and architectural setup of (at least) four Śaiva Tamil temples. These four South Indian venues, closely connected to each other, are, on the one hand, deeply integrated in the local religious history and, on the other, have an enormous impact on related places of worship in South Asia and beyond. The legend is a prime example of the widespread socio-religious phenomenon we call 'Ousting the Devī' (*devī-bahiṣkāra, devī-niḥsāraṇa*). In a four-chapter series, it concludes our collection of sketches of Tamil Devī temples.

The following is a short summary of the said legend, as it can be found in its mainstream version, for example in the pilgrims' guide to the Māṅgāḍu temple by K. K. Moorthy (pp. 226ff), or on advertising internet sites like www.templenet.com/Tamilnadu/maangaadu.html.

Umā covering Śiva's eyes.
Relief on a pillar in the Kāmākṣī temple, Māṅgāḍu

Once upon a time, the goddess Umā (also known as Pārvatī), in a playful mood, covered the eyes of her spouse, Śiva with both hands .

Thereupon darkness spread all over the earth, for Śiva's eyes are the sun and the moon. Gods, sages and men got scared, and Śiva was so incensed that he ruled the following verdict: His Śakti (lit. 'power,' a female deity), in punishment for this humbug, must be reborn and remain on earth. Accordingly, Śiva's Śakti came to life in Māṅgāḍu as Kāmākṣī, meaning, in this context, 'The Eye of Śiva.'

There she awaited Śiva's arrival, for Śiva had promised to marry her to ease the hardships of the banishment. Śiva, though, did not come, and therefore the Śakti started a severe penance. She lit five fires in sacrifice bowls (*homa-*

kuṇḍa) and stood with the big toe of her left foot (*vāmapādāṅguṣṭha*) in the licking flames of the central fire. In this manner she performed penance for a long time.

The legend especially stresses that the goddess performed her penance in a mango grove. Of course, this refers to Māṅgāḍu, which just means 'mango grove,' as the scene of the event. Also, this remark designates Māṅgāḍu as an ancient place of worship in connection with the tree cult and a goddess of fertility, a *yakṣiṇī* ('female demon' or 'nymph').

When Śiva finally became aware of his Śakti's penance, he asked her to proceed from Māṅgāḍu to Kāñcīpuram. There he wished to marry her. And so it happened. In Kāñcīpuram, Śiva appeared in front of the goddess, and they both married under a mango tree.

In her hurry to proceed to Kāñcīpuram, says the legend, the goddess forgot to extinguish the five fires, inside which she had been performing her austerities.

At that time, a famous philosopher, scholar and commentator of holy scriptures, known as Ādi-Śaṃkara

Marriage of Śiva and Kāmākṣī
Frieze on the temple roof in Māṅgāḍu

Ādi-Śaṃkara
Frieze on a pillar in Māṅgāḍu

('Arch-' or first Śaṃkara, traditionally 788-820 AD), travelled throughout India on a pilgrimage. The citizens of Māṅgāḍu, who could not endure the heat exuded by the Śakti's fires, asked him for help. He set up an *Ardha-Meru-Śrī-Cakra*, a magical diagram upon a 'half [flat-topped] Meru mountain.' This Śrī Cakra is said to have banished the blaze, and thus destroyed the heat of the fires.

Still today, a Śrī Cakra is shown in the Māṅgāḍu temple; according to some it is shaped like a turtle (see picture on p. 245).

Also to be seen in the sanctissimum of the Māṅgāḍu temple is an antique statue of a goddess, performing severe penance in the middle of five fires. But this statue – and now we come to the crucial point – is placed just behind another, larger sculpture in front of her – the image of today's main goddess of this temple. In other words, the ancient Kāmākṣī was ousted by a divine parvenu. But who was the upstart?

The new potentate is a golden-coloured, standing goddess. In her right hand she holds a flower with a parrot sitting on it. Her left arm, slightly bent, hangs loosely down to her side. From the point of view of iconography, she thus matches not Kāmākṣī, but the popular mainstream goddess Mīnākṣī of Madurai.

This new statue was inaugurated in a solemn ceremony, a kumbhābhiṣeka, on July 8, 1987, by 'His Holiness Śrī Candraśekharendra Sarasvatī, Śaṃkarācārya and sixty-eighth Jagadguru (Teacher of the Universe) of the Kāmākṣī Pīṭha in Kāñcīpuram', and his successor, the present Śaṃkarācārya Śrī Jayendra Sarasvatī. It was thus invested with the blessings of two Śaṃkarācāryas.

Main shrine in the Kāmākṣī temple in Māṅgāḍu. Kāmākṣī modelled after the features of Mīnākṣī. The elder Devī Vāmapādāṅguṣṭhā, performing penance, is pushed in the background. Devotional picture.

(1) Atlas of an ancient pillar, showing a Śālabhañjikā of the substratum (Kumar, *Masterpieces*, p. 55, plate 2)

(2) Kāmākṣī Vāmapādāṅguṣṭhā 'Standing on the big toe of her left foot.'

To sum up, our reconstruction yields three stages of religious-historical development of the goddess Kāmākṣī in Māṅgāḍu:

(1) In the beginning, on the level of the substratum, there existed an ancient place of worship of a tree goddess of fertility, otherwise called a Śālabhañjikā ('tree-plucker').

(2) Under the influence of Śaiva legends, her gesture of grasping the branch of a tree was reinterpreted as a posture of yoga practice and a suitable aetiological legend was invented. The Śālabhañjikā became Kāmākṣī Vāmapādāṅguṣṭhā.

(3) Kāmākṣī performing penance still belonged to the local substratum. Under the impact of mainstream Śivaïsm she was ousted – pushed in the background – by a lovely popular goddess, now being shaped like the Devī Mīnākṣī of Madurai.

(3) Today's mainstream Kāmākṣī in Māṅgāḍu (devotional picture)

A frieze of Mīnākṣī in her temple in Scarborough. Mīnākṣī's iconography serves as a model for today's mainstream Kāmākṣī in Māṅgāḍu (graphic taken from H. D. Smith/N. Chary: *Handbook of Hindu Gods*..., p. 193).

Date of visit: February 27, 2002, 10:00-12:00.
Address: Sri Kamakshi Amman Devasthanam, Mangadu, Madras 602 101.

Sarasvatī, Kāmākṣī Vāmapādāṅguṣṭhā, Lakṣmī (from left)

Temple tower

Kāmākṣī temple – Māṅgāḍu

Temple entrance

Kāmākṣī Temple, Māṅgāḍu

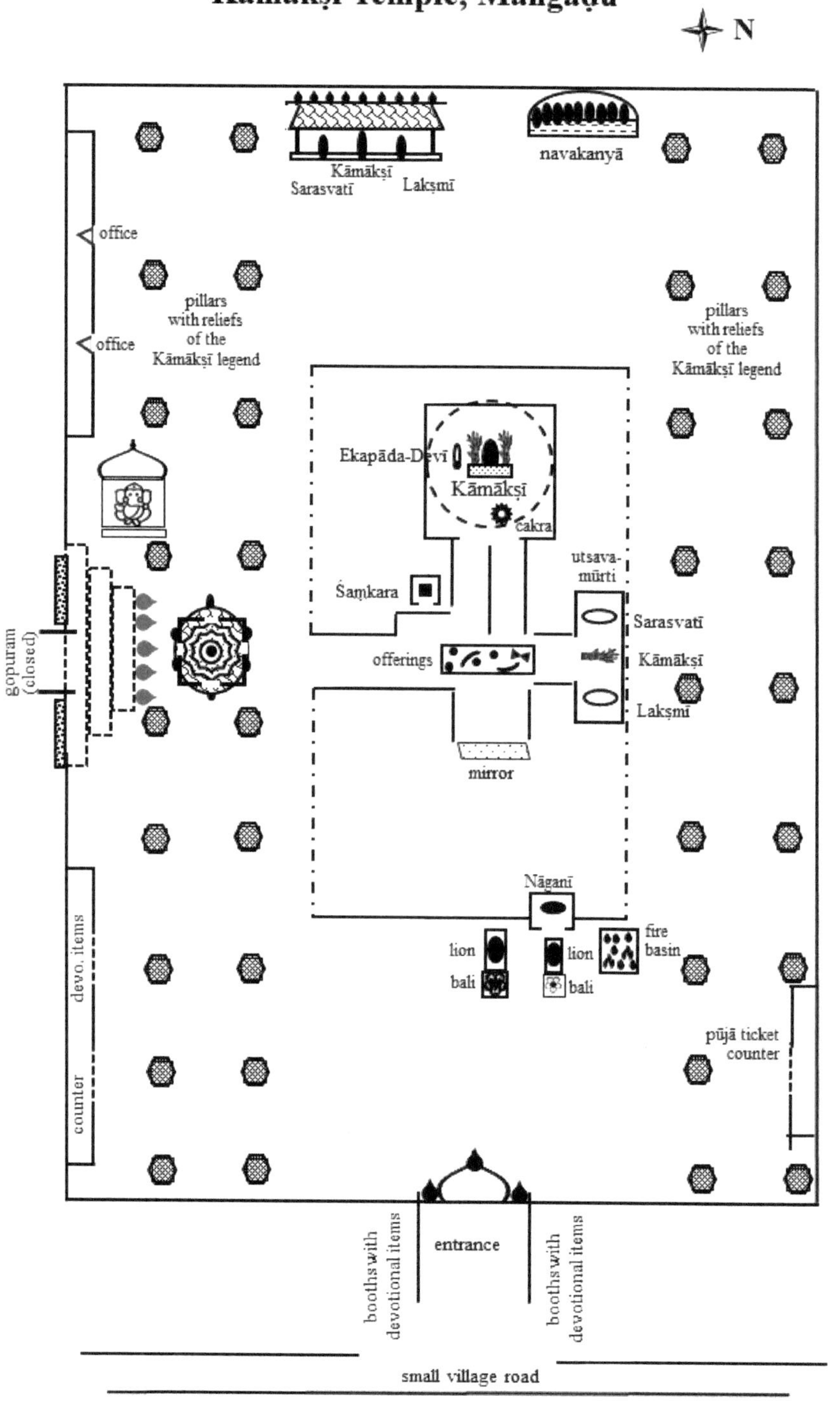

'Ousting the Devī, Part II'
The Ekāmbareśvara Temple in Kāncīpuram

Ekāmbareśvara temple, Kāñcīpuram

This temple is directly connected with the legend of Māṅgāḍu. It is here, in the Ekāmbareśvara temple in Kāñcīpuram, where the mango tree grows, beneath which Śiva is said to have married the Devī when she had finished her penance in Māṅgāḍu and had hurried to Kāñcīpuram. Through this wedding, the god received the epithet Ekāmranātha, 'Lord of the one and only Mango tree.' The temple is sometimes called Ekāmbareśvara temple. (The names do not differ very much from each other: *ekāmba[ra]* is a Re-Sanskritisation of Tamil *ēkampam*, 'name of a Śiva shrine in Conjeevaram,' *Tamil Lexicon* I 553a, < Sanskrit *ekāmra*, 'one mango'; *īśvara* and *nātha* both mean 'lord'.)

The mango tree has its place in the west behind the sanctissimum but still inside the temple compound. In front of this ancient tree, which consists – as the legend goes – of four different

Śiva and Kāmākṣī joining hands during their wedding ceremony

Liṅgāliṅganadevī, Kāñcīpuram, Art Gallery of the Kāmākṣī temple

sorts of mango trees grown together, stands a relatively small shrine. It houses a relief of dark-grey stone which depicts Śiva and Kāmākṣī joining hands during the wedding ceremony.

Three figures are engraved in the black base of this pavilion:

- The Devī embracing the Liṅga (*Liṅgāliṅganadevī*). This depiction refers to the legend concerning the emergence of the Liṅga in the sanctissimum of the Ekāmbareśvara temple (which we will examine below).
- Śiva emerging from his Liṅga (*Śiva Liṅgodbhava*). This effigy represents the Liṅga in the sanctissimum.

Śiva Liṅgodbhava
Śiva emerging from his Liṅga, grasping the goddess's forearm. Frieze in the Art Gallery of the Kāmākṣī temple, Kāñcīpuram; similar to the frieze in the Ekāmranātha maṇḍapa.

• The Devī performing penance, standing on the big toe of her left foot (*Vāmapādāṅguṣṭhā*) beneath a mango tree, as known from the temple in Māṅgāḍu.

It is a popular belief that if a childless woman eats a fruit from this mango tree, she will be blessed with a child (cf. R. K. Das, p. 224). Here, it becomes clear, that an ancient, substratum fertility cult was located on this spot, connected with the tree cult.

In spite of these obviously archaic tree and fertility cults, implicating the worship of yakṣiṇīs (female genii), the sanctissimum of this temple is not occupied by a female deity but by a Liṅga: to be specific, a Liṅga consisting of soil (*pṛthvīliṅga*) or sand (D. D. Shulman, p. 365, n. 66). The temple priests explain this belief by the sandy soil from which the mango tree grows. This statement at least hints at a close connection between Liṅga and the mango tree.

As to the origin of this Liṅga, there exists a narrative with a familiar beginning as it resembles the legend we came to know in Māṅgāḍu (Das, pp. 223f.; Shulman, pp. 51, 172-174).

While Śiva was absorbed in creating, maintaining and destroying the universe, his spouse, the goddess Pārvatī, being in a playful mood, came and covered his eyes. As a result, the natural course of the world came to a stand-still. Enraged, Śiva ruled that, as a penalty for this humbug, his Śakti should be born and remain on earth.

Pārvatī covering Śiva's eyes – relief in the Ekāmbareśvara temple in Kāñcīpuram

Reborn on earth, Pārvatī proceeded to the banks of the river Kampa, performed penance under a mango tree and shaped a Liṅga *out of sand* in order to worship it. Now, Śiva wished to test the seriousness of her veneration. Time and again, he caused very diverse disturbances. Pārvatī, however, always resisted. Thereupon Śiva took the goddess Gaṅgā (a divine personification of the river Ganges) out of his shock of hair and tried to flush Pārvatī's sand-liṅga away by a flood. To save the sand-liṅga, Pārvatī clutched it with her fingernails and pressed it hard to her breasts. The marks of her breasts and her bangles are said to have impressed themselves onto the Liṅga. (Shulman, p. 173) Pleased with her devotion, Śiva was appeased and married the goddess under the mango tree of the Ekāmbareśvara temple.

According to another legend (Das, p. 223f; Shulman, p. 172f), Śiva and Pārvatī were at odds with each other over a game of dice. Śiva cursed the goddess so that she became ugly and had to live on earth. Through severe penance under a mango tree in Kāñcīpuram on the banks of the river Kampa, and with the help of Viṣṇu, the goddess retrieved her beauty. She acquired charmingly beautiful eyes, got the name Kāmākṣī, meaning (in this context), 'She with the loving eyes' and won Śiva's affection anew. They married under the mango tree of the Ekāmbareśvara temple in Kāñcīpuram.

Of course, both legends sanction the ousting of the Devī from the temple, imaginatively explaining why it had become a place of worship dedicated to Śiva. The ancient sanctuary of the substratum, centred around a holy tree and a fertility goddess, was pushed to the background (in fact to the backyard) of the temple, in the west behind the more recent Liṅga in the sanctissimum. The Devī shrine became a Liṅga temple.

Date of visit: Sunday, March 3, 2002, 10:00-12:00.

The mango tree in the Ekāmbareśvara temple in Kāñcīpuram
Devotees performing a pradakṣiṇā (circumambulation)

The Name Kāmākṣī

The current translation of the Sanskrit name Kāmākṣī is: 'She with the Eyes of Love.' This, however, is a simplistic rendering. Another, perhaps preferable, interpretation results from three verses in the *Kāmākṣīśīlakathā*, the 'Narrative of the Nature of Kāmākṣī,' being part of a eulogy of the pilgrimage centre of Kāñcīpuram in the *Brahmāṇḍapurāṇa* (3,4,39,5-6 and 24; ed. J.L. Shastri, Delhi 1983, [1]1973). We read there:

Kāñcīpure pavitre 'smin mahīmaṇḍalamaṇḍane /
keyaṃ vibhāti kalyāṇī Kāmākṣīty abhiviśrutā // 5
dvibhujā vividhollāsavilasattanuvallarī /
adṛṣṭapūrvasaundaryā parajyotirmayī parā // 6

[But] who is she, who shines here in pure Kāñcīpura, the trinket of the world; she, the good one, who is far and wide famous as 'Eye of Kāma (= Śiva)'; she who has two arms, whose body-liana writhes in manyfold happiness, of unseen beauty, made of supreme radiance, the [most] supreme? …

Śiva in his manifestation as Kāma

Śiva-Mīnākṣī temple, Port Louis

jaya jaya jagadamba nityarūpe /
jaya jaya saṃnutalokasaukhyadātri /
jaya jaya Himaśailakīrtanīye /
jaya jaya Śaṃkara-Kāma-vāmanetri // 24

Hail, hail, mother of the world, of eternal form; hail, hail to you, who, when lauded by the many, grants happiness to the world; hail, hail to you, who is to be praised by the Himālayas; hail, hail to you, the left eye of Śaṃkara (=Śiva in his manifestation as) Kāma!

Śiva, whose symbol is the phallus (Liṅga), assumes, in his erotic aspect, the function of the God of Love, Kāma. Śiva is therefore also called Kāma or Kāmeśvara, 'God Love.' The motif of Kāmākṣī being Śiva's left eye, in other words: the 'apple of his eye' or in German, his *Augenstern*, has inspired the legends told in the temples in Māṅgāḍu and Kāñcīpuram, which start out with Kāmākṣī covering Śiva's eyes. Because Śiva's eyes figure elsewhere as sun and moon and, should these celestial bodies be covered so that the earth becomes dark, Śiva then only sees through Kāmākṣī's eyes. Thus, Kāmākṣī has become the 'Eye of Śiva.'

When we assessed the first translation: 'She with the Eyes of Love' as simplistic, the second, 'Eye of Śiva,' appears to be rather educated. While the first rendering stems from the substratum, relying on primitive spiritual feeling, the second belongs to the superstratum, to thoughtful, if not overwrought, spiritual speculation.

A third suggestion perhaps hits the mark. Although it is an assumption, it is not without foundation. If we look once more to Madurai, it might turn out that Kāmākṣī in Māṅgāḍu adopted not only the iconographical attributes from Madurai's Mīnākṣī but also the mode of name giving. The original name of Mīnākṣī came from the substratum; it is handed down as Taṭātakai (Harman, p. 23) and the goddess only received her Sanskrit name at her wedding ceremony (although Mīnākṣī, 'Fish-Eyed,' does not seem a very appropriate name for a popular goddess). Nevertheless, we think it is absolutely feasible that Kāmākṣī only received this Sanskrit name through her marriage, too, it being the traditional transition from the substratum to the mainstream. The language of the substratum must have been some local dialect, therefore 'Kāmākṣī' could just be a Sanskritisation of an unknown local word.

Finally, we may refer to a third goddess, having her domicile in Gauhāṭī, in Assam, the extreme north-east of the Indian subcontinent. Her name is Kāmākhyā. A possible Middle Indic form both of Kāmākhyā and Kāmākṣī would be Kāmakkhā, from which emerges a pattern for a major religious-historical development, one more example of the transition from the substratum to the mainstream.

(Cf. a recent publication on the Ekāmranātha temple in Kāñcīpuram by Schier, 2018; on Kāmākhyā by Stapelfeld, 2001; on Kāmākhyā cf. also Kakati 1989; Dharatīkānta, no date; Barua/ Sreenivasa Murthy, 1965.)

Flagpole (*dhvajastambha*)

Ekāmbareśvara temple, Kāñcīpuram

Temple tower

Temple tank

Ekāmbareśvara temple, Kāñcīpuram

Access road

‘Ousting the Devī, Part III’
The Ekāmbareśvara Temple in Chennai

Kāmākṣī, Ekāmbareśvara temple, Chennai

The Ekāmbareśvara temple in Chennai undoubtedly regards itself as a branch of the Ekāmbareśvara temple in Kāñcīpuram; it also maintains close connections with the Kāmākṣī temple there. A commemorative plaque on the inside of the wall around the temple complex, set up on the occasion of the inauguration (*kumbhābhiṣeka*) of the main gate (*rājagopuram*) on January 29, 1993, explicitly registers that the festivities took place under the patronage of the officiating Śaṃkarācārya of the Kāmākṣī temple in Kāñcīpuram, Śrī Jayendra Sarasvatī.

The abode of the divine couple of Ekāmbareśvara and Kāmākṣī is a rather big city temple in the old part of Chennai near Central Station, enclosed by houses with numerous flats and shops. There is a lively crowd of visiting devotees.

Plaque commemorating the inauguration of the rājagopuram

One enters the temple premises from the street through the main gate, from the east. The entrance to the temple hall, further to the west, is located not directly opposite but some metres askew to the south.

Forecourt between rājagopuram (right) and entrance to temple hall (left)
Facing north; flagpole under renovation

The stucco-reliefs in the roof above the entrance to the temple hall illustrate excerpts from the legend of the Ekāmbareśvara temple in Kāñcīpuram, for example a depiction of the Devī embracing the sand-liṅga and the wedding ceremony of Śiva and the goddess beneath the mango tree.

Friezes above the entrance to the temple hall:

The four Śaiva saints

Wedding ceremony of Śiva and Kāmākṣī

Caṇḍeśvara

Tamil saint Rāmaliṅga

The goddess embracing the sand-liṅga (*liṅgāliṅganadevī*) under the mango tree

These central niches devoted to the sand-liṅga and the wedding ceremony are flanked by the four Śaiva saints (extreme left) and another saint, Rāmaliṅga (extreme right), who is especially popular in South India and famous for his devotional songs, which are said to be induced by divine inspiration.

The remaining frescoes show accompanying deities like the general of Śiva's troops, Caṇḍeśvara and – not represented by pictures here – the divine couple's (Śiva's and the Devī's) sons, Gaṇeśa and Murugan, completed by the popular goddess Durgā and the Somaskanda scene.

Subrahmaṇya with goat-headed companion
Left Ekāmbareśvara temple, right Chennai Museum

On the eastern wall opposite the wedding fresco, between the gopuram and the shrine of Bhairava, just above the beforementioned memorial plate, we come across a niche housing an ancient fresco of Subrahmaṇya with a goat-headed companion. A very similar version of Subrahmaṇya – who is sometimes to be seen with a goat-head (Chāgavaktra) himself – is exhibited in the Chennai Museum.

A frieze in the rājagopuram shows a Kāñcīpuram style Kāmākṣī, with two Śaṃkarācāryas sitting at her feet. In her four hands she holds an open lotus bud (*padma*, lower right), an axe (*paraśu*, upper right), a noose (*pāśa*, upper left) and a sugarcane stalk (*ikṣudaṇḍa*, lower left).

Kāmākṣī
Frieze in the roof of the rājagopuram

The temple hall contains, in its centre, a Liṅga made of black granite. The Liṅga is directed to the east, facing the entrance.

In front of the Liṅga, to the right (seen from the Liṅga to the left), stands another shrine, of equal size, housing the goddess Kāmākṣī, facing south. Her maṇḍapa has its own entrance through a gopuram at the south side, complete with her own flagpole, lotus and lion.

Kāmākṣī, accompanied by goddesses Lakṣmī (extreme left) and Sarasvatī (right, with vīṇā)

Kāmākṣī's own mount, the lion, with lotus bud (*balipīṭha*) and flagpole (*dhvajastambha*)

To sum up, in the Ekāmbareśvara temple in Chennai, the Devī has not been ousted completely. Liṅga and goddess are treated *pari passu*, equally ranking. The Liṅga, according to mainstream tradition, obtained its place in the centre of the temple, facing east. But the Devī stood her ground just beside the Liṅga, with her own shrine of equal size, with a separate south entrance. Theoretically speaking, when visiting this kōvil it should *only* be possible to venerate the goddess – or at least goddess and Liṅga separately and independently from each other.

Times of visit: February 24, 2002, 17:00-18:00, and February 28, 2002, 10:00-11:00 hrs.

Address: *Arulmigu Ekambareswarar Thirukkoil*, 315 Mint Street, Chennai 600 003 (Madras 3), near Central Station.

Rājagopuram
Ekāmbareśvara temple, Chennai

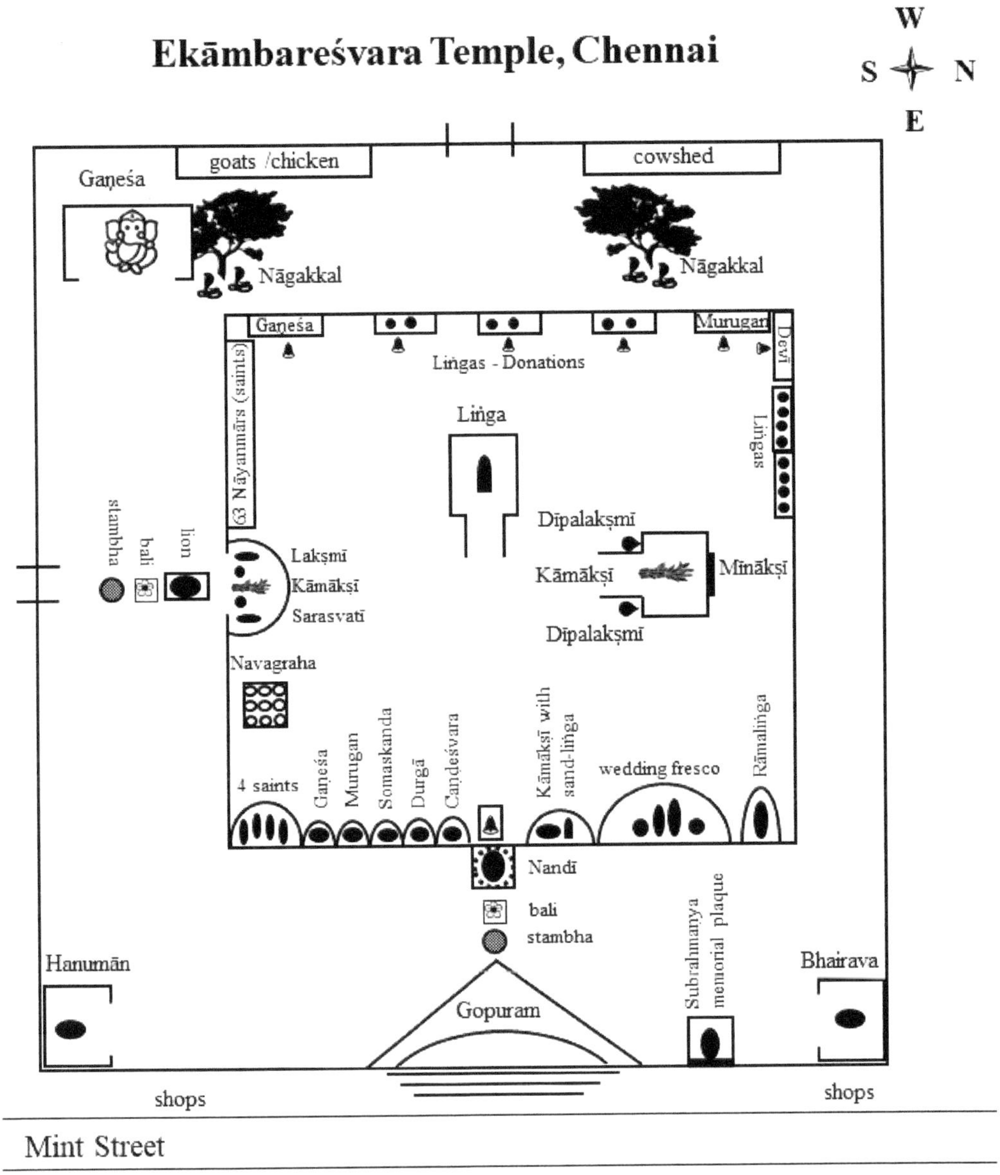
Ekāmbareśvara Temple, Chennai
W
S
N
E
goats /chicken
cowshed
Gaṇeśa
Nāgakkal
Nāgakkal
Gaṇeśa
Murugan
Devī
Liṅgas - Donations
63 Nāyanmārs (saints)
Liṅga
Liṅgas
Dīpalakṣmī
Kāmākṣī
Mīnākṣī
Dīpalakṣmī
stambha
bali
lion
Lakṣmī
Kāmākṣī
Sarasvatī
Navagraha
4 saints
Gaṇeśa
Murugan
Somaskanda
Durgā
Caṇḍeśvara
Kāmākṣī with sand-liṅga
wedding fresco
Rāmaliṅga
Nandī
bali
stambha
Hanumān
Subrahmanya memorial plaque
Bhairava
Gopuram
shops
shops
Mint Street

‘Ousting the Devī, Part IV’
The Kāmākṣī Temple in Kāñcīpuram

Kāmākṣī
Frieze in the roof of the Kāmākṣī temple in Kāñcīpuram

Kāmākṣī of Kāñcīpuram is the Kāmākṣī of Māṅgāḍu who finished her penance there and hurried to Kāñcī to marry Śiva under the mango tree of the Ekāmranātha temple.

Kāmākṣī, ‘Śiva’s (left) Eye,’ sitting between Śaṃkara (Śiva) and Śaṃkarācārya, greets her visitors from the eastern roof of her temple in Kāñcīpuram with a soothing smile. In her four hands the goddess holds a bunch of flowers (lower right), a stylised axe (*paraśu*, upper right), a noose (*pāśa*, upper left) and a sugarcane stalk (*ikṣudaṇḍa*, lower left). The basket-helmet (*karaṇḍamukuṭa*) is adorned with Śiva’s crescent of the moon. Her breasts are partly covered by a band or ribbon, the indigenous ‘bra’ of a forest girl. Heavy earrings and luscious necklaces make her adornment complete.

Śaṃkara (Śiva)

Kāmākṣī's spouse, Śiva, bearing the river Gaṅgā and the crescent in his shock of hair, combines features of two of his manifestations. As the dancing *Naṭarāja* he announces the creation of the universe by shaking the ḍamaru drum and clasping a wriggling cobra; the final destruction is indicated by his holding a flame of fire. Under his right foot he crushes the demon of ignorance, Apasmāra. As *Dakṣiṇāmūrti*, his lower hands show the gesture of preaching (right) and he holds a manuscript (*pustaka*).

Śaṃkarācārya

Closely connected with Kāmākṣī and her temple in Kāñcīpuram is *the* Śaṃkarācārya (traditionally 788-820 AD), also known as Ādi-Śaṃkara, 'Arch-Śaṃkara.' He is said to have soothed the goddess when she raged in her wrathful, destructive aspect as Kālī. Here is the relevant legend (according to C.R. Srinivasan, p. 246; R.K. Das, p. 224f):

Kāmākṣī between Śaṃkara and Śaṃkarācārya

Kāmākṣī, assuming the shape of Kālī by night, used to wreak terrible devastation among the people and country of Kāñcī. Urged on by the citizens, Ādi-Śaṃkara (who had already venerated the goddess as Kāmakoṭi Ambikā) commenced severe penance to appease the furious Devī. He deplored her to refrain from spreading shock and awe. Touched by his deep devotion and prayers, the goddess promised to never leave the temple again without his consent.

Today, a life-sized statue of the Ādi-Śaṃkara is situated in the immediate proximity of the sanctissimum. During the yearly procession of the Great Temple Festival (*mahotsava*), the utsavamūrti ('festival statue') of Kāmākṣī halts in front of this figure in order to symbolically ask permission to leave the temple: 'How strange! The immortal halting for permission from a mortal!', wonders K. K. Moorty in his pilgrims' guide (p. 205).

The Arch-Śaṃkara allegedly stayed in Kāñcīpuram until the end of his life. According to tradition, he also founded a convent school (*maṭha*), where orthodox Hinduism, cult rituals and ritual scriptures are taught.

There are altogether five such 'Places of Knowledge' (*vidyāpīṭha*) all over India. Their heads' statements

Ādi-Śaṃkara
Art Gallery, Kāmākṣī temple

Śrī Jayendra Sarasvatī
Art Gallery of the Kāmākṣī temple in Kāñcīpuram

claim a sense of authority for the spiritual life of the Hindus. Time and again, the Śaṃkarācāryas play a non-negligible role in Indian politics today. In March 2002, the officiating Śaṃkarācārya of Kāñcīpuram, Śrī Jayendra Sarasvatī, intervened as negotiator during a dispute concerning the planned building of a Rāma temple in Ayodhyā. It was explicitly underlined that he – being called a 'seer' by the Indian media – maintains excellent relations with all Indian parties, the right-wing government, the Hindu fundamentalists and the Muslims.

The magical diagram in Māṅgāḍu, called 'Half [flat-topped] Meru Mountain' (*Ardha-Meru-Śrī-Cakra*), which is said to have been installed by the Ādi-Śaṃkarācārya himself, has its counterpart here in front of the sanctissimum of the Kāmākṣī temple in Kāñcīpuram. As entering the temple hall is taboo for non-Hindus, we have to rely on the information given in the relevant literature (R. K. Das, p. 224f; C. R. Srinivasan, pp. 273, 153; K. K. Moorthy, p. 205). A model of this Śrī Cakra, however, can be viewed outside the temple hall, in the north, between the Art Gallery and the Nīm tree. It is not a 'Half Meru' (*Ardha-Meru*), but a complete, towering *Meru-Cakra*.

Ousting the Devī

In the previous chapters, we have witnessed the phenomenon that we call 'Ousting the Devī' on the basis of three temples which are closely connected with the sugarcane goddess Kāmākṣī. Either the temple is directly named after her (like the Kāmākṣī temple in Māṅgāḍu) or after her traditional spouse, Śiva (like the Ekāmranātha temples in Kāñcīpuram and Chennai). In the pilgrimage centre Māṅgāḍu, a fertility nymph, a Śālabhañjikā, belonging to a local substratum tree cult, was ousted by a Śaiva

Meru Cakra
Meru, central mount of Hindu cosmography
Nīm tree in the background

Śālabhañjikā, Art Gallery
Kāmākṣī temple, Kāñcīpuram

Kāmākṣī in the sanctissimum
In the back, on her right, the ousted dryad

goddess who first observed penance in a posture very similar to that of a tree nymph (one arm upright, lower legs crossed or nearly crossed) and was, on her part, ousted by a lovely mainstream goddess (looking like Mīnākṣī from Madurai).

In the Ekāmranātha temple in Kāñcīpuram, the goddess doing penance was ousted from the sanctissimum by her spouse, Śiva, and banished to the temple's backyard. The Ekāmranātha temple in Chennai, a former Devī sactuary, was changed into a Śiva temple, relying heavily on the Ekāmranātha tradition of Kāñcīpuram. So, what can we say then about the religious-historical development of the Kāmākṣī temple in Kāñcīpuram?

As far as we can see, the available depictions of the sanctissimum here show a lovely mainstream goddess of fertility, sitting in the lotus position (*padmāsana*), wielding Śaiva attributes like the axe and the noose as well as rural plants like flowers and sugarcane. This refers to the main goddess in the centre.

In the background, however, not completely vanished from the sanctissimum but pushed to the rear, a standing divinity holds her ground. She seems to be a hybrid between an archaic tree nymph, as branches grow out of her head and shoulders and a penitent standing on her left leg. The right lower leg is bent upwards to her navel, exactly like the Devī doing penance in Māṅgāḍu.

The ousted tree nymph or dryad.
Branches growing out of her head.
Devotional picture.

Vāmapādāṅguṣṭhā Devī, Kāñcīpuram
Frieze in the big gopuram

Of course this original goddess who today stands in the rear is the same Devī who, according to the Māṅgāḍu legend, hurried from Māṅgāḍu to Kāñcīpuram as soon as Śiva had promised to marry her there. So the conclusion is inescapable that the Kāmākṣī in the background, in Kāñcīpuram, is a direct offshoot or scion of the Kāmākṣī in Māṅgāḍu – one might even call them identical. And in the same way as in Māṅgāḍu, this more ancient, original goddess has been ousted by a popular mainstream figure resembling the model in Madurai.

The Mīnākṣī-like Kāmākṣī of Kāñcīpuram, once having superseded the outdated tree nymph and having conquered the central place in the sanctissimum, seems to feel quite comfortable in her new mainstream surroundings. Some pictures show her sitting in the middle between two serving subsidiaries, namely Lakṣmī, the goddess of fortune and Mīnākṣī, just to underline the cross-regional relations to Māṅgāḍu and Madurai.

Time of visit: March 2, 2002, 10:00-12:00 hrs.

Kāmākṣī, accompanied by Lakṣmī to her right and Mīnākṣī (wearing the red sari)

A class visiting the Kāmākṣī temple in Kāñcīpuram

Flagpole with Nandī, Kāmākṣī temple, Kāñcīpuram

Temple tank and gilded dome above the sanctissimum in the middle.
Art school left of the temple hall. Kāmākṣī temple, Kāñcīpuram, from the west

Kāmākṣī Temple, Kāñcīpuram

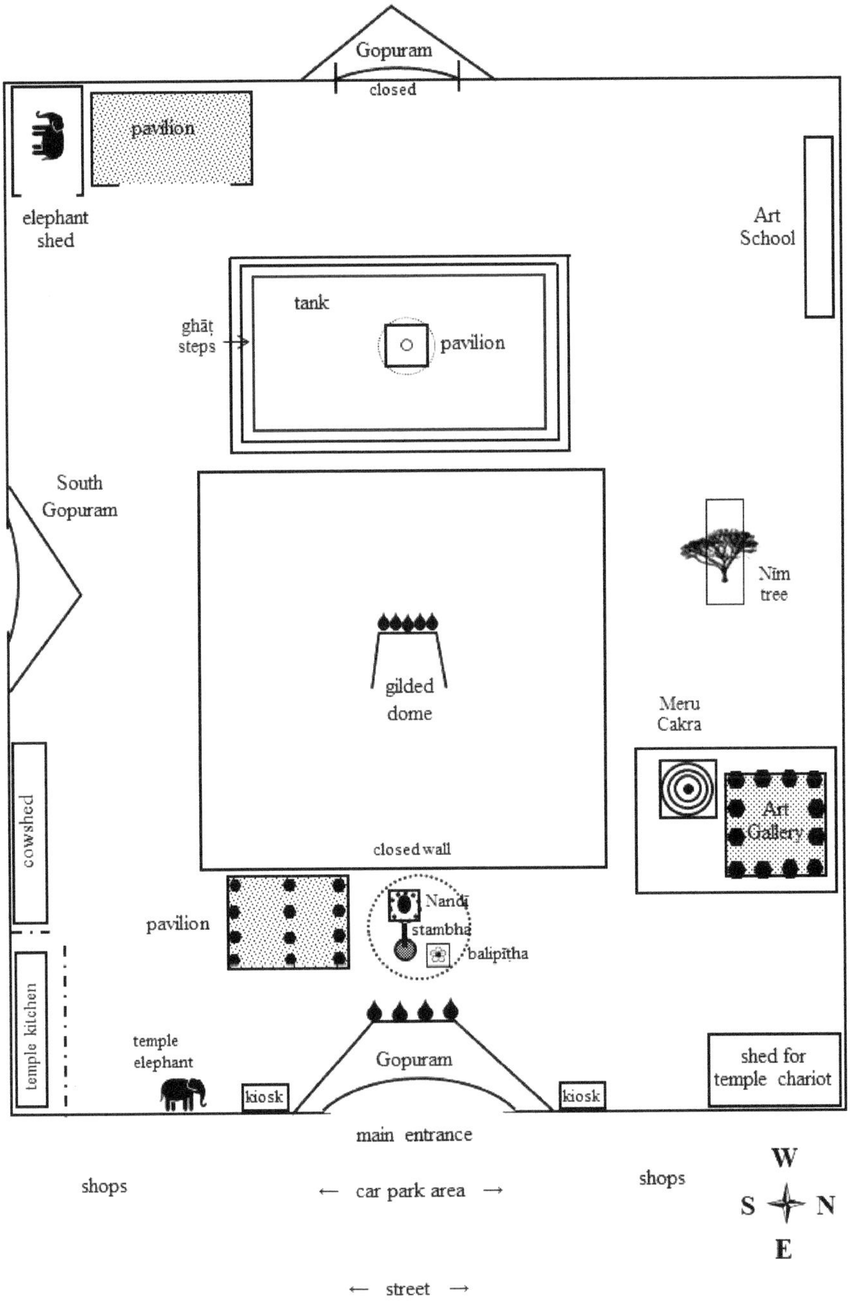

A Note on the Southern Orientation of Devī Temples

Whereas the temples dedicated to Gaṇeśa, Murugan or Śiva tend to face east, Devī temples present an exception: they are, originally and typically, orientated to the south.

The best example can be seen in the relatively recent Durgā temple in Toronto where Durgā faces the midday sun. In remarkable contrast stands the Kālī-Ambā Temple in Beau Vallon, Mauritius, which actually faces north. However, as Mauritius lies in the southern hemisphere, at high noon, the sun shines from the north! We dare say that this temple, too, follows the traditional precept.

There are four temples that had originally been orientated to the south, but were re-directed to the east in the process of transforming them into the present-day devasthānas. These are the temple for Kāmākṣī in Māṅgāḍu, for Ekāmbareśvara in Chennai and the Munneśvara temple in Chilaw. Although their modern iṣṭadevatās, mostly Śiva or his Liṅga, respectively, all face east, the ancient shrines for the original goddesses, which are still preserved, testify to their primary southward alignment. In the Kāmākṣī temple in Kāñcīpuram, the position of the Śrī Cakra in the north (also the Devī's place) and of the additional gopuram in the south corroborate our hypothesis of a later re-adjustment.

There are two temples which follow practical obligations. The Kālī kōvil in Negombo is orientated towards the busy Sea Street in the east, so the access is easier. The situation is the same as far as the Muṭṭu-Mārī-Ambā Temple in Negombo on the opposite side of Sea Street is concerned. But after all, the ancient Durgā shrine, which seems to be the original place of worship here, faces south. The modern temple was only built later.

Emigrant temples are often set up in locations quite alien to their present destination, for example in former storehouses, so that the orientation of the temple is predetermined. Such is the case with the Nāgabhūṣaṇī temples in Scarborough and in Frankfurt – both looking east – or with the Mīnākṣī temple in Scarborough, set up in a former cottage (north).

Generally, we observe a tendency initiated by the mainstream Gaṇeśa, Murugan and Śiva temples. These must be orientated to the east and thus, draw the newly erected Devī temples in the same direction. Some examples are the Mārī-Ambā temple in l'Escalier and the Draupadī temple in Riambel, both in Mauritius. But this does not change the orientation of the ideal type of sanctuaries for the goddess which remains the south.

Śiva Temples

‘Śiva and Mīnākṣī’
The Arul Migu Sockalingum Meenatchee Ammen Tirukkōvil in Port Louis

Front view of the temple

The temple is located at a short distance outside the centre of Port Louis, in what looks like an industrial area. Hill chains, extinct volcanos and fields of sugarcane plantations start immediately to the south-east. The temple was founded in 1854 (T. Ammigan: *Tamils in Mauritius*, p. 7). Our temple guide, Jessen Armoogum, a young Mauritian of Tamil descent, tells us that the temple was recently renovated – which is obvious at first sight. The gopuram (temple tower), which is about 11.5 metres tall, was built because of the following events: A rich donor, challenged by some very important legal business, vowed that, if he was acquitted, he would put a substantial sum at the temple trustees’ disposal for renovating the *Arul Migu Sockalingum Meenatchee Ammen* temple (a creolised version of its Tamil appellation).

Temple society's logo

He won the case and donated one million Mauritian Rupees (about € 43.000) to the restoration of the temple paintings and six million (€ 258.000) for the erection and artistic structuring of a gopuram. The gopuram was created by temple architects (*śilpaśāstrī*) from Jaffna, Sri Lanka, who spent two years in Mauritius fulfilling this contract. Their company logo is attached to the gopuram's base.

Arul Migu Sockalingum Meenatchee Ammen Tirukkōvil literally means 'The Temple of Lord Beautiful (= Śiva) and Mīnākṣī, the Mother Goddess (*ammaṉ*).' (Tamil *aruḷmiku*, 'lord'; *cokka-liṅkam*, 'of beautiful form', *liṅkam* < Sanskrit *liṅga*).

The renovated temple was re-inaugurated in a solemn celebration on January 19, 2001 during a four-week-long ceremony.

A special pūjā in honour of the god Śiva is performed each Friday at 6 pm.

Jessen Armoogum was still quite overwhelmed with the edification following the celebration of the last Mahāśivarātri ('Great Night of Śiva'), which culminated this year 2001 on February 21. It had been the first important festival on the calendar after the formal re-inauguration of the temple.

Two plates with the company logo

Gopuram

Ritual Purity and Non-Hindu Visitors

On the left of the temple entrance, a sign is affixed forbidding tourists from entering the temple. Nevertheless we are allowed to enter the inside of the temple together with our guide.

He had warned us at the beginning of the tour that admission would not be possible and had justified his objection by stating that the devotees, before they approach the deities for pūjā, had not eaten any meat for a week and that they had ritually cleansed themselves and taken a shower before. Whether our reposte that we were vegetarians and had also taken a shower in the morning changed his mind, is debatable to say the least.

Be that as it may, we were only allowed to enter the temple after the group of tourists, who were present too, had left the temple premises in order to avoid unnecessary discussions, as J. Armoogum explained.

Jessen Armoogum, temple guide

In addition, the brahmin on duty would first have to finish his own pūjā and leave the temple. The brahmin, J. Armoogum added, a Tamil from Jaffna, was very scrupulous and objected to tourists setting foot inside the temple – a notion not shared by the more liberal temple society.

The Temple History – A Hypothesis

Inside the temple, our guide gives explanations as to the single statues in their shrines or maṇḍapas. Here it becomes quite clear that the main deity of this temple is by no means the goddess Mīnākṣī but the god Śiva, who presides in his manifestation, the Liṅga made of black granite, in the sanctissimum.

The underlying religious-historical, or rather religio-sociological, phenomenon that we call 'Ousting the Devī' had already interested us in the previous section on Devī temples, mainly through the example of the sugarcane goddess Kāmākṣī. This process – a struggle for predominance – is often indicated by temple appellations consisting of a double name. We recall the *Vinayagur Seedalamen Temple* in Beau Vallon, also situated in Mauritius. There, the goddess, Śītalā-Ambā, presides in the samctissimum and not Vināyaka, the 'Remover of Obstacles,' the elephant-headed god Gaṇeśa, although he is mentioned first in the kōvil's name (*Vinayagur Seedalamen Temple*).

J. Armoogum states that the locally fixed granite statues, like the Śivaliṅga, cannot be removed because they are irremovably set into concrete. As to Śaiva temples, this idea seems to be plausible since Śivaïtic places of worship are initially built around or above natural objects; that is why they cannot be moved. Our guide continues to explain that if people do wish to move a sthalamūrti, for ritual grounds, they firstly have to bring a cow which must pull at the statue, so that it can be taken away by a human being.

It is not very probable that J. Armoogum has experienced such a 're-moval' of deities personally; his information seems to be grounded on hearsay. His account, however, is an indication that in the course of the historical development of the temple a redistribution of its statues has taken place. As a matter of fact, previous to the re-inauguration of the *Sockalingum Meenatchee Ammen Temple* on January 19, 2001, at least one other formal ceremony had been performed, a 'mahākumbhābhiṣeka,' on November 17, 1989. On the occasion of this celebration, the temple society (*Hindu Maha Jana Sangham*) published a special brochure (see Bibliography under *Arul Migu Sockallingum…*). The reason for this earlier ceremony must have been a new building, re-building, or extension of the temple.

It is our hypothesis that in the course of the development of this temple, the goddess Mīnākṣī, who once had her place in the sanctissimum, was ousted from the main shrine and had to move into a side-maṇḍapa. To prove this assumption, more research in Mauritian archives, if possible in collaboration with the temple society, is necessary. Nevertheless, a preliminary outline of the temple history can be drawn, to explain how a *Meenatchee Ammen* temple, that of a mother goddess, could become a *Sockalingum Meenatchee Ammen* temple, i.e. a Liṅga sanctuary, consecrated to Śiva, where the goddess Mīnākṣī plays a hardly-recognisable part.

The first Indians to arrive in Mauritius were banished convicts.

C. Anderson: *Convicts in the Indian Ocean*, pp. 6-10. – As to literature on the history of Indians in Mauritius see also 'Notes' at the end of the last chapter 'The Jyotirliṅga Temple at the Grand Bassin in Mauritius.'

They were followed, soon after the abolition of slavery in 1834, by contract labourers who had been enlisted (or kidnapped) in India to work on the sugarcane plantations in Mauritius. Whereas the convicts partly came from socially higher strata of the Indian society, the contract labourers were mainly poor peasants or belonged to other socially lower strata, forced by financial poverty to leave their Indian homeland. Highcaste Hindus were seldom bothered by lack of money and the laws of ritual purity forebade them from travelling abroad. The deprived plantation labourers imported their rural village and mother goddesses, as is shown by the majority of the temples on Mauritius: They are dedicated to Mārī-Ambā, Śītalā-Ambā, Draupadī-Ambā, Kālī-Ambā, or to the juvenile, handsome god Murugan, who is closely connected with the mother goddess. Accordingly, all over Mauritius emerged mostly small places of

Plain shrine for Gaṇeśa, Mauritius

veneration. Examples can still be found today, like a simple Gaṇeśa shrine *en route* between Point-aux-Roches and Rivière de Gallets, in the very south of the island.

Some of those recruited labourers became overseers on the plantations, independent owners of small shops or merchants later on, predominantly in the spice business. In the course of time, they accumulated some modest affluence. (R.B. Allen: *Slaves, Freedmen, and Indentured Laborers in Colonial Mauritius*, pp. 136ff, 179ff). Afterwards, on the fringes of today's capital Port Louis, Tamil merchants built a temple in honour of Mīnākṣī, the famous South Indian mother goddess. Reflecting the confusion concerning the temple's main deity, T. Ammigan (*Tamils in Mauritius*, p. 7) writes: 'A temple dedicated to Lord Śiva was built by the traders in 1854 at Nicolay Road, Port Louis, bearing the name of Shri Sokalingum Meenatchee Ammen Temple. This temple is now [1989!] a magnificent example of Dravidian sculpture.' This remark implies that the temple certainly looked much more modest in 1854.

Gradually, the former Mīnākṣī-Ambā temple was enlarged, rebuilt, 'improved.'

Gaṇeśa, Śiva, Pārvatī (aka Mīnākṣī), Murugan, Nandī (from left)

The Hindu-Tamil community attached to the temple improved itself simultaneously. The first temple brahmin officiated until 1925. The temple society (*Hindu Maha Jana Sangham*) was founded in 1944 (*Arul Migu Sockalingum…*, p. 14f). The provincial village cult of the mother goddess was transformed in favour of supraregional mainstream Śivaïsm, meaning the new deities were the high-god Śiva, his spouse, Pārvatī and their two sons, Gaṇeśa and Murugan (aka Subrahmaṇya).

In a religio-historical perspective, we can assume a transformation very much like this: the independent goddess Mīnākṣī-Ambā was identified with Śiva's spouse, Pārvatī. Through this identification, Mīnākṣī was deprived of her independence; she became an aspect, the female attribute of the encompassing deity, Śiva. Having become Pārvatī, the goddess was now only entitled to a place *beside* her spouse. This theological transformation was reflected in the architectural transmutation of the temple too. Instead of the statue of the Devī, a Liṅga of black granite moved into the central sanctissimum of the kōvil, the symbol of the god Śiva in his sublime manifestation. The goddess, however, was not totally banished from the temple. Being Pārvatī, she was assigned a separate maṇḍapa beside the shrine of Murugan at the north-side, richly decorated with a dome on top of the roof, depicting diverse manifestations of the goddess.

Brāhmaṇī Kāmākṣī Mīnākṣī Lakṣmī Mohinī

Friezes of goddesses on the dome on top of Pārvatī's shrine

We would like to conclude our hypothetical outline by our thoughts on the Mīnākṣī-Sundareśvara temple in Madurai (Tamil Nadu, India). The ancient temple had been destroyed by the muslims in 1310, except the shrines of Mīnākṣī and Śiva. The remaining architectural parts were then concentrated in one big temple complex. (R.K. Das, *Temples of Tamilnad*, p. 58.) Although the sanctuary of the goddess Mīnākṣī is situated in today's Mīnākṣī-Sundareśvara temple in the immediate vicinity of the god Sundareśvara, it is not at all incorporated or even subordinated to it. Quite the contrary, the devotees enter the temple complex via an entrance which leads in a direct line to Mīnākṣī's shrine and celebrate their pūjā in front of the Devī first, before they proceed to Sundareśvara's maṇḍapa. This arrangement strongly suggests an initial sanctuary of a mother goddess with an adjunct shrine of her juvenile lover. Historically, this also explains the wedding of Mīnākṣī and the god Sundareśvara, which is celebrated annually in March/April. We recognise here a festival of fertility, which must be interpreted as a 'holy wedding,' a *hieros gamos*, the wedding of the mother goddess with her juvenile lover for the cyclical regeneration of the vegetation. (Cf. M. Meisig, *Der Kult der Großen Mutter in Indien?*, p. 101ff.) Incidentally, it is worth mentioning that the shrine of Sundareśvara is placed to the left of the goddess, at the usual place of the statue of young Murugan in Śaiva Tamil temples.

In Port Louis, something similar happened to the development in Madurai, where, after the destruction by the muslims, both sanctuaries, that of the goddess and of her juvenile lover, were integrated into one big temple complex, trying to establish the whole complex as *one* sanctuary of the god Śiva. This plan failed however and the temple primarily remained a place of veneration for the goddess who was too strongly rooted in her local native surroundings.

It was different with the development of the Mīnākṣī temple in exile, however. In Port Louis, Mauritius, the shrine of a mother goddess, who was alienated from her local homeland, could no longer exist on the ground level of the substratum, but was transferred to the mainstream layer in order to elevate it to a rebirth as a Śiva temple. Due to the emigrant situation in Mauritius, one could even go so far as to nearly completely obliterate (except the insertion of the goddess in the temple name and the outward depictions of the Devī on the temple roof) the traces of the erstwhile mother goddess, Mīnākṣī.

The Subsidiary Deities

Having concentrated on the protagonists, Śiva and Mīnākṣī, we do not wish to finish our sketch of the temple in Mauritius's capital without at least a glance at some minor deities of this sanctum. The visitor enters the exterior temple premises through the gate under the gopuram which is guarded on both sides by two sentinels, heavily armed with ax, trident, club, etc., richly adorned with jewellery, sacred thread, Śaiva tilakas and tripuṇḍras, each keeping a lion down under his foot.

Sentinels at the gate

Having passed the gate, one sees two shrines on the right side, in the north-eastern corner. One houses another guardian deity, viz. Śiva in his manifestation as Bhairava, the 'Terrible,' the other is inhabited by the Nine Planets (*Navagraha*).

Turning to the opposite, south-eastern corner, we observe a fine-looking belltower.

Nine Planets

Proceeding through the middle of the forecourt, we stand in front of the obligatory triad of lotus bud (*balipīṭha*), flagpole (*dhvajastambha*) and the main god's mount (*vāhana*), the bull.

Belltower

Śiva Dakṣiṇāmūrti, frieze on top of his shrine, and his granite statue at the outer temple wall

At the southern outside wall of the temple building we pass the maṇḍapa of Śiva Dakṣiṇāmūrti, always facing south, his right hand showing the gesture of preaching.

Turning around the south-western corner of the temple hall, we see the peacocks' cages to the left (west) and attached to the temple wall is the shrine of Caṇḍeśvara, the 'Fierce Lord,' known as general of Śiva's troops.

Caṇḍeśvara, frieze on top of his shrine

Murugan riding his mount, the peacock Accompanied by his consorts Vallī and Devānī

The passage-way to the north is decorated by the abode of the festival statues of Śiva's son, Murugan, the war-god, accompanied by his two consorts, Vallī and Devānī.

Paying a visit to the interior of the temple hall once more, our attention is captured by a fancy painting under the ceiling. If you let your eyes glide from left to right, you see an elephant's head. From right to left, you see that of a bull.

Time of visit: April 6, 2001, 11:00-13:00 hrs.

Address: Sockalingum Meenatchee Ammen Temple, Nicolay Rd, Port Louis, Mauritius.

Picture puzzle

Arul Migu Sockalingum Meenatchee Amman Temple
Port Louis, Mauritius

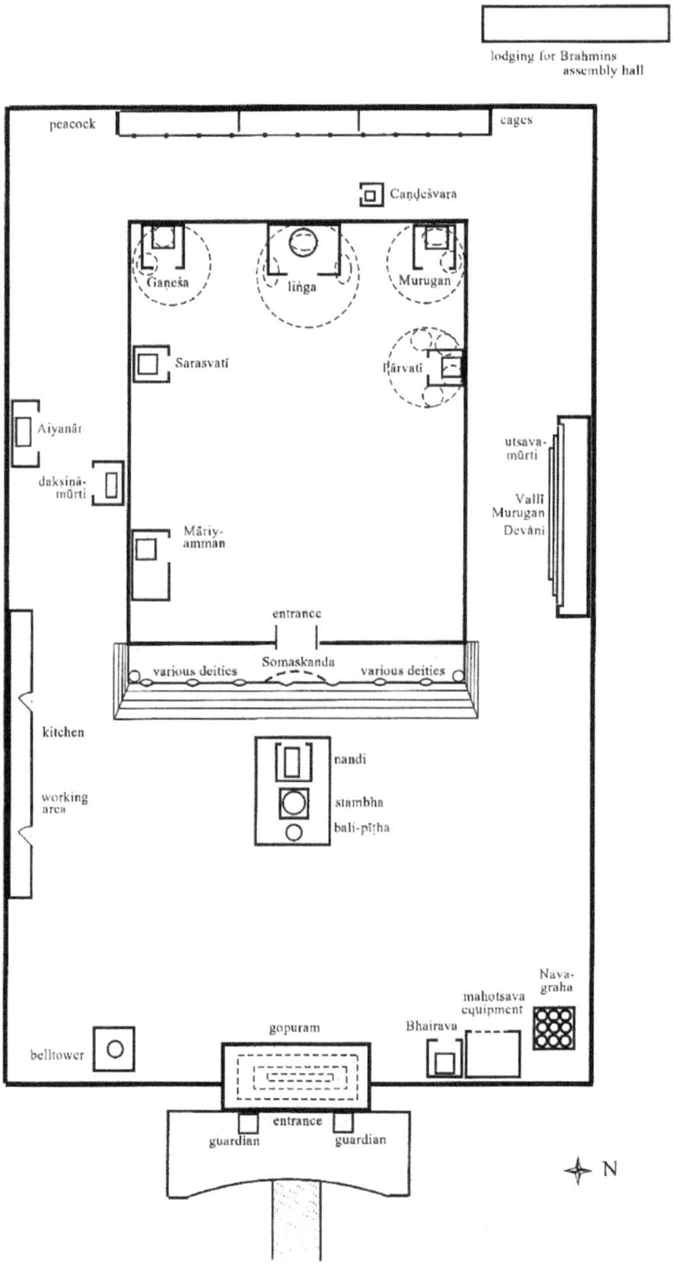

‘First Lord and Mother of Beauty’ The Munneśvara Temple in Chilaw

First Lord and Mother of Beauty
Śivaliṅga and Vaḍivāmbikā
Sanctissimum, Munneśvara temple, Chilaw

The island of Ceylon (the name derives from Pāli *Sīhala*, Sanskrit *Siṃhala*) was famous for pearl fishery already at the times of the Chinese Buddhist pilgrim-monk Fǎxiǎn 法顯. He started his pilgrimage to India in 399 A. D. It lasted 18 years, while he traveled, mostly walking on foot, from China anti-clockwise around the Himālayas, to India, the homeland of Buddhism, to see the historical places where the Buddha was born, preached and died. From the ancient harbour town of Tāmralipti south of modern Kolkata, on the Bengal coast, the Chinese monk sailed on a merchant-ship, in a south-westerly direction, propelled by the winterly north-east monsoon, on to *Siṃhala Dvīpa*, the 'Island of Ceylon.' Here is a quotation from his travelogue (Taishō no. 2085, vol. 51, p. 864c9-15):

彼國人云。相去可七百由延。其國本在洲上。東西五十由延，南北三十由延。左右小洲。乃有百數。其間相去，或十里，二十里，或二百里。皆 統屬大洲 。多出珍寶珠 。有出摩尼珠，地方可十里 。王使人守護 。若 有採者，十分取三。

bǐ guó rén yún, xiāngqù kě qībǎi yóuyén. qí guóběn zài zhōu shàng. dōng xī wǔshí yóuyén, nán běi sānshí yóuyén. zuǒyòu xiǎo zhōu, nǎi yǒu bǎi shǔ. qí jiān xiāngqù, huò shí lǐ, èrshí lǐ, huò èrbǎi lǐ. jiē tǒng shǔ dà zhōu. duō chū zhēnbǎo zhū. yǒu chū móní (muâ-ńi) zhū, dìfāng kě shí lǐ. wáng shǐ rén shǒuhù. ruò yǒu cǎi zhě, shí fēn qǔ sān.

> *The people of this country say that the distance [from Tāmralipti to Ceylon] is about 700 yojana. Their native country lies on an island, which measures from east to west 50 yojana, and from south to north 30 yojana. On both sides – like the entourage of a prince – there are small islands, 100 by number. Some are 10 miles distant from each other, some 20 miles and some 200 miles. But as to their government, they are all subject to the main island. Many of them produce jewels and pearls. Some produce* maṇi-*pearls ('jewel'-pearls, which can be pierced to tie them on a necklace), in an area of about 10 miles. The king orders men to supervise it. If some [pearls] are collected, he takes three out of ten.*

The 100 islands mentioned by Faxian refer to the sound (sometimes called 'Adams Bridge') between Rameshvara in India and Talaimannar in modern Sri Lanka where there are several small islands to be seen. Faxian must have got the impression that the whole island of Ceylon was encircled by other little islets, which it is not.

The Munneśvara temple is situated right on that coast where Faxian landed on Ceylon. Today, Śiva is the main god who is worshipped in this sanctum. But represented in this temple is a goddess, too, by a bronze statue in the sanctissimum. In addition, there is a granite statue of the same goddess in a separate shrine. Her name is Vaḍivāmbikā, 'Mother of Beauty.'

Interestingly, there exists a legend which bears a striking resemblance to Faxian's account of the king who demands a third of the pearls collected by the pearl-divers. The legend culminates in the following passage:

> *'During the ancient days a queen named Alli Arasani ["White Lotus"] made three separate heaps of the proceeds of pearl fishery, one for Mīnākṣī of Madurai, one for Śrī Vaḍivāmbikā of the Munneśvara temple and one for herself.'*

S. Arumugam (*Some Ancient Hindu Temples*, p. 42) comments: 'This Māhātmya [legend] seems to connect Vaḍivāmbikā with pearl fishery. Perhaps the original goddess ensured good crops for pearl diving and safety for the pearl divers during their dangerous work.'

Evidently, S. Arumugam takes it for granted, that the goddess Vaḍivāmbikā is not only a guardian goddess of pearl-fishery but also that she – and not Śiva – was the original deitiy, the 'original goddess' of the Munneśvara temple.

Vaḍivāmbikā
Utsavamūrti being carried in a procession around the sanctissimum

Today, it is a Śivaliṅga that represents the main god, Śiva, in the sanctissimum of this magnificent devasthāna. It is carved out of black granite and Vaḍivāmbikā has become an accompanying goddess. Her figurine is cast in bronze, which makes it an utsavamūrti, a festival statue; it may be removed from its usual place. On the arrival of our first visit to the Munneśvara temple in Chilaw, her mūrti (statue) had indeed been taken away out of the mūlasthāna and was being carried in a procession around the exterior passageway of the temple, attended by twelve brahmins. It was followed by a large crowd of pious believers, paying homage. On our next visit, the figure had safely returned home to the sanctissimum, to her place between Śivaliṅga and Cakra.

Devotees following
the bronze statue during the procession

Vaḍivāmbikā, modern, bronze statue, between Liṅga and Cakra
Facing east

Vaḍivāmbikā, ancient, granite statue, independent shrine
Facing south

The stone Liṅga, the bronze statue of Vaḍivāmbikā and the Cakra (which is also cast in bronze) are all three placed in the main shrine in the extreme west of the temple hall, facing east. They look along the middle passageway, at Śiva's mount (Nandī), lotus bud and flagpole at the entrance to the hall. This is what we suggest calling the east-west axis of the sanctum.

But there is also a second axis in this kōvil that runs from north to south. At its south end towers the largest gopuram, which is unfinished. It is devoid of any statues or reliefs and it is not coloured yet. At the opposite end, the visitor finds himself confronted with another statue of Vaḍivāmbikā. This one is actually made of granite, – facing south, in a shrine built in the northern wall.

Situated on this north-south axis between the granite Devī and the gopuram, we find a remarkable feature embedded in the ceiling: a time-worn yantra. It consists of nine square fields with a lotus in the centre, which is surrounded by four other lotuses and four large fish. Around this big yantra we see a frame, depicting two fish nudging a lotus.

Ancient yantra in the ceiling, north-south axis, two fish nudging a lotus

Ancient yantra
A lotus in the centre, surrounded by four other lotuses and four fish

There cannot be any doubt that the north-south axis represents the more antique, perhaps the original layout of the temple: (1) The granite statue, clearly ancient, which demonstrates the original majestic power of the goddess. (2) The imposing unfinished gopuram and (3) the archaic yantra.

As mentioned above, the yantra, the magical diagram, in the ceiling of the Munneśvara temple contains a lotus, flanked by fish. These attributes corroborate Vaḍivāmbikā's close affinity with the sea.

One of the most threatening risks the pearl-divers take – beside the obvious dangers of their occupation – is fish attacks under water. Therefore, the guardian deity of the pearl-divers, Vaḍivāmbikā, is petitioned to protect against this menace, too. This easily explains the appearance of fish in the temple's yantra on both sides of the lotus.

All these features along the north-south axis are special, thus suggesting antiquity, even originality. Today's Śiva-Munneśvara temple must once have been a Devī temple, dedicated to the main goddess Vaḍivāmbikā (Tamil *Vaṭivāmpikā*), 'Mother Beauty.' The Śivaliṅga in the modern main shrine, whom the goddess just accompanies, is but a secondary development.

The name *Munneśvara* needs an explanation, too. Tamil *mu<u>nn</u>esvaram*, Tamil-Sanskrit *munneśvara* (*munnā-īśvara*) must not be confused (Bastin, p. 22) with skt. *muni-īśvara* and the gods who go under this name. This would be skt. *munīśvara*, anglicised as 'Muneeshwaram', with a single 'n' and double 'ee', meaning 'Lord of the Ascetics', i. e. Śiva). Munneśvara, in contrast, means 'the First (tam. *munnā*) Lord' which is traditionally interpreted as the temple where Rāma first (*munnā*) worshipped the Lord (Śiva). We would rather interpret it as: 'the temple of the First (= highest) Lord' (cf. Tamil *mu<u>nn</u>ava<u>n</u>*, 'the first Being, God', *Tamil Lex.*). Munneśvara is said to be the first Īśvara temple, the other four in Sri Lanka being (according to K. Ashokkumarrajah, our temple informant) (2) Koneśvara (in Trincomalee), (3) the Īśvara temple in Mannar, (4) the Nakuleśvara temple near Jaffna and (5) the Īśvara temple in Galle.

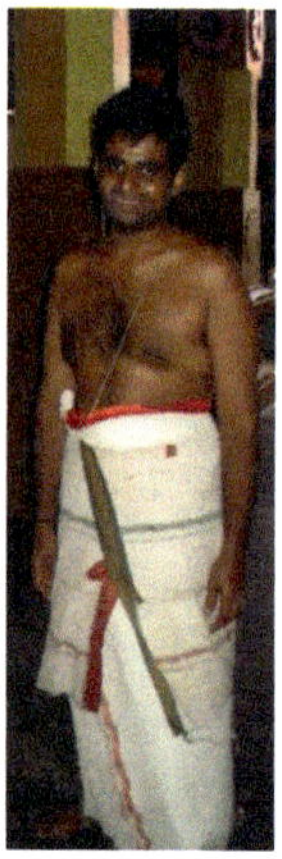

Mr. R. Subramaniam, temple brahmin

Mr. K. Ashokkumarrajah

Our interviewee was Mr. K. Ashokkumarrajah, journalist (The Associated Newspapers of Ceylon Limited, Thinakaran [Dinakara] Tamil National Daily/Weekly).

Asked if he was the temple trust manager (since he was sitting in the temple office) or one of the trustees, K. Ashokkumarrajah told us that the Munneśvara temple is not managed by a regular temple trust but that there is only one trustee. We assume that this one trustee is the temple's Chief Priest. His name is mentioned on the 'official' heraldic card of the Munneśvara temple as 'R. S. Karthikeyan, Chief Incumbent Priest, Sri Munneswara Devasthanam, Chilaw.' (Bastin's main informant, cf. p. xii).

Twenty brahmins work permanently in the Munneśvara temple. Two of them were kind enough to function as our guides: Mr. R. Muraleetharan and Mr. R. Subramaniam. We are highly indebted to all three of our informants, their valuable support and information is much appreciated.

Mr. Subramaniam, when we met him again in 2008 in Negombo, had by now become chief priest of the Muṭṭu-Mārī-Ambā temple in Sea Street, Negombo.

Main entrance, east front
Munneśvara temple, Chilaw

Minor deities and auxiliary genii

So far, we have focussed on the protagonists of the pantheon. We would now like to have a look at the subsidiary and auxiliary actors, of whom the Munneśvara temple has plenty at its disposal. Of course, we cannot present them all.

Having entered the temple through the eastern main gate, we find the shrine of the Sun god (*Sūrya*), immediately to our left, complemented by the shrines of the Moon (*Candra*) and the guardian Bhairava on the right.

When we now look along the east-west axis of the temple, we will notice the obligatory triad of flagpole, lotus bud and Śiva's mount Nandī.

Dhvajastambha, balipīṭha and Nandī
Gaṇeśa shrine to the left, Murugan right

Gaṇeśa, granite

Pañcamukha
Five-headed Gaṇeśa in his gallery

These three objects of devotion are placed in the middle between two large pavilions – Gaṇeśa, to our left, and his half-brother Murugan to the right. The sidewalls in front of them are decorated with galleries presenting depictions from their mythology.

Murugan gallery

Kāmākṣī
Two attendants with fly-whisks

When we now proceed along the passageway between the temple hall and the outside southern wall, we will reach, halfway after the east-west axis, the gates that mark the south-north axis. To our left, we notice the tall gopuram, to our right the door with a view on the granite statue of Vaḍivāmbikā.

Above the door, a Devī is enthroned who we have discussed in greater detail already, viz. the sugarcane goddess Kāmākṣī. This statue of Kāmākṣī did not yet exist in Cartman's times (*Hinduism in Ceylon*, 1st ed. 1957, pp. 90-96). Apparently, the goddess has become so popular since then that she received the honour of a place as subsidiary to Vaḍivāmbikā.

Śiva Dakṣiṇāmūrti

Two deities do belong to every Śiva temple, to the right and left of the sanctissimum, accommodating the main statue and these are: the preaching Śiva Dakṣiṇāmūrti (the 'Southern Statue') and the general of Śiva's troops, Caṇḍeśvara. Here in the temple of the 'First Lord', they inhabit their maṇḍapas, where they are to be expected, at the proper places in small pavilions at the outside walls of the mūlasthāna, Śiva Dakṣiṇāmūrti in a niche in the south and Caṇḍeśvara in the north.

Caṇḍeśvara

Durgā Mahiṣamardinī

The northern wall along the outer passageway is decorated with well-assorted, exquisite murals, depicting scenes taken from Hindu mythology.

Opposite the shrine of Caṇḍeśvara, we find the goddess Durgā, conquering the 'Buffalo Demon' Mahiṣāsura, killing him with a lance she has received from the gods. Durgā especially is petitioned for protection, because she, 'anytime when the world is distressed by demons will descend and destroy the enemy.' (Cf. V. Moeller, *Mythologie…*, article *Durgā*, p. 64).

Narasiṃha, the man-lion Avatāra
Stepping out of the split column, mauling the demon Hiraṇyakaśipu

The next image, the god Viṣṇu's fourth Avatāra, the man-lion Narasiṃha, belongs to Vaiṣṇava mythology. Nevertheless, it has made its way into a Śiva temple. The man-lion is depicted mauling the demon named Hiraṇyakaśipu, 'Gold-Rug.' The legend runs as follows:

At the end of the Golden Era, the god Viṣṇu, in the shape of a man-lion, once more executes his act of rescuing the Hindu religion. The demon Hiraṇyakaśipu has gained a favour from the god Brahmā, that he can be killed neither by man nor animal, neither inside a house nor outside, neither by daytime nor by night. That is why he gets more and more carefree and impudent, proclaims himself as king over all beings and establishes a régime of injustice, until finally gods and men demand his elimination. Hiraṇyakaśipu has a son called Prahlāda, a fervent devotee of Viṣṇu. His devotedness infuriates his father Hiraṇyakaśipu, – being a demon he is a natural-born enemy of the gods. One day, in twilight, father and son are just standing in the entrance to the house, so it is neither day nor night, neither are they located inside the house nor outside – the pious Prahlāda once more praises Viṣṇu's omnipresence. His father derisively queries whether Viṣṇu might also be found inside the column in front of him. Mischievously, Hiraṇyakaśipu kicks the column; then and there the pillar splits open, out steps Viṣṇu in his Avatāra as man-lion: neither man nor animal and therefore able to conquer the demon, Hiraṇyakaśipu, despite his being protected by

Śiva in his manifestation as Śarabheśvara
Mauling Viṣṇu's Avatāra Narasiṃha

Brahmā's favour. The man-lion mauls the demon, law and order (dharma = religion) are saved again. Prahlāda, the pious son and worshipper of Viṣṇu, inherits his father's kingdom and rules justly and in a god-fearing way.

After this excursion into Vaiṣṇava mythology we proceed to the next fresco. It shows Śiva in his rather unusual manifestation as Śarabheśvara, 'Lord of the Śarabha beasts.'

The Śaiva devotees have declared their favourite and high god Śiva to be the lord of those Śarabhas and have invented a legend according to which Śiva, in his manifestation as Śarabheśvara, the 'Lord of the Śarabhas,' humiliated Viṣṇu's terrifying Avatāra Narasiṃha, the man-lion (Moeller, p. 166).

Śiva can be recognised by his shock of matted hair bearing the crescent and the heavenly river Gaṅgā. His four hands wield (clockwise from upper right): axe, antelope, fire and a cobra. As Śarabheśvara, he has two wings and eight lion-legs (two of them growing from the animal's back).

The lion-eater's front paws maim the man-lion Narasiṃha in the same way as Narasiṃha had once maimed the demon Hiraṇyakaśipu.

The *Ṛg-Veda*, the most ancient collection of Old Indian hymns (around 1.500 B.C.), recalls (8,100,6) a fabulous monster called Śarabha. The word is related to the English 'hart,' or German 'Hirsch.' The beast has eight legs, two wings and devours lions and elephants. Kālidāsa, the greatest Sanskrit poet and dramatist, also devoted a stanza (1.54) of his most popular poem *Meghadūta* ('Cloud Messenger,' around 410 A.D.) to the animal. The thunder cloud, hovering over the Himālayas, is advised to be careful of the Śarabhas who will mistake the cloud (because of its appearance) for an elephant and will jump and try to maim it. But the cloud will destroy the monsters and fell them with hail storms.

As we have reached the main entrance again, our circumambulation through the Munneśvara temple in Chilaw will be concluded here, near the shrine of the Nine Planets. Many devotees visit the temple mainly to satisfy these astrological bodies. Their statuettes are venerated in a shrine situated according to tradition, in the north-east. In the same corner we also find the Spring Pavilion, which houses most of the bronze effigies of the temple. The temple chariot (*ratha*), upon which they will be carried around the temple during the Great Festival (*mahotsava*) stands in between.

Times of visit: April 6, 2006, about 12:00-13:00 hrs.
April 20, 2006, 10:00-12:30 hrs.
Address: East of Chilaw (Sinhala 'Halāvata'), about two kilometres on the road to Kurunegala.
www.srimunneswaradevasthanam.com.

Belltower, north-west corner

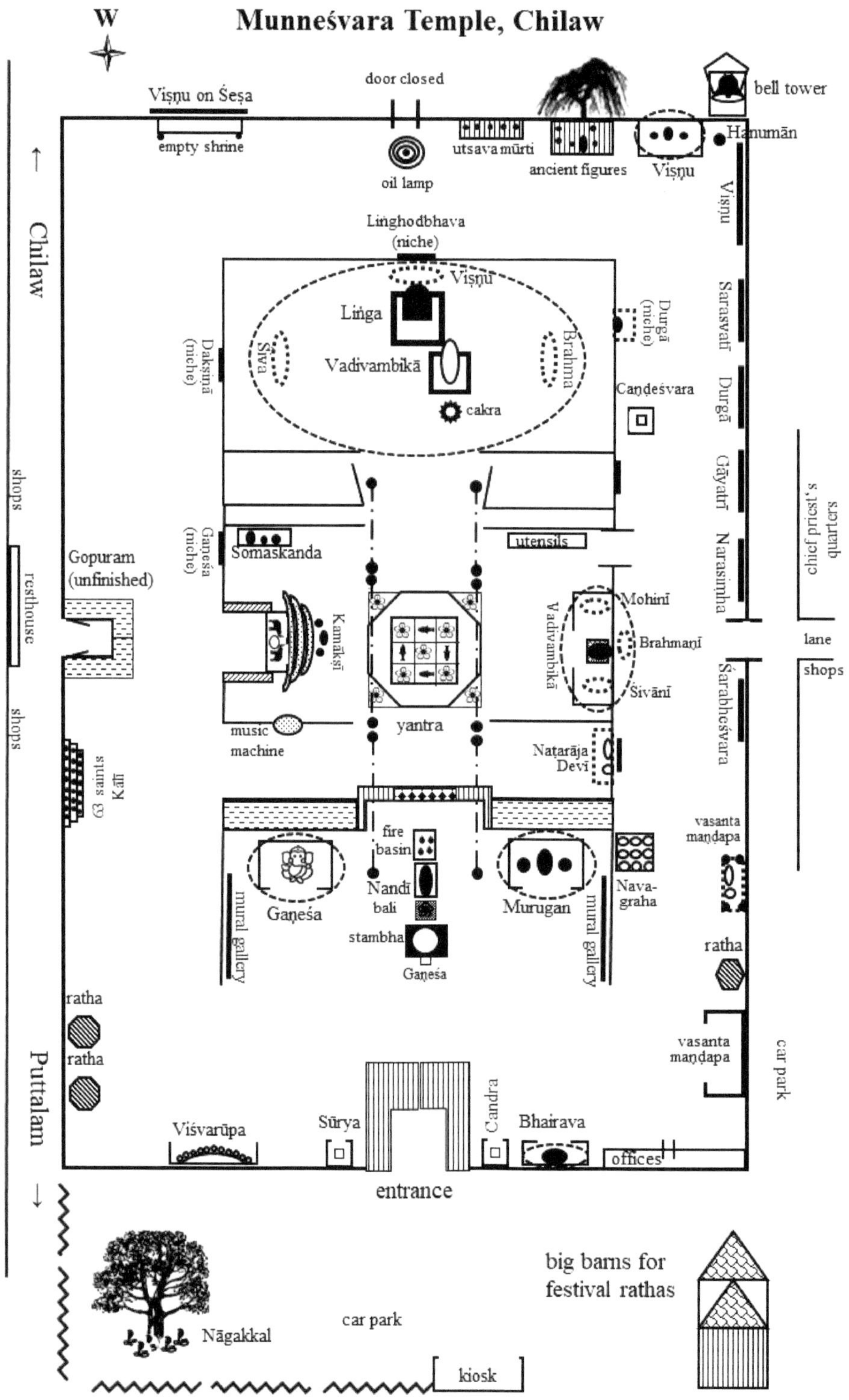
W
Munneśvara Temple, Chilaw
Viṣṇu on Śeṣa
empty shrine
door closed
oil lamp
utsava mūrti
ancient figures
Viṣṇu
bell tower
Hanumān
Viṣṇu
Sarasvatī
Durgā
Gāyatrī
Narasiṃha
Chilaw
shops
resthouse
shops
Linghodbhava (niche)
Viṣṇu
Liṅga
Vadivambikā
cakra
Śiva
Brahma
Dakṣiṇā (niche)
Durgā (niche)
Caṇḍeśvara
Gaṇeśa (niche)
Somaskanda
utensils
Gopuram (unfinished)
Kamākṣī
Vadivambikā
Mohinī
Brahmaṇī
Śivāṇī
yantra
music machine
Naṭarāja Devī
63 saints
Kālī
chief priest's quarters
lane
shops
Śarabheśvara
vasanta maṇḍapa
fire basin
Nandī
bali
stambha
Gaṇeśa
Gaṇeśa
Murugan
mural gallery
mural gallery
Nava-graha
ratha
ratha
ratha
vasanta maṇḍapa
car park
Puttalam
Viśvarūpa
Sūrya
Candra
Bhairava
offices
entrance
big barns for festival rathas
Nāgakkal
car park
kiosk

'Regular Rites'
The Kipling Śiva Temple

Kipling Śiva Temple, Etobicoke, Canada
East front, entrance with outdoor Liṅga

The *Kipling Śiva Temple* in Etobicoke near Toronto, Canada, was founded in 1992. The present building was purchased in 1999. The mortgage still stands at 400.000 CAD.

The temple, measuring about 50 x 30 square meters, is set up in a former workshop floor with glass windows. Heating is provided by a booming machine resembling a canon.

The interior fitting and decoration of the temple is still under construction. A third of the temple hall area behind the sanctissimum is separated as a construction site. Behind the barrier, the Gaṇeśa shrine is completely masoned, plastered with sculptures but not painted or coloured. The Śivaliṅga maṇḍapa is bare brickwork. The construction work is making slow progress for lack of money. The porter's lodge and kitchen are so far only bricked, but not plastered.

The temple society consists of six members. Regular visitors are workmen – not very affluent – from the industrial area where the temple is situated. The kōvil is predominantly visited by Sri Lankan Tamils who immigrated as refugees to Canada since 1987. All over the country there are approximately 300.000 of them.

The whole of Brydon Drive, where the temple is located, is lined by car repair and fittings shops. Besides the temple stands the assembly place of a Christian sect, which was being visited on the Sunday morning by believers of presumably African origin. A special feature of this Tamil temple is the fact that it is also frequented by non-Tamil Indian Hindus, for instance Panjabis. That is why the sign on the outside above the temple entrance is labelled not only in Tamil (*Civa<u>n</u> kōvil*), but also in North Indian Nāgarī script (*Śiva mandir*) and English.

There is an outdoor Liṅga shrine in front of the main entrance. It was set up so that prospective visitors, in case the temple is closed, do not leave frustrated, but at least have the opportunity to perform their pūjā in front of the Liṅga in that pavilion.

Liṅga shrine, outdoors

The Temple Staff

Our interlocutor is Mr. Balakrishna Shastri, brahmin, from the Tanjore District, Tamil Nadu. He has been living in Canada for 21 years.

Mr. Balakrishna Shastri
Temple brahmin and operator

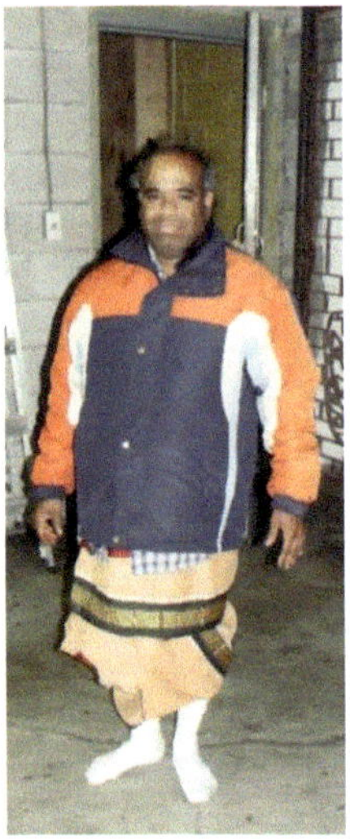

Mr. Balakrishna Shastri is the sole priest and the driving force behind the temple. He performs religious duties outside the temple too, paying home visits for instance.

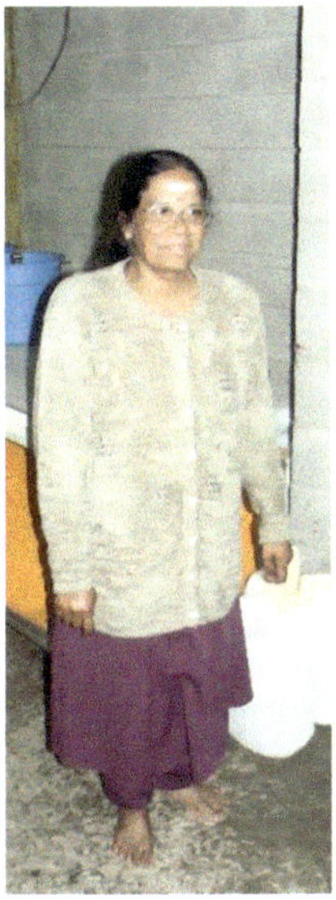

He is assisted in the temple by a female volunteer who collects the pūjā and donation bills, for example.

Another helper assists in the kitchen. A twenty-year-old young man plays spiritual music from a tape recorder, activates the electronic drums and knells the bell to emphasise the highlights of the pūjā.

Responsible for spiritual music

One member of the temple community sang Śaiva stotras (praise hymns) in Sanskrit during the whole pūjā, referring to a booklet in Tamil script.

Reciting Sanskrit stotras

Temple Statues – Liturgy

The temple statues are partly made of granite (Bhairava, Navagraha, Caṇḍeśvara, Dakṣiṇāmūrti, Murugan with consorts, Nandī and Balipīṭha), partly of white marble (Śiva, Gaṇeśa, Durgā, Kṛṣṇa and Rādhā, the Rāma group), or of some brownish stone, perhaps a natural, irregularly shaped soap stone (Liṅga). There is no flagpole (*dhvaja-stambha*).

During our visit, Balakrishna Shastri is performing the nityānuṣṭhāṇa-pūjā, the 'Veneration by Regular Rites.'

Following this, we had the opportunity to witness an anna-prāśanam, 'the ceremony of giving a new-born child food to eat for the first time, one of the 16 saṃskāras [*rites of passage*] performed between the 5th and 8th month (usually in the sixth, *Manusmṛti* 2.34) with preliminary oblations to fire' (Apte).

Finally, a short Gaṇeśa pūjā was performed, hosted by an elderly couple. There were about thirty devotees present, mainly young people..

Anna-prāśanam

Feeding a baby the first solid food (rice)

Sequence of the Nityānuṣṭhāṇa Pūjā

The Sanskrit term *nitya-anuṣṭhāna* can be translated as 'regular rite' or 'every-day ceremony'; *nityānuṣṭhāna-pūjā* accordingly as 'veneration of deities by regular ceremonies.' The simple, unsophisticated ritual had the following sequence: firstly, each granite statue was doused with cold water – a ritual cleanse.

For this purpose, Balakrishna Shastri had enfolded his hips in a reddish-yellow bath towel, decorated by a sun motif, for protection, instead of his dhōtī. He only donned his ritual robe again after the ablution. The figures of the deities were cleansed in the following order: Bhairava, Navagraha, Murugan, Caṇḍeśvara, Dakṣiṇāmūrti, Nandī and finally the Liṅga. After the ablutions, milk was poured over the Liṅga. A tilaka was then painted on the forehead of the statues and they were dressed.

The donning of the Liṅga was performed behind a lowered curtain. When the curtain was drawn and the richly decorated Liṅga presented, the event was accompanied by a drum roll, bell-ringing and enthusiastic exclamations from the devotees.

The congregation then performed a pradakṣiṇā, a circumambulation, through the temple hall, commencing with Gaṇeśa, while the oil lamps were swung. In front of the Liṅga, the pūjā tickets were collected by the assistant and passed on to the brahmin who inserted the respective name in his prayers.

Dousing the Nine Planets with water… and dressing them again

Caṇḍeśvara in a fresh cloth

Gaṇeśa pūjā

Dressing Murugan

Bhairava, recognisable by his trident and dog

Śiva's mount Nandī and lotus bud

Śiva, holding trident and ḍamaru drum, his necklace a cobra, in his hair the crescent, to the back gushes the heavenly river Gaṅgā.

Nandī, Śiva's mount, the white Zebu bull

Ḍamaru, Śiva's drum

Nandī, the granite statue or sthalamūrti

Oblations for Śiva

Dousing the Liṅga with milk

Painting a tilaka on the Liṅga

The Śivaliṅga in full splendour

Enthusiastic exclamations

Folding the cloth for the Liṅga

Reading the names of devotees
to the Śivaliṅga

The ceremony was concluded by clapping the hands three times in front of Caṇḍeśvara. Balakrishna Shastri informed us that Caṇḍeśvara recognises the respective devotee by the lines on his or her hand and reports the individual's good or bad deeds to Citragupta, secretary of Yama, judge of the afterworld.

Śiva's blessing
Painting a tilaka on the devotee's forehead

We wish to conclude this chapter with an appropriate tale from the Sanskrit folktale collection *Kathāsaritsāgara* ('Ocean of the rivers of stories', 12,72,319ff). It shows how popular such true-to-life tales are in religious, Hindu contexts and also in secular life. The Kipling Śiva temple plays its part through spreading such Old Indian folktale traditions, even overseas. The tale relates how the Ceylonese thief Singhavikrama cheated death.

Singhavikrama has come up with the theory that of all the gods, Yama, judge of the dead, is the only important one. However, experience teaches that as a rule such a high authority is harder to approach than a subaltern. Therefore, our rascal made oblations only to Yama's secretary, Citragupta.

Finding this remarkable, Citragupta one day disguises himself as a brahmin, sets off to Ceylon and visits the thief to put him to the test. Instantaneously, the thief asks the alleged brahmin to chant a prayer in favour of the afterworld secretary and, as Citragupta hesitates, he even leaves him his wife. As a result, Citragupta (who cannot resist), reveals a secret holy place where the power of death does not reach.

Speedily, the thief heads off to the rescuing island but he cannot enjoy his immortality for long. Yama lures the rebel away from the wellness temple with the help of a beautiful nymph. Reluctantly, the thief must appear before Yama's tribunal.

But even then, our imp has cunningly calculated what to do. The secretary whispers to him that when he, the thief, is asked if he wishes to first enjoy the reward of his good deeds in heaven and repent in hell afterwards, or the other way around, he should choose the first possibility, i.e. beatitude on call. Being in heaven, he then should refrain from all indulgences and instead, collect through penance and sacrifice (which up there would not be too challenging) so much merit that his debt would thus be settled.

So it happens. The rascal leads such an exemplary life in heaven that even the god Śiva is touched, the thief is actually spared from going to hell, 'and Yama kept still.'

Time of visit: Sunday, October 23, 2004, 11:30-14:00 hrs.
Address: 80 Brydon Drive, Etobicoke, ON M9W 4N6.
tel. 416-742 8484.

Durgā, riding her lion and enjoying her favourite treat: lime fruit

Murugan, Kṛṣṇa, Rāma
Altar and shrines

Frieze on the future Gaṇeśa shrine, not painted as yet

Kṛṣṇa and Rādhā

Temple hall, view to the west

The Rāma group: Hanumān, Rāma's brother Lakṣmaṇa, Rāma and his spouse Sītā

Temple hall, view to the north-east

Kipling Shiva Temple, Toronto

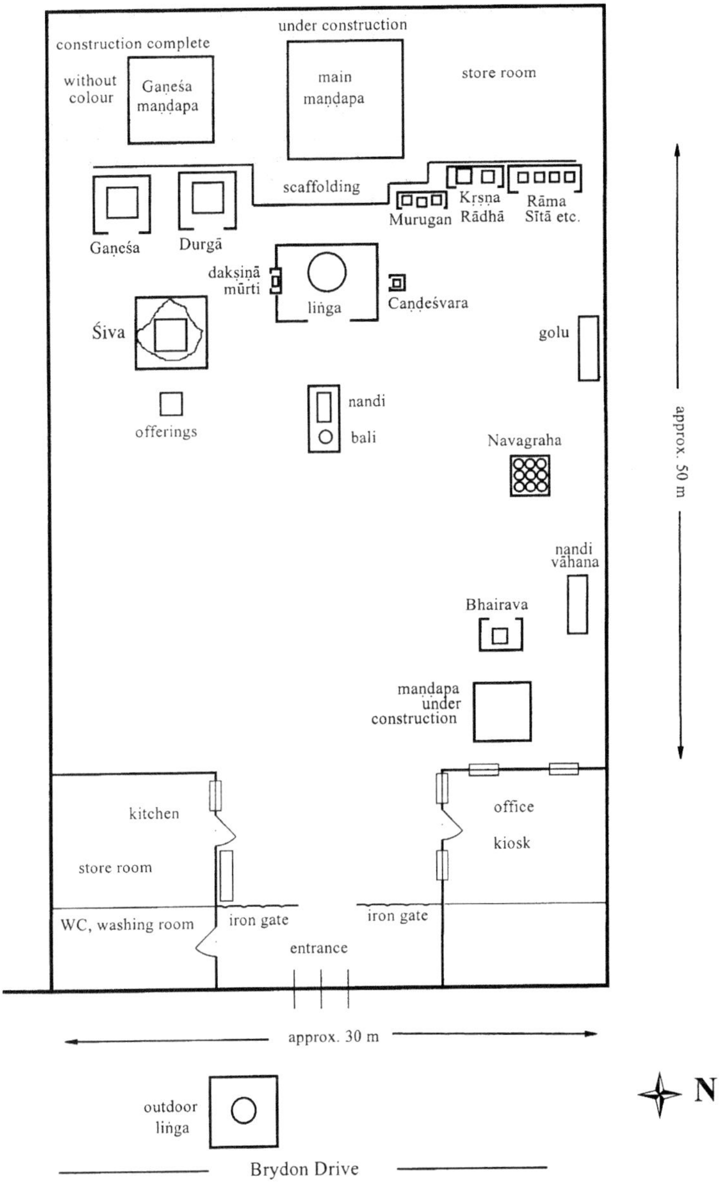

‘Between Folk Religion and Universal Religion’ The Jyotirliṅga Temple at the Grand Bassin, Mauritius

The temple from the lake side

Mauritius: A Historical Survey

The island of Mauritius, which belongs geographically to Africa, culturally however to Asia, is moulded by its peripheral location at the end of the world. Until the rise of steam navigation, the island in the Indian Ocean was of the greatest strategic importance for transcontinental sailing vessels. The entire shipping route, from Europe to South, South East and East Asia through to Japan, went around the Cape of Good Hope, so that Mauritius – not least because of its freshwater supplies – was an indispensable harbour between Madagascar and Ceylon.

That is why Mauritius had been known to Arabian seafarers since the 10th century. In 1512, the Portuguese Mascarenhas discovered the uninhabited island for the Europeans. Since then its history has been characterised by the struggle of the colonial powers for supremacy. In 1598, the Dutch named the island after their governor Prince Maurice of Nassau. The French came in 1715 and in 1735, their governor Mahé de Labourdonnais founded the capital, Port Louis. Although the advent of the British was to be felt from 1748, the Code Napoléon, i.e. the French Civil Code, was introduced in 1808. In 1810, the French had to capitulate in the face of the British but in 1814, the French and the British divided the archipelagos of the Western Indian Ocean between them. The neighbouring island Réunion went to

France, Mauritius, Rodrigues and the Seychelles fell under British sovereignty. Since 1968, Mauritius has belonged to the Commonwealth as a sovereign state. The first Prime Minister, Seewosagur Ramgoolam, was of Indian descent, as his name reveals. The Republic of Mauritius was formed in 1992.

ABBOO RAMASAMY
Abboo Ramasamy, 384,535, arrived on the *Zenobia* from Madras in 1878. He was aged 30, 5'9" tall and a vannia from North Arcot. He came as a single man with his cousin, Kistnappa and was registered as an Old Immigrant in 1884.
Abboo died at Grand Port in 1892.

PUTEEAH RAMSURRUN
Puteeah Ramsurrun, no. 269,263, had arrived on the *Bushire Merchant* from Calcutta in 1860. She was then a 19 year old, a Gowalla by caste, 4'9 tall, from Sairpur, Gazipur. She returned on the *Australesea* on 15.4.1887. Her photograph was taken in 1885.

Indian convicts

In 1814, at the beginning of British rule, Mauritius had 78.000 citizens, 80% of whom were slaves. In addition, during the years 1814-1837, convicts from India arrived as the British colonial rulers immediately began to use Mauritius as a penal colony (in Hindi *kālāpānī*)[1] (see notes at the end of this chapter). 'Between 1814 and 1837, some 1.500 Indian convicts, including just six women, were shipped to Mauritius from the Presidencies of Bengal and Bombay and the island of Ceylon.'[2]

The Indian prisoners were employed for road construction and clearing of ebony woods. 'After their arrival in Mauritius, the convicts were put to labour in public work projects, which included clearing land, quarrying, building and repairing roads and bridges.'[3] They thus prepared the requirements for the successful cultivation and transportation of sugarcane: 'Their labour was also crucial in building the communications necessary for the development of the sugar industry which placed Mauritius at the centre of global trading networks.' (Loc. cit.)

After the end of the era of sailing, the island lost its importance as an overseas harbour. From that point on, Mauritius became more and more a sugarcane plantation, in possession of a few sugar magnates. After the abolition of slavery in 1834, these sugar barons recruited substantial numbers of contract labourers from India, probably on account of the good experience they had had with the Indian convicts.[4] Up to the present day, the population of Mauritius is about 60% of Indian descent. Hindi is, after Creole, the most popular colloquial language. Official and press idioms, however, are in the colonial languages – French and English. These are, still today, not understood, let alone spoken, by the majority of the citizens.

So the Mauritian population predominantly consists of descendants of slaves, convicts and plantation labourers.[5] The largest group by far, the aforementioned 'indentured labourers,' were recruited by the sugar barons' agents to escape poverty in their Indian home villages. Some youths were actually kidnapped and abducted. The general consciousness of this injustice is still quite evident, as the following sentences from a Mauritian folktale show; they are taken from a collection of popular 'Tales', written by a Mauritian of Indian descent, Ramesh Ramdoyal:[6]

> In his younger days his father used to tell his children stories of his native village in India, and of the life he had led there. They heard how he was lured from his village to the island of Mauritius by the lying words of the dream merchants:
> "Come, come, brave men! Come and see the beautiful lands beyond the black waters! Come, brave lads, sprung from the loins of tigresses! Come forth and let fortune smile on you! Put down your name for a trip to *Maricha Nagar*, a paradise on earth. Money is in the air there, as there are fishes in the sea. You have only to cast your net to catch it all up!"
> 'Mauritius was on everybody's lips,' his father told them. 'People could hardly wait to go there. Old men, young men, people of every type and description, all flocked to the recruiting centres. Some fools even offered money to get a contract.'
> 'In this way,' sighed his father, 'I signed my name. And this is how I came to *Maricha Nagar*.' Manohar's father talked about the terrible voyage, the crossing of the *kālā pānī* (the black waters), the endless back-breaking work and the inhuman treatment.
> 'It was like living in hell. We had lost everything dear to man. We had lost our freedom, and were made to work like animals. But, my children, if it is true they have enslaved our bodies, they have not broken our spirits. They have not taken away from us our faith, or our honour, or our dignity. As long as we still have these, all is not lost. The night is very long, but the dawn will surely break one day.'

The plantation labourers of Indian descent have been alienated from the culture and tradition of their ancestors for several generations. From the beginnings, i. e. since the first decades of the 19th century, the emigrants founded Hindu temples.[7] The first place of worship of the 'Goddess Amman' on Mauritius is said to be the Mārī-Amman temple, founded in 1811, near the hamlet Terracine (close to Souillac in the extreme south).[8] (The present temple construction is more recent; it was erected in 1962.) But after their emigration to Mauritius, the connection to their relatives and friends in India was cut forever for the impoverished Indian field labourers. For them, there existed no opportunities to travel. Any contact whatsoever with their homeland was out of the question.

Over the last decades, we have observed a kind of renaissance of the Hindu Mauritian temple cult. A couple of shrines were renovated, like for example the *Arul Migu Sockalingum Meenatchee Ammen Tirukkōvil* in Port Louis (see p. 283), an indication of the revival of interest in and desire to know more about the religious traditions during a time when they are threatened by immersing into oblivion. But then, compared with Hindu temples in the Indian homeland, an important difference becomes obvious. For example in Mauritius, there has been an innovation that structurally changes Hinduism. Under the conditions of migration, Hinduism is compelled to open itself up. While many orthodox Hindu temples in India still close themselves in elite fashion against alien influences, most of the temples of Hindu emigrants demonstrate cosmopolitanism. On the one hand they seek connection to Indian traditions when, for instance, Mauritian temple societies engage brahmins and traditional architects (*sthapati*) coming from India and Sri Lanka. On the other hand they endeavour to attract crowds of pilgrims and non-Hindus. The religious life of the Mauritian Hindu population shows clearly how their culture is characterised by the *search for the lost tradition – À la recherche de la tradition perdue*. This feature is fundamental to the understanding of Mauritian emigrant Hinduism.

Grand Bassin and Jyotirliṅga temple

One of the central and most relevant problems of humanities related to contemporary Asia can be outlined by the statement that presently, under the radically altered conditions of modern life, regional folk religions are in the process of changing into trans-regional

View from the temple over the Grand Bassin

universal religions. As part of this transition, the Jyotirliṅga temple at the Grand Bassin in Mauritius deserves special interest. At this cultic place, one can observe how Hinduism, originally a folk religion (or rather a conglomeration of heterogeneous folk religions) confined to India, has in no way become extinct beyond the Indian homeland, nor banished to the kālāpānī. Instead it has accomplished a radical and far-reaching metamorphosis into a universal religion. In the process of this astonishing development, even the Mauritian Jyotirliṅga temple plays a forerunner's part. Here, we observe Hinduism in one of its most progressive manifestations.

Nevertheless its spiritual core remains *traditionally* Hindu. This is proved by its location at a natural shrine. Śaiva kōvils are built around a natural holy place, as opposed to Vaiṣṇava shrines where Viṣṇu's idol is placed into the building.[9] Śaiva temples arise around a conspicuous object of nature as their centre, for example around a curiously-formed stone which has been venerated since time immemorial as a Liṅga, the symbol of the high god Śiva.

This typical location of Śaiva temples, centred around an age-old sanctum, concurs with the nature of orthodox Hinduism as a folk religion which is inseparably linked to local traditions, being and remaining accessible only to persons who are actually born at these locations. New temples, however, founded overseas, far from the homeland, cannot get hold of local religious traditions. Temple founders, for example, have to place their statues of Hindu deities into an already existing building, say, a former profanely used warehouse, which now becomes a sanctum. This is the normal case for most emigrant Tamil temples (refer to the Siddhi-Vināyaka temple in Hamm, p. 9ff, or the Varasiddhi-Vināyaka Devasthānam in Toronto, p. 13ff). These temple statues are then declared to be sthalamūrtis, 'local[ly fixed] statues' which must never leave their shrine again. The fixation of the sthalamūrtis in certain locations can be understood as a reflection of the ancient holy objects of nature.

Then again, whole rock formations can be chiselled to become a Śaiva temple, so that the natural object itself is changed into a sanctuary, as might be observed in the case of several examples in Māmallapuram (also Mahābalipuram) in Tamil Nadu, or the cave temple of Elephanta[10] on an island off the shore of Bombay (today Mumbai).

The Jyotirliṅga temple shows the characteristics of a traditional Śaiva sanctum, as well as of an emigrant temple. On the one hand, it is located not only at, but even *in* a natural site, a lake, which is venerated as a holy place. On the other, an artificially moulded Liṅga has been brought inside and was installed there as a sthalamūrti, surrounded by a number of utsavamūrtis ('festival statues').

The foundations of the Jyotirliṅga temple have been laid into the crater lake of a volcano in the south-west of the island, the 'Grand Bassin', presumably the most ancient religious object of nature in Mauritius. The fresh water has been considered an ominous place by the Mauritians for generations. In Hindi this pond is called *Parī tālāb*, 'Fairies' lake,' and is venerated by the

Mauritian Hindus as a holy, even the most holy lake of Mauritius. The following legend narrates, how the 'Fairies' lake' is supposed to have gained its religious significance as a Hindu place of pilgrimage. Although a legend, there does seem to lie a certain amount of historical events at its root:[11]

> In the course of time many people came from India to work the land. They came hoping for a better, fuller life. But they soon realised that the system under which they had agreed to work was no better than slavery. They worked from dawn to dusk under very harsh conditions. Yet, although the system crushed their bodies, it did not succeed in stifling their spirit. They drew comfort and inspiration from the example of Rāma, the glorious king of Ayodhyā, who after fourteen years of exile in the forest, came back to his kingdom to re-establish the principles of truth and justice.
>
> In the same way his followers hoped that their days of exile would one day come to an end, and that they would inherit a world where all men, women and children lived in love and peace with one another. In the meantime they did their best to recreate on the island some of the traditions and pageantry of their old motherland. But, though they continued to observe their customs, they could not travel to the sacred waters of the Ganges, to which they used to make annual pilgrimages on the occasion of the Mahāśivarātri festival. The river Ganges was very, very far away…
>
> In those days there lived a man by the name of Jhummungeer (note in the original: 'An authentic character, more commonly known as Jhummun Gossagne [Gosvāmī]'). *He had been kidnapped* [our emphasis] on the banks of the Ganges *when he was thirteen and brought over to Mauritius to work in the fields*. All his life he was haunted by his memories of the Ganges. The villagers thought he was a little mad and never took him seriously, but one night he had a wonderful dream. He dreamt he was bathing in the river Ganges. Suddenly a mighty current pulled him down and swept him for days on end through a channel under the sea. When he came to the surface he found he was in an enchanted lake inhabited by heavenly fairies. The lake was set in a deep forest and on one side there was a hillock in the shape of a temple.
>
> 'Jhummungeer,' the fairies told him, 'you are the first mortal who has journeyed from your beloved Ganges in India to this lake in Mauritius. As you have seen, the two waters are in truth but one and the same. *You and your people can quench your spiritual thirst in this very lake.* You need no longer miss the holy Ganges that you have left behind. Go forth, Jhummungeer, and find the lake.'
>
> Jhummungeer woke up. He told everyone in the village about the holy lake, but nobody believed him. They thought he was mad. Yet there was something in his madness which was infectious. And so it happened that, one morning, Jhummungeer and three followers set out in a bullock cart in search of the lake. They travelled the entire length and breadth of the country until, finally, they discovered the lake in the place now known as Grand Bassin. At night Jhummungeer climbed to the top of the temple-shaped hillock and there, in the clear moonlight, he saw with his own eyes the fairies he had seen in his dream, singing and dancing on the lake.
>
> For a long time afterwards the 'mad' Jhummungeer and his friends went from village to village talking about the fairy lake and raising money to build a mandir (temple) at Terre Rouge, Bois Pignolet. When the mandir was completed, a large group of people set out with Jhummungeer on a pilgrimage to the fairy lake. They took with them water that had been brought all the way from their ancient Ganges.
>
> As they made their way, hundreds and thousands of people from the villages joined them until, by the time they reached the lake, it seemed that never before had there been on the island such a large gathering of people. When they saw the lake – how pure its water was, how serene and peaceful everything looked – they had no

doubt in their minds that the lake was indeed blessed by the presence of fairies. They called it the *Pari Talao* (the Lake of the Fairies [*parī tālāb*]). They poured the water from the Ganges into the lake to the accompaniment of chants and prayers. *There, as they stood on the banks of Pari Talao, they heard the mystical call of the Ganges.* They began to sound their gong and their cymbals and their drums, in joy and rapture, till the skies throbbed and the echo filled their aching hearts with peace and happiness. They brought back with them in copper *lotas* (jars) some of the precious water from the lake. And, for the first time in this country, the water of Pari Talao was poured at Bambhola's (note 'another name for Shiva') feet in the mandir they had newly built. *From then on they could make their annual pilgrimage to the fairy lake, and their years of exile were over.*

Hanumān, the monkey hero-god

Gaṅgā Mātā

The ground-water sea is also called Ganga Talao (Hindi *Gaṅgā tālāb*),[12] the 'lake Gaṅgā,' in contrast to the river Gaṅgā; it must be taken into account that in India all rivers can be called Gaṅgā or be considered as Gaṅgā. In Mauritius, moreover, there exists the belief that – as has been described in the legend – a kind of tunnel, 'a channel under the sea,' is leading to the Indian river Gaṅgā. The longing for a connection of emigrant Hinduism – for the spirituality in the Indian homeland – manifests itself in this folk belief. As Hinduism is compelled to live on far from its homeland, it needs an umbilical cord to 'Mother Gaṅgā,' to *Gaṅgā Mātā*, the geographical centre of Indian religion. In the water of the lake, directly in front of the Jyotirliṅga temple, a colossal statue of the goddess Gaṅgā

Mātā faces the holy shrine; beside her is her 'bodyguard' (to quote the temple newspaper), a towering statue of Hanumān.

This tunnel to India virtually becomes a symbol for the transition of Hinduism from a folk religion to a universal religion. Its function is to sanction the Hindu cults overseas. The necessity does really exist: in the 19th century, the ban on travelling was still valid for orthodox Hindus and could result in being expelled from one's own caste, since the traveller would pollute himself through the contact with meat-eating and alcohol-drinking barbarians.

There is a naive aetiological legend too, accounting for how the lake is supposed to have come into existence: Śiva is said to have visited the island, and some drops of Gaṅgā water – Śiva carries the goddess Gaṅgā in his ascetic plaits – fell from his shock of matted hair down to the ground:[13]

> *The legend of Grand Bassin.*
>
> *In times past, when gods and goddesses used to travel by the Puṣpak Vimān, the god Shiva showed to his wife Parvati the splendid places created by Brahma, the god of creation. After having admired so many wonders of the Earth, the ship of Parvati and Shiva reached a small island in the Indian Ocean. Entranced by the beauty of the island and the emerald sea surrounding it, Parvati asked Shiva to land on it. Going from the eastern side of the island, they reached the southern coast. But in the course of landing, a few drops of Ganga (which Shiva carries on his head...) happened to fall into a crater, which was immediately transformed into a natural lake. The water of the Ganga asked Shiva not to forsake it on this desert island. Shiva promised that, in the course of time, men coming from the banks of the Ganges would settle in the island and would come every year in pilgrimage to the natural lake to collect its water which they would then present to him as an offering. Thousands of years later, the prophecy of Shiva became true. And every year, one half of the entire population repair in pilgrimage to the lake of Grand Bassin on the occasion of the festival of Mahashivaratree.*

This aetiology is moulded after the legend of the origin of the Puṣkara lake in Rajasthan, the most important place of worship of the god Brahmā, an oasis in the middle of the desert Thar, about ten kilometres north-west of the city of Ajmer. In Sanskrit, *puṣkara* means 'blue lotus.' Traditionally, the name of the place of pilgrimage, Puṣkara, is explained in the analogy wherein the flower (*puṣpa*), has fallen out of the hand (*kara*) of the god Brahmā. According to the legend of the origin of Puṣkara, the god Brahmā is said to have thrown (with his 'hand lotuses,' in ancient times at the end of the Satyayuga, the Golden Era), a lotus flower from Brahmā's heaven down to the earth, in order to purify the world. The lotus flower hit the ground three times, thereby exuding 'pure water.' This is the origin of the three lakes of Puṣkara which can be seen there during the monsoon season.

The Jyotirliṅga in the sanctissimum

Foundation and Inauguration of the Jyotirliṅga Temple

The construction of the Jyotirliṅga temple as it currently appears is connected with the erection of the central cult object in the middle of the temple, the Śivaliṅga or Jyotirliṅga. It is a sthalamūrti, a fixed, permanently installed idol. It is not only the Liṅga itself, which has been chiselled out of a block of black marvel in a single piece, but also the base and the Yoni in which it rests which symbolises Śiva's female aspect.

The stone was manufactured by the Geeta Marble Company in Delhi, India. It originates from the hills of Rajasthan. The Liṅga, including base and Yoni, weighs about seven metric hundredweight (363 kg), is one metre (exactly 101,6 cm) long, half a metre (50,8 cm) wide and ¾ metres (76,2 cm) tall. On February 8, 1989, it was transported to Mauritius by air cargo, arrived at the Jyotirliṅga temple on February 26 and was let down through the temple roof to its present position. Consecrated with holy water from the Gaṅgā in India and the Gaṅgā Tālāb in Mauritius, on February 28 it was given one thousand pounds of rice as a food offering and on Wednesday, March 1, 1989, fruits, honey, curd and ghee were donated.

The *Mauritiuseshwar Nath Shiva Jyotirlingam Temple* – Sanskrit *Mauriśeseśvara-Nātha*, a manifestation of Śiva the 'Leader, Lord of Mauritius' – was built after only one month had passed and parts of a former temple structure were included. Its foundations rest on concrete pillars in the water of the lake. The inauguration ceremony lasted from March 3-5, 1989. The three days of prayers and mantra recitations were led by a brahmin from Nepal called Acharya Umanath Sharma Shastry, in the presence of the Prime Minister, the Rt Honourable Sir Aneerood Jugnauth and his wife, Lady Sarojini Jugnauth. The inauguration rituals were performed by Mr J. R. Dayal and his wife, who still both preside over the temple society today. After the end of the ceremony, on the third day, from 2 p.m., the public had free access to the temple.

The Thirteenth Jyotirliṅga Temple

Traditional Śaivism recognises twelve 'Jyotirliṅga' temples, i.e. temples in which stones designated as Liṅga ('sign'; 'phallus') are venerated as symbols of the god Śiva in his luminous form (Sanskrit *jyotis*, 'light'). As early as in Kālidāsa's Sanskrit poem *Kumārasaṃbhava* (2.58), at the beginning of the 5th century A.D., Śiva is called *paraṃ jyotiḥ*, 'the highest light.' The Jyotirliṅga temple at the Grand Bassin in Mauritius is, in the devotees' opinion, the thirteenth Jyotirliṅga temple to exist in the Hindu world and also the first and only one outside India. The acceptance of this emigrant temple by the twelve orthodox temples in India remains uncertain; it does not appear on the homepage (www.templenet.com/jyotir.html) of the Indian temple organisation.

The names of the twelve orthodox Jyotirliṅgas (or rather of the temples built around them) on the Indian subcontinent are mentioned on a huge copper plate on the left of the sanctissimum. The inscription is written in creolised, defective Sanskrit. In the following, we give, in the left column, the transliteration of the original and in the right column the text as it would read in correct Sanskrit:

SHRI GANESHAYA NAMAH ATH Trayodash Jyotir lingani	śrīgaṇeśāya namaḥ/ atha trayodaśajyotirliṅgāni //
Savrashtey Somnathanch MalliKarJunam Shishailey VJainyam MahaKalam OmKaram Amleshwarm	saurāṣṭre *somanāthaṃ* ca śrīśaile *mallikārjunam*/ ujjayinyāṃ *mahākālam* oṃkāre *māmaleśvaram*//
Paralyam Vaidnathanch DaKinyam BhimshanKaram Setubandhe tu Ramesham Nagesham DaruKavaney	paralyāṃ *vaidyanāthaṃ* ca ḍākinyāṃ *bhīmaśaṃkaram*/ setubandhe tu *rāmeśaṃ* *nāgeśaṃ* dārukāvane//
Varanasyam tu Vishwesham TrayambaKam Gautametatey Himalaye tu Kedaram Ghusmeshameh Shivalaye	vārāṇasyāṃ tu *viśveśaṃ* *tryambakaṃ* gautamītaṭe/ himālaye tu *kedāraṃ* *ghiṣaṇeṣaṃ* ca śivālaye//

Dwadash Jyotir lingani Santi Nepal Bharatey Trayodasham Mauritiuseswaram Mauriseh Sarva Vishrutam	dvādaśajyotirliṅgāni santi nepālabhārate/ trayodaśaṃ *mauriśaseśvaraṃ* [mauriśeśaṃ] mauriśe sarvaviśrutam//
Etani Jyotir lingani Sayam Pratah Pathenarah SaptaJanma Kritam Papam Smarnenah Vinashyati	etāni jyotirliṅgāni sāyaṃ prātaḥ paṭhen naraḥ/ saptajanmakṛtaṃ pāpaṃ smaraṇena vinaśyate//

Translation

'Obeisance to the illustrious Gaṇeśa! Now the thirteen Jyotirliṅgas [will be enumerated]: In Saurāṣṭra (i.e. Gujarāt) the Somanātha[-liṅga], in Śrīśaila Mallikārjuna, in Ujjayinī Mahākāla, in Oṃkāra Māmaleśvara, in Paralī Vaidyanātha, in Ḍākinī Bhīmaśaṃkara. in Setubandha (=Adam's Bridge) Rāmeśa, in the forest of Dārukā Nāgeśa, in Benares Viśveśa, Tryambaka on the banks of the Gautamī (= Godāvarī), Kedāra[nātha] in the Himālayas and Ghiṣaṇeśa in Śivālaya, – these are the twelve Jyotirliṅgas in Nepal and India. The thirteenth is Mauriśaseśvara ('Lord of Mauritius') in Mauritius, [and this is] the most famous of them all. One shall recite these [names of] the Jyotirliṅgas in the morning and in the evening. The evil done in seven rebirths: it will be extinguished by [such] recitation.'

Translation with Notes

Obeisance to the illustrious Gaṇeśa! Now the thirteen Jyotirliṅgas [will be enumerated]:

In Saurāṣṭra (i.e. Gujarāt) the Somanātha[-liṅga], – the well-known temple of Somnāt (Patan) near Veraval in Gujarāt, cf. 'Murray' = L.F. Rushbrook Williams: *A Handbook for Travellers in India, Pakistan, Nepal, Bangladesh and Sri Lanka (Ceylon)*. 22nd edition, John Murray, London 1982, p. 284.

In Śrīśaila Mallikārjuna – the Mallikārjuna temple in Śrīśaila, east of Kurnool in Andhra Pradesh; Murray, p. 481f.

In Ujjayinī Mahākāla, – the Mahākāleśvara-Tempel in Ujjain in Madhya Pradesh.

In in the forest of Dārukā Nāgeśa, – the Dārukā temple near Dwarka (Dvārakā) in the extreme north-west of Kathiawar on the coast of Gujarāt, Murray, p. 288.

In Benares Viśveśa, – = Viśveśvara ('Biseswar') or Viśvanātha temple, also 'Golden Temple,' Murray, p. 163.

Tryambaka on the banks of the Gautamī (= Godāvarī), – in 'Trimbak' at the spring of the Godāvarī, west of Nasik, about 100 km north-west of Bombay, see Murray, 'Temple of Trimbakeswar,' pp. 117f.

Kedāra[nātha] in the Himālayas, – about 100 km north-west of Hardwar in Uttar Pradesh; Murray, p. 366.

And Ghiṣaṇeśa in Śivālaya, – the name of this temple is mentioned in Devanāgarī on the website of *http://www.templenet.com/Maharashtra/grish.html*. In Latin script one also finds 'Grushneshwar.' The mentioned homepage continues: 'Grishneshwar is also known as Ghushmeshwar … It is located at a distance of 11 km from Daulatabad near Aurangabad in Maharashtra ... near Ellora.'

– These are the twelve Jyotirliṅgas […] .

(See also Moeller, p. 18.)

Kālī

Heterogeneous Pantheon

The central cult object in the Grand Bassin Jyotirliṅga temple is surrounded by a considerable number of subordinate deities. A Nāga, a cobra deity, has his body wrapped threefold around the Liṅga and spread his seven heads with splayed hoods over it. Unlike Liṅga and Yoni the snake is painted in bright colours. There are more stone statues, like for example snake stones (*nāgakkal*), the Nine Planets (*Navagraha*), but also Śiva's mount, the white zebu bull Nandī (which can be found directly between the sanctissimum and the lake at the main entrance of the temple hall). There are other statues made of soapstone or painted plaster.

The Jyotirliṅga temple with its surrounding temple structures shows the characteristics of all the three levels of Hinduism: the cults of the (1) *substratum* are represented as well as (2) *mainstream* Hinduism, and also influences of the (3) *superstratum*. On the level of the substratum we find the aforementioned snake and planet cults, also the veneration of the Great Goddesses (*Devī*), which are known to have emerged from rural mother goddesses and tree or vegetation genii. On the mainstream level, the Grand Bassin temple surpasses all the other temples in Mauritius, and probably most of the other shrines outside India, by the complexity of its pantheon. It comprises several varieties of Hinduism, by no means only Śaivism, since Viṣṇuism, Kṛṣṇaism, even Brahmanism are represented here, as a separate shrine is dedicated to Gāyatrī, Brahmā's second spouse. Tāntrik influences are added on the level of the superstratum, for example by the well-known Śaiva Tāntrik, Satya Sai Baba

The snake stones – Nāgakkal

(who will appear below in connection with the belief in miracles at the Grand Bassin)

By its widespread pantheon, the Jyotirliṅga temple differs from the places of worship of South Indian Tamil emigrant Hinduism, which only contain a limited Śaiva inventory of deities. In their centre we will mostly find Pārvatī's son Gaṇeśa or Śiva's son Skanda (Murugan), or the goddess herself in her substratum manifestations as Mārī-Ambā, Kālī-Ambā, Sītalā-Ambā or Draupadī-Ambā, as Mīnākṣī or Kāmākṣī. Unlike them, the Jyotirliṅga temple at the Grand Bassin endeavours to gather a pan-Hindu ensemble. Nor is its temple society presided by Tamil affiliated, but rather by Hindi speaking Mauritians with North Indian ancestors. Nevertheless there are unmistakable South Indian influences. The temple operators do not encapsulate themselves in a provincial

Nāgendra
The central snake stone, detail

niche, but are rather desirous, by the diversity of their pantheon, to express their universalistic attitude.

Durgā

Without dwelling extensively on single divinities, the most prominent of them will be mentioned now. In the east of the temple premises, still high above on the road next to the stairs leading downwards towards the lake, there is a place of veneration of Kālī; down beneath the stairs, directly at the lake front, a group of three snake stones (*nāgakkal*) with statues of Ādiśeṣa, Nāgendra and Kaliṅga (?). We proceed to the temple hall, which is situated at the south side of the lake

Lakṣmī-Nārāyaṇa (Viṣṇu and his spouse)

and opens up to the north, facing the water (the Jyotirliṅga, however, is exactly orientated to the east, according to the precepts). On entering the temple hall, we now find at its east end a statue of Durgā. The next shrine, of the Nine Planets (*Navagraha*), is de-

Kṛṣṇa and Rukmiṇī

signed with extra care. Lakṣmī-Nārāyaṇa (i.e. Viṣṇu and his spouse) and the corresponding couple of Kṛṣṇa and Rukmiṇī frame the Liṅga on the right and left sides. The western annex

The hero Vīrabhadra

houses the Buddha (as Avatāra of Viṣṇu), the hero Vīrabhadra, the six-headed Kārttikeya (otherwise known as Skanda or Murugan) and the other

Great Goddess, Kālī. Outside the temple hall, right on the lake front, rises a monumental trident of Śiva; next to it stands the abovementioned monkey hero, Hanumān. A figurine of Brahmā's second spouse, Gāyatrī, is located behind a pane of glass in a separate pavilion.

Belief in Miracles

The idea of proselytising is alien to traditional Hinduism, a religion that people are born into by their caste affiliation, without any possibility of conversion whatsoever. Notwithstanding, the missionary activities of the Jyotirliṅga temple, in accordance with the universalistic approach of the sanctum, are an important aspect of its spiritual life. In order to attract masses of pilgrims, the temple operators advertise their sanctum at prominent media places, hinting at miracles, which they claim to happen regularly at this holy place, – in continuation of the ominous legends around the Grand Bassin (such as those already mentioned above). The devotees give accounts like the following of such supernatural apparitions (p. 3, col. 2-4, special edition of the temple newspaper *The Eye*):

As soon as the Liṅga was installed, on March 2, 1989, at about 5 p.m., a heavy thunderstorm broke right above the Grand Bassin and caused a power cut in the whole area. Just as Mr J. R. Dayal, during the inauguration ceremony called 'Rudra Abhiṣeka,' lighted the *mahā jyoti*, the 'Great Light,' in front of the central ritual pot (*kalaśa*), the heavenly light in the form of lightning forced its way through the temple roof and penetrated the Śivaliṅga. 200 devotees outside the temple could feel the flash of lightning in their umbrellas. At the moment when Acharya Umanath Sharma Shastry recited the Śivapurāṇa in the temple hall, 21 bulbs above the Śivaliṅga lighted up despite the power failure. Thereupon, accompanied by a 'pleasant, graceful and empowering sound', the whole illuminating system of the temple came into life. The copper plates in the temple roof became aglow in fluorescent red. Water dropped spontaneously at the foot of the Śiva trident. The print of a right foot of an adult appeared on the silk cloth which lay upon the Śivaliṅga. This footprint then formed the shape of Gaṇeśa, an elephant's head. Thereafter, a tremendous shower let the water of the lake rise until the island in the middle of the lake was covered. For one hour, access to the Grand Bassin was blocked on account of the over-flowing rivers.

Gāyatrī

An apparition of Kālī?

'The whole happening was witnessed by people of different religious belief.' (p. 13, col. 3) By way of this supernatural event and the authority of Acharya Umanath Sharma Shastry, the Jyotirliṅga, according to Hindu belief, had been established and sanctioned. The spot where the lightning had penetrated the Liṅga is marked by a sign of white ashes (*tripuṇḍra*). Such miracles had allegedly happened earlier in India too.

On the eighth day of the inauguration ceremony the water pot (*kalaśa*) which represents Gaṇeśa is said to have acquired the shape of an elephant's head, including trunk and tusk (Gaṇeśa only has one tusk). A snake and a Svastika also manifested themselves on the Liṅga.

In the short history of the temple such miracles are said to have occurred over and over again. One of the most impressive was the seeming manifestation of Śakti Kālī in the fire of the oblation with ghee during the *āhuti* ceremony in the sacrificial basin. A

B. B. (Satish) Dayal

photograph of this event is kept in the temple, on which the contours of a shape similar to Kālī's could only be guessed at in the flames of the oblation.

The Indian Tāntrik Satya Sai Baba performed another miracle on March 4, 2000, as the highlight of the Mahāśivarātri festival of that year. At 7

Satya Sai Baba

p.m., in front of a raptured crowd, he had let an oval golden Liṅga emerge from his mouth:

> *Emergence of the Linga from Bhagavan's Body.* After these speeches, the great moment arrived when Bhagavan ['god', meaning Satya Sai Baba] rose from the chair at 5.15 p.m. to deliver His Sivarathri Sandesh ['message on the occasion of the Śivarātri festival'] to the eagerly awaiting devotees... Bhagavan concluded His Divine Discourse at 6.30 p.m. ... Thereafter, the students of Prasanthi Nilayam and Brindavan Campuses as also from Anantapur Campus started the night-long Sivarathri Bhajan. When Bhagavan sat in the chair, all eyes were fixed on Him. Though He was moving His right hand with the rhythm of the Bhajans, signs of Lingodbhava were visible on His face. Bhagavan started drinking more and more water. The devotees held their breath when signs of the emergence of the Linga from Bhagavan's body became prominent. The much awaited moment arrived at about 7.00 p.m. when with a forceful movement an oval-shaped golden Linga emerged from Bhagavan's mouth, sending the hundreds of thousands of devotees into raptures. Holding the Linga in His right hand, Bhagavan showed it to all the devotees first from the platform and then by moving between the rows of devotees. It was the greatest moment in the lives of the assembled devotees when they witnessed this soul-elevating divine phenomenon. Bhagavan left the Sai Kulwant Hall for His resident [read: residency] at 7.20 p.m. Night-long vigil and Bhajans continued with deep devotional fervour. (The Eye, p. 19, col. 4-6).

Pilgrim Tourism: The Temple as Economic Factor and Political Issue

Every year in February/March at the Mahāśivarātri festival, two days before the new moon of Phālguna, the last month of the hybrid moon-sun calendar of the Hindus (in the year 2001, this date fell on Wednesday, February 21), pilgrimage tourism reaches its peak when approximately 300.000 devotees, not only from Mauritius but also from overseas, flock to the Grand Bassin. The temple society promotes this mass tourism by expressly welcoming non-Hindus, too, wooing them by hinting at the alleged miraculous powers of the lake and the temple:

> Spiritual tourism or cultural tourism is an important sector of tourism. In Mauritius let it be said that Mauritiuseswar Nāth Temple is a pioneer in the field. Because of its location, its architecture, sanctity and miraculous powers people flock to this holy abode of lord Shiva. Bus loads, car loads of tourists make it a point of to visit this temple... Grand Bassin and in particular Mauritiuseswar Nath is an unavoidable tourist spot. It is an essential part of any tourist itinerary. A puller of crowds! Mauritiuseswar Nath

> is the centre of attraction day in and day out all through the year. (*The Eye*, p. 3, col. 2). Special flights are chartered from Africa, Asia, Europe and other countries for the Mahashivaratree-festival. (*The Eye*, p. 13, col. 4).

Once more the universalistic tendency manifests itself, which of course has unmistakable profane consequences for the temple organisation, as the income brought by the masses of pilgrims make the temple an important economical factor. And the remarkable financial attraction inevitably enhances its political relevance. For instance, the former Mauritian government under Prime Minister Navin Ramgoolam set up a 'commission of enquiry,' presided over by the judge Bernhard Sik Kuen, to get economical control over the temple. Obviously, mass spirituality and profanisation are mutually dependent.

The details communicated above as to the temple history are taken from '*The Eye*. Weekly Newspaper.' (No. 14, February 16-22, 2001; no imprint, published from Port Louis, Mauritius). The information to be found therein was supplemented by Mr. B. B. (Satish) Dayal, brother of the founder and he himself is also co-founder of the temple. Our extensive conversation (which lasted approximately 1½ hrs) was conducted mainly in Hindi, occasionally in English, since Mr Dayal preferred Hindi, which he spoke much more fluently than English. His colloquial language is Creole, as is usual in Mauritius. Although Mr Dayal is clearly of Indian descent, he definitely calls himself Mauritian. His Indian

Śiva's mount, the zebu bull Nandī

ancestors are supposed to have come from Gujarāt but he has no connection to them anymore.

Universalism

What lends the Mauritian Jyotirliṅga temple its eminent religious-historical importance, is the inescapable fact that here, Hinduism has clearly accomplished the step from a folk religion to a universal religion. We have verified this contention by at least seven aspects: (1) the religious-geographical border location at the end of the world, far from its folk-religious homeland; (2) the oligations of the emigrant situation, which replaces orthodox encapsulation by exoteric world-openness; (3) the pan-Hindu diversity of the pantheon; (4) the inclusion of members of all Indian regions, descendants of North- and South Indians; (5) the missionary work; (6) the business management including mass tourism; and (7) the opening up and appealing to non-Hindus.

The existence of Hindu emigrant temples on all five continents shows that in the meantime, Hinduism has expanded from a *folk religion* into a *world religion*. It has long since given up its folk religious confinement to South Asia. It has even gone one step further: the *world religion* has become a *universal religion*. The universalism of Hinduism is not a claim, but a reality. The temple shall explicitly be a home not only for Hindus, but for mankind:

> A temple is an abode of God. All human beings are children of the same God. In Mauritiuseswar Nath the plain truth is that people of all conditions are respected and honoured. (*The Eye*, loc. cit., p. 3, col. 3)

द्वादशज्योतिर्लिङ्गानि सन्ति नेपालभारते ।
त्रयोदशं मौरिशेशं मौरिशे सर्वविश्रुतम् । ।

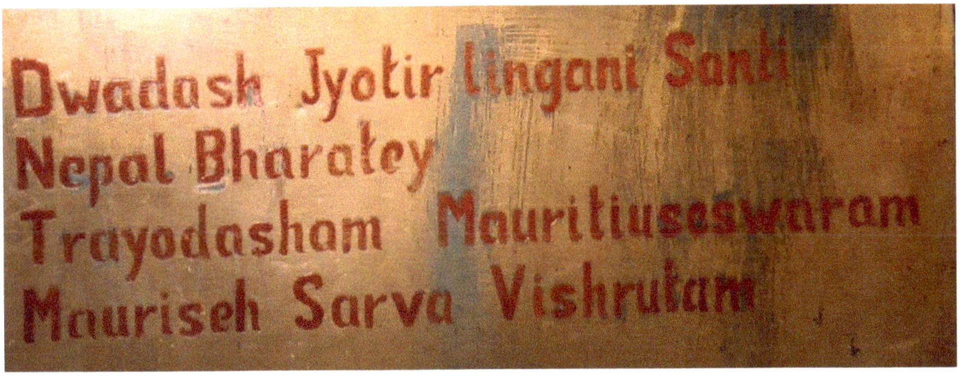

Time of visit: April 6, 2001.
Address: *Mauritiuseshwar Nath Shiva Jyotirliṅgam Temple*, Grand Bassin, Mauritius.

Notes

1 Cf. Clare Anderson: *Convicts in the Indian Ocean. Transportation from South Asia to Mauritius, 1815-1853*. London 2000.
2 Anderson, *Convicts*, p. 6.
3 Loc. cit., p. 6.
4 Cf. loc. cit., p. 7.
5 Richard B. Allen: *Slaves, Freedmen, and Indentured Laborers in Colonial Mauritius*. Cambridge University Press, Cambridge 1999. – Marina Carter: *Servants, Sirdars and Settlers*. Indians in Mauritius, 1834-1874. Oxford University Press, Delhi 1995. – Jean Benoist: *Hindouismes Créoles. Mascareignes, Antilles*. Editions du Comité des Travaux historiques et scientifiques (C.T.H.S.), Paris 1998.

Śiva's trident (*triśūla*)

6 Quoted from Ramesh Ramdoyal: *More Tales from Mauritius*. Macmillan Press, London 1981, p. 38. The author (born 1939) was former 'Director of the Mauritius Institute of Education'. After elementary education in Port Louis, he graduated from universities in Dublin, Oxford and London; see R. Ramdoyal: *Festivals of Mauritius* (Ed. de l'Ocean Indien). Stanley, Rose-Hill 1990, p. 169.
7 See Marion Meisig: *Tamilischer Hinduismus auf Mauritius. Der Mīnākṣī-Tempel in Port Louis*. In: Mitteilungen für Anthropologie und Religionsgeschichte (MARG), Bd. 14. Ugarit-Verlag, Münster 2001, pp. 251-274.
8 See T. Ammigan: *Tamils in Mauritius*. Proag Printing, Port Louis (Mauritius) 1989, p. 6.
9 Cf. U. Schneider: *Einführung in den Hinduismus*, 1989, p. 137.
10 Cf. Ulrich Schneider: *Towards a Sculptural Programme at Elephanta*, in: id.: *Opera minora* (Beiträge zur Indologie, 39). Ed. Marion Meisig. Wiesbaden 2002, pp. 232-243.
11 Again quoted from R. Ramdoyal: *More Tales from Mauritius*, 1981, pp. 27-29.
12 GANGA TALAB: 'An ancient volcanic crater which has become a lake in the forests of the central highlands. It is the sacred lake of the Mauritian Hindus who believe that it emanates from the sacred river Ganga in India. Since the time of French colonisation, the lake, called Grand Bassin, was shrouded in mystery and legend. A famous European traveller, J. Milbert, published a book in 1812 in which he mentioned that the inhabitants of the island looked with fear and awe upon this lake that never dried up and whose depth seemed impossible to measure. They even believed that monstrous eels which could swallow human beings or possibly even stags lived in the lake. When the Indians who settled in Mauritius discovered the lake, they believed it had divine attributes like the river Ganga in India…' (Sydney Selvon: *Historical Dictionary of Mauritius*. African Historical Dictionaries No. 49. The Scarecrow Press, Metuchen, N.J./ London 1991 [rev. ed. of: *Historical Dictionary of Mauritius* by Lindsay Rivière, 1982], p. 78).
13 Sydney Selvon/ Issa Asgarally/ Abhimanyu Unnuth: *Mauritius: its People, its Culture. The Tourist's Practical Guide*. Translated by Henri Brunel. Printed by MSM, Les Pailles, Mauritius 1988, p. 35.
14 Cf. K. Meisig: *Shivas Tanz*, 1996, p. 94. – Cf. also Aditya Malik: *Das Puṣkaramāhātmya: ein religionswissenschaftlicher Beitrag zum Wallfahrtsbegriff in Indien* (Beiträge zur Südasienforschung, Südasien-Institut Universität Heidelberg, 155). Steiner, Stuttgart 1993.

Jyotirlinga Temple, Grand Bassin, Mauritius

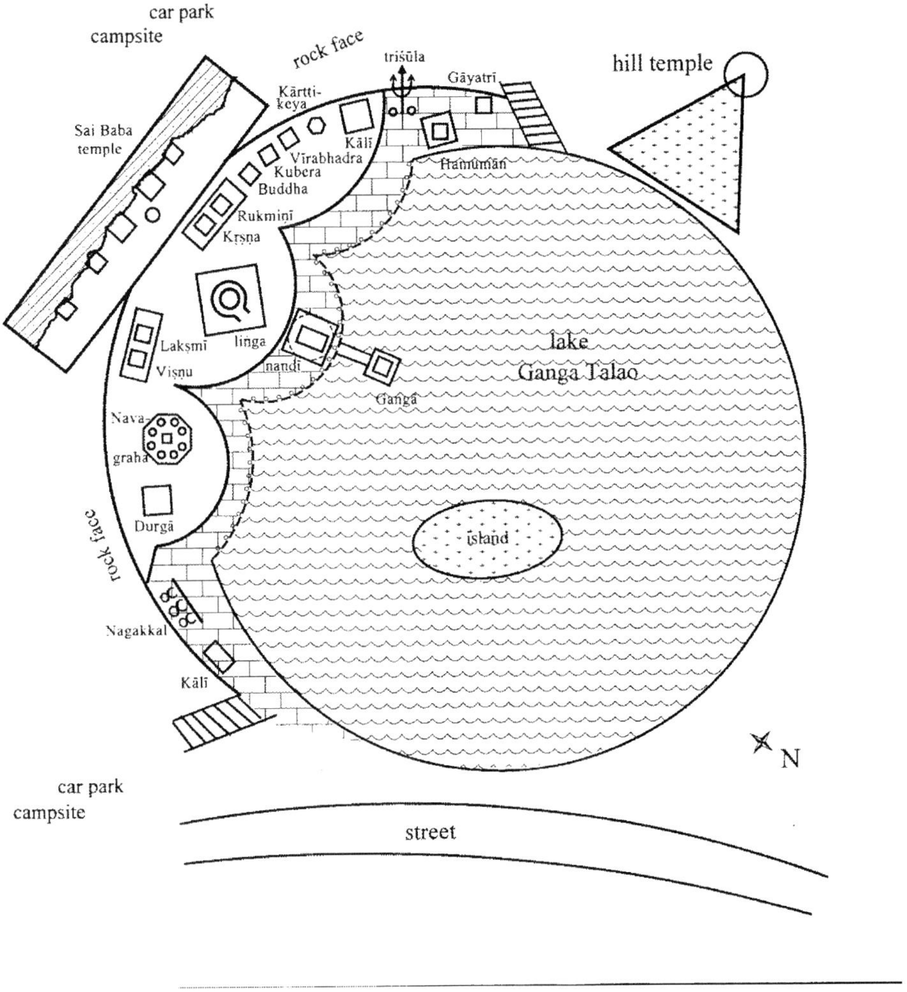

Appendix

'The Nine Planets'
Epicentre of Astrology

Pavilion of the Nine Planets, Murugan temple, Hamm
Viewed from the south: red Mars in the front centre

The Nine Planets (Navagraha) are not astronomical but astrological bodies. They do consist of the five astronomical planets visible with the naked eye, namely Mercury, Venus, Mars, Jupiter and Saturn but are complemented by the Sun and Moon and two 'grahas' ('grabbers') called Rāhu and Ketu: Rāhu is the devourer of the Sun and Moon during eclipses and Ketu is the demon of comets and meteors. They are said to be identical with the ascending and descending nodes of the moon.

The traditional place of the Nine Planets (Skt. Navagraha, Tam. Navakkirakam) is somewhere along the northern temple wall. The nine statues will be there even if the orientation of a temple deviates from the orthodox eastern direction, like, for example, in the Māṇikya-Vināyaka temple in Bambalapiṭiya, which faces west.

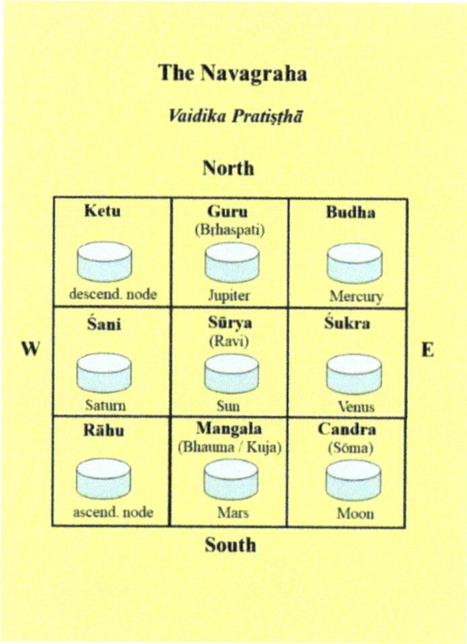

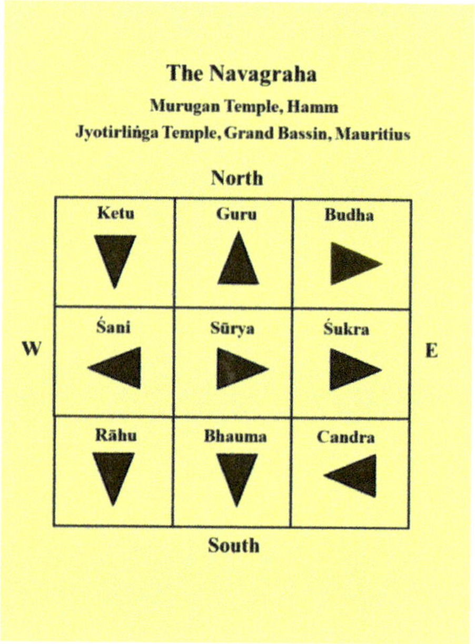

While the main deity is the spiritual centre of a Tamil temple, the Nine Planets can be regarded as its astrological epicentre.

Some devotees will visit a temple with the sole objective of venerating the Nine Planets. They believe them to be extremely powerful in a magical sense. This is especially true for Saturn who is widely feared for his supernatural influence.

For demonstration purposes we have selected two shrines of the Nine Planets: the first in the Murugan temple in Hamm, because it is set up in accordance with most of the modern mainstream temples and the second in the Jyotirliṅga temple at the Grand Bassin in Mauritius. These give an impression of the extreme iconographical differences which can be met with in Tamil temples.

Apart from the iconography (Moeller, p. 79), the *arrangement of statues* in both these temples follows the Vedic position (*vaidika-pratiṣṭhā*). It runs like this: beginning with Saturn (Śani) in the west, then Ketu in the north-west, followed by Jupiter (Guru or Bṛhaspati) in the north, Mercury (Budha) in the north-east, Venus (Śukra) in the east, the Moon (Candra or Soma) in the south-east, Mars (Maṅgala, Bhauma, Kuja or Aṅgāra) in the south, Rāhu in the south-west and the Sun (Sūrya or Ravi) in the centre. (In some temples, Rāhu and Ketu have swapped places.)

None of them must face another: Saturn turns to the west, Ketu faces south, Jupiter north, Mercury east, Venus also east, the Moon west, Mars south, Rāhu south and the Sun is always orientated to the east.

Saturn – Śani

The Statues in Detail – Murugan Temple in Hamm

Saturn. His Sanskrit name Śani is derived from *śanaiś-cara*, 'going slow.' His day of the week is Saturday. He is clad in black. In front of a halo, he stands before his mount, a crow or raven. Like all the other 'planets,' his head is helmed with a basket-crown (*karaṇḍamukuṭa*), he is adorned with a necklace of beads and wears the sacred thread (*yajñopavīta*) over his left shoulder.

In his upper hands he holds an arrow and a bow, in his right lower hand, a trident, and his left lower hand shows the gesture of granting boons (*varada*).

Ketu

Ketu. 'Meteor,' Comet.' He represents the descending node of the moon, i.e. the point in the orbit of the moon where it crosses the ecliptic (the seeming orbit of the sun) from north to south. He is also known as the 'dragon's tail.' Ketu is the demon of meteors and comets.

Girded with an orange cloth, he stands in front of a lion, beneath the hoods of a five-headed cobra, which is spread like a halo behind and above his head. Like Saturn and all the others, he wears a basket-crown, a necklace of beads and the sacred thread.

The hands of his two arms are folded in veneration (*añjali*).

Jupiter – Guru or Bṛhaspati

Jupiter. His Sanskrit name Guru means 'heavy'/'grave,' and is an appellation for dignified persons, especially the teacher, the guru. It is related to the Latin *gravis* (see Mayrhofer).

His day of the week is Thursday. Dressed in a yellow cloth, he stands in front of his mount, the elephant, being twice as tall as the animal.

As to the attributes in his hands: his upper right balances a rosary (*akṣamālā*), his upper left has a vessel filled with holy water (*kamaṇḍalu*); his lower right holds a rod (*daṇḍa*) and his lower left grants boons (*varada*).

Mercury – Budha

Mercury. His Sanskrit name Budha derives from the same verbal root √*budh* as the appellation Buddha. Both mean the 'Awoken One.' When rising as a morning star, Mercury can only be observed very early, just before daylight.

His day of the week is Wednesday. Dressed in a lime green cloth, he stands in front of his mount, the lion.

In his upper hands, he wields a sword (right) and a shield. With his lower right hand, he leans on a club, while his lower left shows the gesture of granting boons (*varada*), in the same way as all the other planets do, except Rāhu and Ketu, who fold their two hands (all their companions have four) in veneration (*añjali*).

Venus – Śukra

Venus. His Sanskrit name Śukra is masculine, the 'Bright One' or the 'White One.'

His day of the week is Friday. Clad in white, he stands in front of his mount, the horse.

The male Venus holds exactly the same attributes as Jupiter – rosary, water-pot and rod (*daṇḍa*) – also showing the gesture of fulfilling wishes (*varada*).

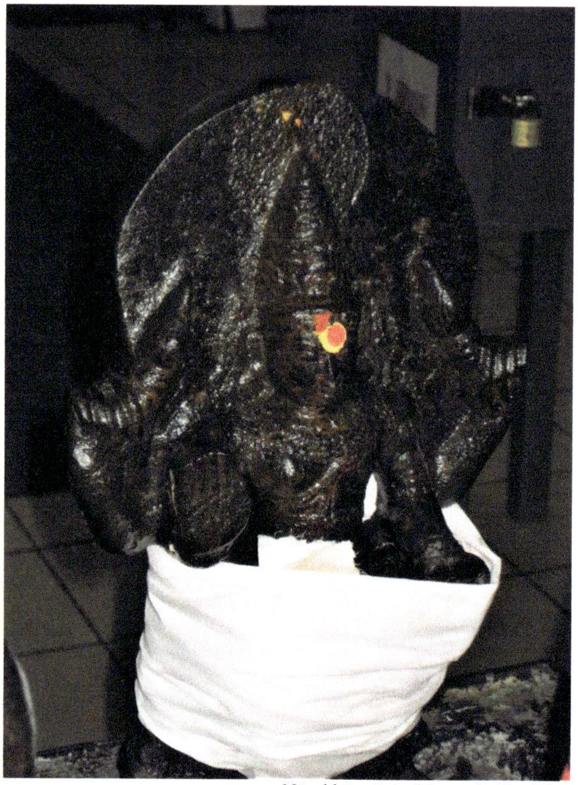

Nāgabhūṣaṇī-Ambā temple, Frankfurt

Moon – Candra

Moon. Candra, the 'Shimmering' or 'Gleaming One,' is dressed in white. His day of the week is – also according to the Hindu calendar – Monday. He stands upon his chariot, which is drawn by ten antelopes.

His halo is shaped like the crescent, lying on its back (which, in tropical India and Sri Lanka, the crescent actually does).

In his upper hands he holds a lotus bud each. The lower right hand – open palm held out to the observer, fingers upright – shows the gesture of providing freedom from fear (*abhayada*). The lower left – open palm, fingers downwards – grants boons (*varada*).

Mars – Maṅgala or Bhauma or Kuja or Aṅgāra

Mars. His Sanskrit name Maṅgala can be translated as '[Bringer of] Luck.' He is dressed in a red cloth. His day of the week is Tuesday.

Standing in front of his mount, a goat, his lower left hand indicates the granting of boons (*varada*). With his lower right he leans on a club. His upper left balances a trident on the index and middle finger. Upon the same two fingers of the upper right hand dangles a lotus bud at the point of the stem.

Rāhu

Rāhu. His name has been interpreted since Vedic times as the 'Grabber.' He is the demon who grabs and devours the Sun and Moon during eclipses. Being Ketu's counterpart, he represents the ascending node of the moon, i.e. the point in the orbit of the moon where it crosses the orbit of the sun from south to north. He is also known as the 'dragon's head.'

His colours are greyish, shadowy; here he is clad in pale violet. His trunk ends in a noticeable dragon's tail. His mount is a parrot. The hands of his two arms are folded in veneration (*añjali*).

Sun – Sūrya

Sun. Sūrya, as the sun-god is called in Sanskrit, stands in the centre of the Nine Planets, always facing east. He is dressed in red. His day of the week is – also according to the Hindu calendar – Sunday. The chariot of the Sun is drawn by seven (otherwise mostly five) horses.

His halo can be described as a disk with points and marked by sun-beams.

His four hands show the same attributes and gestures as that of the moon: two full-blown lotus flowers, granting of fearlessness and boons.

Sūrya – the Sun god
Varasiddhi-Vināyaka Devasthānam, Toronto

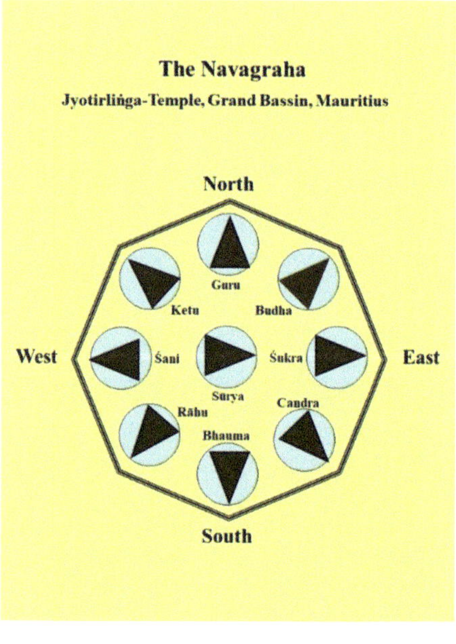

Jyotirliṅga Temple in Mauritius

The setup and orientation of the Navagraha statues in the Jyotirliṅga temple at the Grand Bassin are identical with what we have found in the Murugan temple in Hamm but the rest is nearly completely different. We will present the iconography of the statues in the same order as before, starting with Saturn in the west, proceeding clockwise, to conclude with the Sun in the centre.

Saturn – Śani

Differing from what we observe in most of the Tamil emigrant temples, where all the statues of the Nine Planets are chiselled out of granite, only four of these figures in the Jyotirliṅga temple are made of this black stone: Saturn, Ketu, Mercury and Rāhu.

Saturn sits on a bull, has a halo around his head and sports a moustache. He is decorated with a string of black beads, spread above his head and flowing down over the shoulders. He wields a sword with his right hand and the left holds a shield before his chest.

Ketu is headless, an extraordinary depiction which is explained by the following legend: the dragon-shaped demon Rāhu drank from he forbidden potion Amṛta, the nectar of immortality. The Sun and Moon informed Viṣṇu about this sin and the god severed Rāhu's immortal head and placed it in the sky, where it devours the Sun and Moon during the eclipses, wreaking its vengeance. Ketu, the decapitated but immortal leftovers of the demon's body – also called 'the dragon's tail' – causes the meteors and comets. – That is why the lower trunk of the statue runs into the bent body of a dragon, with a fish's head at its end.

Ketu

Ketu is decorated with a long string of beads, which runs all the way from around his neck over the inside of his two left elbows down to the floor. A hip-long cloth is hung over his shoulders. His upper right hand wields a sabre above the stump of his slain neck and his upper left holds a shield. From his lower right hangs a rosary and the lower left hand begs the devotee to stick a devotional flower between thumb and fingers (*kaṭaka-hasta*, 'crab-hand'; Moeller, p. 100 with illustration 24).

Jupiter – Guru or Bṛhaspati

Jupiter is depicted by a figurine of ochre soapstone. He sits on his elephant in front of a halo. A long string of yellow beads is laid around him, encircling the elephant too from trunk to toe. He sports a necklace of pearls and a moustache. His basket-helmet is adorned with a yellow tilaka. In the hands of his four arms he holds, from the lower right clock-wise, a rod (*daṇḍa*), an open lotus, a mirror (*darpaṇa*) and a rather large bowl filled with grains.

Mercury – Budha

Mercury sits on his lion in front of a halo. He is decorated by a necklace and a moustache. A long string of large yellow and lime-green beads surrounds both his body and the lion, from mane to hind feet. In his four hands he wields, from lower right clockwise, rod (*daṇḍa*), trident (*triśūla*), battle-axe (*paraśu*) and a metal lance (*śakti*), which is stuck into the 'crab-hand' (see explanation under *Ketu*) of the stone figure.

Venus has no halo around his head. His statue is made of white marble. He sits on his mount, the horse. Both steed and rider are decorated with a long string of thick, white beads.

Venus – Śukra

Moon – Candra

In his lower right and upper left hand he holds a lotus flower. His upper right hand swings a fly-whisk (*cāmara*), an insignia of royalty. His lower left 'crab-hand' is empty.

The *Moon*, made of white marble, sits on an antelope, which drags a long string of thick white pearls. There is a halo around his head and he sports a moustache. In his hands he holds, again from the lower right clockwise: a lotus flower, a fly-whisk, a battle-axe and the 'crab-hand' is empty.

Mars rides a goat and his pearls are red. All other features are the same as the Moon's.

Mars – Maṅgala

Rāhu

Rāhu is represented only by the demon Rāhu's head, lurking behind the lying crescent which it is about to devour. As to the different depictions of Rāhu and Ketu in the Murugan temple in Hamm and in the Jyotirliṅga temple at the Grand Bassin, we can recapitulate (now that all four statues have been discussed) that their treatment in the Jyotirliṅga temple sticks to the Purāṇic legend (as summarised above under *Ketu*): Here, Rāhu's head is severed and Ketu only appears as the demon's dragon-tailed trunk, the head slain. The statues in the Murugan temple have swapped these motifs, inasmuch as Rāhu is tailed and Ketu has the dragon's five cobra heads.

The crescent behind which Rāhu lurks, lies on a chariot. This divine carriage is driven by a charioteer and drawn by a lion or tiger without mane. Rāhu has *no* halo around his head, sports a moustache and is decorated with a long string of thick black beads.

Sun – Sūrya

The *Sun*, his statue made of white marble, has a halo around his head and a moustache. He sits on a five-headed horse and is decorated with a string of red beads.

His lower right hand grants freedom from fear (*abhayada*), his upper right swings a fly-whisk, the upper left wields a battle-axe and the lower left 'crab-hand' (*kaṭaka-hasta*) is empty.

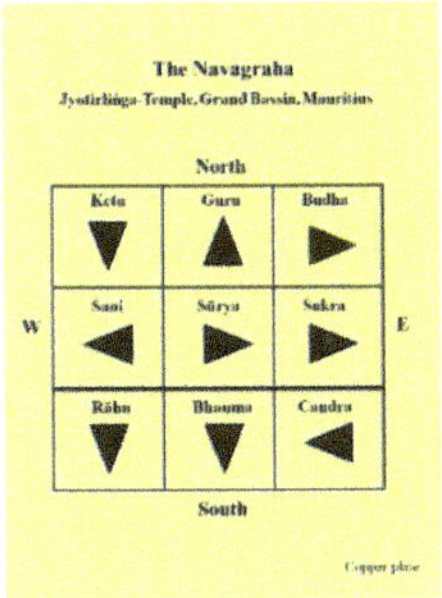

Copper plate in the Jyotirliṅga temple, turned 90° to the right, showing the symbols of the Nine Planets; Saturn (Śani) left centre = west, Jupiter (Guru) top centre = north, etc.

Of the thirty-three temples in our collection of sketches there are only six that do not come with a pavilion for the Navagraha. These six are without exception very small, mostly remote village or suburban temples in Mauritius (Mārī-Ambā in l'Escalier, Vinayagur-Seedalamen and Kālī in Beau Vallon and Draupadī in Riambel). All the others, like for example, the Kalpaka-Vināyaka temple in Frankfurt or the Mārī-Ambā temple in Negombo, proudly present the pavilion of the Nine Planets as the astrological hub of the sanctuary.

Kalpaka-Vināyaka Kōvil, Frankfurt

Mārī-Ambā temple, Negombo

Putan Budha	Cukkiran Śukra	Cantiran Candra
Viyāḷam (Kuru) Bṛhaspati	Cūriyan Sūrya	Cevvāy Bhauma
Ketu	Canīsvaran Śani	Irāku Rāhu

The Nine Planets, Government Museum Patna, India
12th century

The most ancient depiction of the Nine Planets that we came across was in the Government Museum Patna in Uttar Pradesh, India. It originates from the nearby city of Gorakhpur and is dated in the 12th century AD.

The frieze shows the dragon-tailed Ketu on the very right side. Next to him we discern Rāhu with the large head. The sun-god Sūrya can be recognised in the centre by his horse-chariot beneath.

The Five Laws of Magic

(1) Contact is contagious
(2) *pars pro toto* – The part for the whole
(3) *similia similibus* – Similar effects by similar causes
(4) Magic of words
(5) *opus operatum* – Deeds work by themselves

sparśaḥ saṃcārī – bhāga eva sarvam –
tulyais tulyāni – mantraiḥ kārmaṇam – karma kṛtavat

Tamil temples are deeply rooted in the beliefs of magic. That is why we wish to conclude our collection of sketches with a survey of the magical world-view. Our guideline will be a paragraph from Ulrich Schneider's introduction to Buddhism (*Der Buddhismus. Eine Einführung*, ^{3}1992, p. 58).

The magical approach is not at all limited to Tamil temples, nor is it an overcome relic from the primitive thinking of stone-age gatherer-hunters. As a matter of fact, all of us, provided that we are prepared to observe ourselves critically, will detect in our subconscious behaviour the more or less obvious remnants of this pre-religious or even – if we define magic as part of religion – religious approach.

According to Schneider, the magical world-view can be described by five laws, namely: (1) Contact is contagious. (2) Pars pro toto – the part for the whole. (3) Similia similibus – similar effects by similar causes. (4) The magic of words. (5) Opus operatum – deeds work by themselves.

We will try to illustrate these five laws of magic by examples taken from the world of Tamil temples. We are going to repeatedly refer to the Toronto Durgā temple's motto, or rather its uncompromising admonition to visitors, which appears on the kōvil's website reading 'No Shoe · No Jacket · No Photo · No Video · No Cell Phone.'

No shoe! – Why is the visitor advised to leave his footwear in front of the temple entrance? The answer will lead us to the first of our Five Rules of Magic.

1) Contact Is Contagious

Magical thinking divides the world into two spheres: sacred and profane. The temple belongs to the sacred, the world outside to the profane. The border between these areas is clearly defined: the temple gate is carved out of massive wood and created by robust workmanship. This border must not be transgressed without former purification, for the sacred is pure, the profane impure. One must not confuse hygienic cleanliness with ritual purity. You might clean your shoes of all mud and waste as diligently as possible but they would still remain magically impure and you would not be allowed to wear them inside the temple. The aura of the profane cannot be removed, it will cling to their fabric. Their profane nature would still pollute the holy sphere of the temple. This is the reason for the law of magic being placed at the beginning, the start of a tour of a temple. This law reads: *Contact is contagious*.

Do not touch! The aura of a powerful personality is transferred by contact. The devotee donates food to a deity, like bananas. It is not only customary, but part of the ritual, that the devotee might be given back the leftovers of the deity's meal, which are called prasāda (Sanskrit for 'mercy' or 'clemency'). When the brahmin in the *Vinayagur Seedalamen Temple* in Beau Vallon gave us four bananas out of the prasāda of Devī Śītalā, this was not just a host's friendly gesture but a ritual act. We were given the opportunity to partake of the goddess's divine power. – When the devotees in the Nāgabhūṣaṇī-Ambā temple in Frankfurt are reluctant to take back the saris they have previously donated to the goddess, it is not only because the clothes are defiled with coconut milk or greasy with offered ghee. These saris have been worn by Nāgabhūṣaṇī-Ambā, they have come in close contact with the Devī and are therefore charged with her divine power. – The granite Liṅga in the Jyotirliṅga temple at the Grand Bassin in Mauritius had to be transferred from the area of the profane to the sphere of the sacred by consecrating it with water from the Gaṅgā in India, which is considered a holy river and also from the Gaṅgā Tālāb in Mauritius, which the Hindus respect as the most ancient sanctuary of the whole island of Mauritius. It is only by means of the holy water that the profane stone receives its divine aura.

No jacket! – Brahmins officiate in the temples not only barefooted, but always stripped to the waist. The Subrahmaṇya-Svāmī temple in Colombo even extends this rule to visiting laymen by a sign that reads MALES DO NOT ENTER WITH UPPER CLOTHES. The Toronto Durgā Temple is more relaxed when forbidding just jackets. One additional reason for these restrictions is to mark the border between the spheres of the profane and the sacred. But there is, furthermore, the superstitious belief that demons hide in the folds of clothes and must not involuntarily be brought in. – Japanese Shintō temples (Shintō 神道 meaning 'The Way of the Spirits') do not have rectangular entrances; you always have to wind around at least one bend or corner. In this way, it is made difficult for evil spirits to enter the holy premises. The same phenomenon can be observed in the Vināyaka-Śītalā-Ambā temple in Beau Vallon, Mauritius. The entrance to the shrine of the nāgakkals does not lead directly to the holy objects but is set apart, so that you have to turn around the end of a wall to come in. – This superstition, by and by, belongs to the field of animism rather than to the rules of magic. The world of magic is quite independent from any gods or supernatural beings. Its laws and rules do work by themselves, no matter who employs them. Anybody can use them, he only needs the know-how.

(2) Pars pro toto – The Part for the Whole

No photo! – This ban leads us directly to another magical law. It reads: *pars pro toto – the part for the whole*. The lines of the hand, for example, are considered an exact and reliable microcosm of the whole person. – When the devotees complete their circumambulation of the statues by venerating Caṇḍeśvara in his tiny shrine in the Canadian Kipling Śiva temple, they do that because, as the brahmin informs us: 'Caṇḍeśvara recognises the respective devotee by his or her lines of the hand and reports the individual's good or bad deeds to Citragupta, secretary of Yama, judge of the afterworld.' – Footprints are seen as identical with a person or a god like Śiva (as in Kālidāsa's poem *Meghadūta*, verse 1.58) as well as their shadow. Photographs are a kind of shadow, a chāyārūpa. The picture is not only a part but equivalent to the whole person. Clothes or dolls can replace a real individual. What makes the thing dangerous is that such parts of a person – an effigy, a photo – or similar representatives can be used for conjuring or casting evil spells. It is the fear of abusing photos of the deity that induces this ban on taking photographs.

The ban is extended to *videos* as well, for these are just an advanced technical development of producing shadows, or photos. Naturally, *cell phones* are included here, for they also enable the user to shoot photos and videos, not to mention the noise of continuous one-sided conversation that is apt to strongly bother meditating devotees.

(3) Similia similibus – Similar Effects by Similar Causes

Here, we have reached the third of our laws: *similia similibus – similar effects by similar causes*. The underlying idea is that of an analogy of microcosm and macrocosm. What is done in the microcosm, must have its effects on a macrocosmic scale as well. Such an analogy works especially with respect to past and present, corresponding in a religious context to the mutual interference of myth (in the past) and ritual (in the present). – To quote another example: in the Kāmākṣī temple in Māṅgāḍu we read on a sign (in somewhat broken English which is nevertheless quoted here for the sake of authenticity): *It is said that Sri Kamakshi performed her tapas* ['penance'] *and got married* [to] *Sri Ekambareswar* [Śiva] *at Kanchi. Therefore if any unmarried girl, who comes and offer vows to Sri Kamakshi, the worshipper will also get married. This is a known fact in this area.* Or on a similar sign in the Ekāmranātha temple in Kāñcīpuram: *It is popular belief that a childless woman, if she eats a fruit from this mango tree, will be blessed with a child.* The events in the past – Śiva having married the goddess – must affect the present in that a worshipping girl will find a husband and she will become pregnant with a child. Respectively when she venerates the tree goddess of fertility, a dryad, by eating a fruit from her mango tree. – A maṇḍala or Śrī Cakra – both Sanskrit terms meaning 'circle' – is an especially powerful instrument of magic which is why it is also named yantra, 'instrument.' A maṇḍala or yantra is an effigy, a representation of a whole temple. Therefore, it can be used to banish deities and to force them to act according to the priest's wishes. That is why the brahmin in the Mīnākṣī temple in Scarborough, Canada, has the – in his own words – 'highest respect' for this tool; he even wears a small yantra in shape of an amulet around his neck. Tilakas and tripuṇḍras (the three horizontal lines of Śaiva bhaktas), which are extensively made use of in worshipping holy statues, are similar symbols of magical power.

(4) Magic of Words

The fourth law of magic is the *magic of words*, spells like the mantra *om*. Mantras are – so to speak – spoken yantras. The *homo religiosus* uses mantras to achieve his means even against the resistance of divine powers. – During our visit to the Toronto Durgā temple, a Navakoṭi ('Ninety Million') ritual was being performed. A certain mantra was repeated ninety million times by four brahmins in the sanctissimum, a time-consuming process indeed, lasting for months. Because a mantra is a magical spell, it can be used for conjuring. Consequently, mantras are often kept secretly. The studies of an orthodox Hindu youth, a brahmacārī, are concluded by a consecration (*dīkṣā*), after which he receives the sacred thread (*yajñopavīta*). During this ritual, his teacher, the guru, whispers his personal mantra, his 'gurumantra,' in his ear. – A sub-form of the *magic of words* is the magic of names: secret names play an important role. Bījamantras, 'seed-syllables,' are magical formulas that equal the names of certain deities. For example, Agni, the Fire god, is identical with the syllable *ran*, the goddess Kālī with the syllable *krīm*, Sarasvatī, the goddess of speech, arts and science, with *aim*, etc.

(5) Opus operatum – Deeds Work by Themselves

The fifth and last law of magic reads *opus operatum – deeds work by themselves*. A magical deed is compelling – resistance is futile. This rule can be applied to all the other four laws of magic, with which it works together and makes them effective. Curses and penance are striking examples of the effectiveness of magical acts. – Let us once more return to the goddess Kāmākṣī and her cults in Māṅgāḍu and Kāñcīpuram: According to local legends, Śiva cursed the goddess so that she became ugly and had to live on earth. In Māṅgāḍu, to quote the relevant legend, 'she awaited Śiva's arrival, for Śiva had promised to marry her to ease the hardships of the banishment. Śiva, though, did not come and therefore the Śakti started severe austerities. She lit five fires in sacrifice bowls (*homakuṇḍa*) and stood with the big toe of her left foot (*vāmapādāṅguṣṭha*) in the licking flames of the central fire. In this manner she performed penance for a long time.' Śiva, compelled by the Devī's penance, had to come and marry her. Magic effects unconquerable pressure.

The age-old rule of *do ut des* ('I give so that you may give') makes use of the *opus operatum*, as well. It is applied in the Scarborough Durgā temple

– as we have seen – to encourage visitors to donate for stone tiles for the floor, by the statement: 'If you are generous yourself, the goddess will be generous to you.'

The consequences of the Five Rules of Magic can be unexpectedly extreme; they extend far and wide even into most mundane fields: *opus operatum*...

et

OPERIS FINIS

Bibliography

Apte, Vaman Shivaram: *The Practical Sanskrit-English Dictionary*. Revised and Enlarged Edition (Reprinted from the Revised and Enlarged Editon, Poona 1957). Rinsen Book Company: Kyoto ^{2}1986.

Arul Migu Sockallingum Meenatchee Ammen Tirukkovil. [Temple newspaper] Published by the Hindu Maha Jana Sangham on the occasion of the Maha Kumbabhishegam of Arul Migu Sockalingum Meenatchee Ammen Tirukkovil, Port Louis, Mauritius, 17th November 1989.

Arumugam, S.: *Some Ancient Hindu Temples of Sri Lanka, Where I Have Worshipped*. 2nd edition, Mary Martin: Colombo 1982. [The traditional viewpoint of an educated devotee; full of useful, reliable and often confirmable information.]

Ayyar, P. V. Jagadisa: *South Indian Shrines*. (Illustrated). Revised and enlarged edition. New Delhi 1982.

Barua, B. K./ Sreenivasa Murthy, H. V.: *Temples and Legends of Assam*. Bombay 1965.

Bastin, Rohan: *The Domain of Constant Excess. Plural Worship at the Munneshvaram Temples in Sri Lanka*. New York, Oxford 2002. [Uncritically dependent on the questionable statements of his informants; some useful details, but unreliable; registers only English literature.]

Bechert, Heinz: *Mythologie der singhalesischen Volksreligion*. In: *Wörterbuch der Mythologie*, ed. H. W. Haussig. I. Abt.: *Die alten Kulturvölker*, 8. Lieferung. Stuttgart 1974-82.

Bhattacharyya, Narendra Nath: *The Indian Mother Goddess*. New Delhi ^{2}1977 (rev., enl.; ^{1}1970).

Bunce, Frederik W.: *An Encyclopaedia of Hindu Deities, Demi-Gods, Godlings, Demons and Heroes*. With Special Focus on Iconographic Attributes. Illustrations by G. X. Capdi. 3 vols. New Delhi 2000.

Carter, Charles: *A Sinhalese– English Dictionary*. Colombo, new printing, 1965.

Cartman, James (Rev.): *Hinduism in Ceylon*. Colombo 1st ed. 1957.

Das, R. K.: *Temples of Tamilnad*. Bharatiya Vidya Bhavan: Bombay 1964.

Dharatīkānta: *Kāmāmākhyā-tīrtha*. Gauhāṭī, no date [in Bengali].

Glasenapp, Helmuth v.: *Heilige Stätten Indiens*. Die Wallfahrtsorte der Hindus, Jainas und Buddhisten, ihre Legenden und ihr Kult. München 1928.

Gonda, Jan: *Die Religionen Indiens: II Der jüngere Hinduismus*. Stuttgart 1963.

Harman, William P.: *The Sacred Marriage of a Hindu Goddess*. Bloomington, Indianapolis 1989.

Jouveau-Dubreuil, G.: *Archéologie du Sud de L'Inde*. Tome 1: *Architecture*, tome 2: *Iconographie*. Paris 1914.

Kakati, Banikanta: *The Mother Goddess Kamakhya*. Publication Board Assam: Guwahati 1989 ([1]1948?, preface March 3, 1948).
Kollar, Peter L.: *Symbolism in Hindu Architecture. As Revealed in the Shri Minakshi Sundareswar*. New Delhi 2001.
Kumar, Jitendra: *Masterpieces of Mathura Museum*. Mathura 1989.
Mayrhofer, Manfred: *Etymologisches Wörterbuch des Altindoarischen*. 3 vols. Heidelberg 1992-2001.
Meisig, Konrad: *Shivas Tanz. Der Hinduismus* (Kleine Bibliothek der Religionen, hrsg. v. Adel Theodor Khoury, vol. 4). Herder: Freiburg, Basel, Wien 1996. Reprint 2003.
Meisig, Konrad: *Das Kastensystem des Hinduismus*. In: Wer ist mein Nächster? Die Antwort der Weltreligionen, hrsg. v. Adel Th. Khoury und Peter Hünermann (Herder Taschenbuch, vol. 1512), Freiburg, Basel, Wien 1988, pp. 11-58.
Meisig, Konrad: *Ayodhyā. Probleme der religionswissenschaftlichen Auseinandersetzung mit dem Hindu-Fundamentalismus*. In: Jahrbuch für Religionswissenschaft und Theologie der Religionen, vol. 3. Oros Verlag: Altenberge 1995, pp. 126-141.
Meisig, Konrad: *„Mutter Indien" (Bhāratamātā). Zur Personifizierung kosmologischer Vorstellungen im politischen Hinduismus*. In: Zeller, Dieter (ed.): *Religion im Wandel der Kosmologien* (Religionswissenschaft, vol. 10). Peter Lang: Frankfurt a. M. 1999, pp. 281-285. – Also in: Mitteilungen für Anthropologie und Religionsgeschichte (MARG), vol. 14, 1999, Ugarit-Verlag: Münster 2001, pp. 131-140.
Meisig, Konrad: *Neuere Entwicklungen im Hindufundamentalismus*. In: Mitteilungen für Anthropologie und Religionsgeschichte (MARG), vol. 14, 1999, Ugarit-Verlag: Münster 2001, pp. 219-228.
Meisig, Konrad: *Tamilischer Hinduismus in Deutschland. Ein Rundgang durch den Vighneśvara-Tempel in Hamm (Westfalen)*. In: Mitteilungen für Anthropologie und Religionsgeschichte (MARG), vol. 14, 1999, Ugarit-Verlag: Münster 2001, pp. 229-249.
Meisig, Konrad: *Krieg und Gewalt im Hinduismus*. In: *Krieg und Gewalt in den Weltreligionen. Fakten und Hintergründe*. Ed. Adel Theodor Khoury, Ekkehard Grundmann, Hans-Peter Müller. Herder: Freiburg, Basel, Wien 2003, pp. 67-82, 132f.
Meisig, Konrad: *Der Jyotirliṅga-Tempel am Grand Bassin, Mauritius. Hinduismus von der Volksreligion zur Universalreligion*. In: Zecher, Reinhard (ed.): *Unterwegs mit und in der Philosophie. Festschrift für Karl Anton Sprengard*. Hamburg 2003, pp. 245-260.
Meisig, Konrad: *Hinduismus im Exil*. In: Sitzungsberichte der Leibniz-Sozietät, ed. 66, Jahrgang 2004, pp. 5-27.
Meisig, Konrad: *Zehn Jahre nach Ayodhyā. Fundamentalistische Gewalt in Gujarat im Frühjahr 2002*. In: Mitteilungen für Anthropologie und Religionsgeschichte (MARG), vol. 17, 2005, Ugarit-Verlag: Münster, pp. 79-89.

Meisig, Konrad: *Der Highgatehill Murugan-Tempel in London-Archway: ein Zentrum des Auswanderer-Hinduismus.* In: Mitteilungen für Anthropologie und Religionsgeschichte (MARG), vol. 17, 2005, Ugarit-Verlag: Münster, pp. 217-236.

Meisig, Marion: *Tamilischer Hinduismus auf Mauritius. Der Mīnākṣī-Tempel in Port Louis.* Vortrag bei der 29. Studientagung der Deutschen Religionsgescichtlichen Studiengesellschaft, Münster, vom 18.-20. Juni 1999. In: Mitteilungen für Anthropologie und Religionsgeschichte (MARG), vol. 14. Ugarit-Verlag: Münster 2001, pp. 251-274.

Meisig, Marion: *Die Verdrängung der Devī: vier Hindutempel in Madras und Umgebung und ihr Einfluß auf den Kāmākṣī-Tempel in Hamm-Uentrop.* In: Mitteilungen für Anthropologie und Religionsgeschichte (MARG), vol. 17. Ugarit-Verlag: Münster 2005, pp. 91-115.

Meisig, Marion: *Die Grammatik eines Śaiva-Tamil-Tempels. Zur Ikonologie hinduistischer Emigranten-Tempel.* In: Mitteilungen für Anthropologie und Religionsgeschichte (MARG), vol. 19. Ugarit-Verlag: Münster 2006.

Meisig, Marion: *Der Kult der Großen Mutter in Indien.* In: Jahrbuch für Religionswissenschaft und Theologie der Religionen, vol. 2, Herder: Freiburg, Basel, Wien 1994, pp. 88-113.

Michell, George: *Monuments of India.* I: *Buddhist, Jain, Hindu.* Middlesex 1989.

Moeller, Volker: *Die Mythologie der vedischen Religion und des Hinduismus.* In: *Wörterbuch der Mythologie.* Ed. H. W. Haussig. Stuttgart no date [1966].

Moorthy, K. K.: *Sarvam Sakti Mayam. A Mini-Compendium of 300 Sakti Temples.* Message Publications: Tirupathi A. P. 1997.

'Murray', see: Williams, L.F. Rushbrook.

Pathmanathan, S.: *Murukaṉ the Divine Child: The Kantacuvāmani Temple at Nallūr.* In: *Lanka*, 5, 1990. Ed. Peter Schalk. Uppsala 1990, pp. 80-102.

Raghavan, M. D.: *Tamil Culture in Ceylon. A General Introduction.* Colombo [1974?].

Rao, T. A. Gopinatha: *Elements of Hindu Iconography.* Paragon Book Reprint Corp.: New York 1968.

Scherer, Anton: *Gestirnnamen bei den indogermanischen Völkern.* Heidelberg 1953.

Schier, Kerstin: *The Goddess's Embrace. Multifaceted Relations at the Ekāmranātha Temple Festival in Kanchipuram.* Wiesbaden 2018.

Schleberger, Eckard: *Die indische Götterwelt. Gestalt, Ausdruck und Sinnbild. Ein Handbuch der hinduistischen Ikonographie.* Köln 1986.

Schneider, Ulrich: *Einführung in den Hinduismus.* Darmstadt 1989.

Schneider, Ulrich: *Towards a Sculptural Programme at Elephanta*, in: U. Schneider: *Opera minora* (Beiträge zur Indologie, 39). Ed. Marion Meisig. Wiesbaden 2002.

Schumann, Hans Wolfgang: *Buddhistische Bilderwelt.* Köln 1986.

Shulman, David Dean: *Tamil Temple Myths. Sacrifice and Divine Marriage in the South Indian Śaiva Tradition.* Princetown University Press: New Jersey 1980.

Smith, H. Daniel/Narasimha Chary, M.: *Handbook of Hindu Gods, Goddesses and Saints.* Delhi 1991.

Srinivasan, C. R.: *Kanchipuram through the Ages.* Delhi 1979.

Stapelfeldt, Sylvia: *Kāmākhyā – Satī – Mahāmāyā. Konzeptionen der Großen Göttin im Kālikāpurāṇa.* (Diss. Tübingen 1998) Frankfurt a. M. 2001.
Tamil Lexicon. Published under the Authority of the University of Madras. 6 vols. University of Madras: Madras 1936.
Williams, L. F. Rushbrook: *A Handbook for Travellers in India, Pakistan, Nepal, Bangladesh and Sri Lanka (Ceylon).* 22nd ed. John Murray: London 1982.

Index of Names and Subjects

Glossary of Frequently Used Terms

We use religious and scientific terms in their Sanskrit version, treating them like genuine English words but in their linguistically correct transliteration and with diacritical marks (not puja, but pūjā; not rishi, but ṛṣi). Anglicised loanwords like juggernaut are very scarce. Names are capitalised, for example Śiva, Navagraha, South India.

balipīṭha: a granite lotus bud in front of the main shrine; literally: a seat (*pīṭha*) for the deity upon which offerings (*bali*) can be laid out.
Cakra: see *yantra*.
Devī: goddess.
gopuram: temple tower above the main entrance gate.
kōvil: temple.
kumbhābhiṣeka: inauguration.
Liṅga: a phallus, usually made of stone, symbolising Śiva.
mālā: garland.
maṇḍapa: shrine, pavilion.
māyā: the cosmic illusion.
mūlasthāna: see sanctissimum.
mūrti: statue.
Nāga: a snake deity, cobra.
nāgakkal: snake stone.
Navagraha: the Nine 'Planets': Mercury, Venus, Mars, Jupiter, Saturn, Sun and Moon, Rāhu (devourer of Sun and Moon during eclipses) and Ketu (demon of comets and meteors).
pradakṣiṇā: a circumambulation in veneration of a deity, keeping it to the right.
pūjā: veneration ceremony, prayer ritual.
ṛṣi: seer, sage.
Śaiva: Śivaïte, Śivaïtic.
sanctum: temple.
sanctissimum (*garbhagṛha*, *mūlagarbha*, *mūlasthāna*): the main shrine of a sanctum or temple.
Ṣaṇmukha: 'Having six heads,' a manifestation of Murugan.
sthalamūrti: 'place-statue,' always remains in its shrine, usually made of black granite.
tilaka: 'a mark made with sandalwood or unguents' (Apte), mostly on the forehead.
utsavamūrti: 'festival statue', may be removed from its place, usually made of bronze.
Vaiṣṇava: Viṣṇuitic; a follower of Viṣṇu.
yantra: a magical diagram symbolising a temple, usually used for banishing deities.